THIS IS YOUR **PASSBOOK**® FOR ...

INFORMATION TECHNOLOGY SPECIALIST IV

NATIONAL LEARNING CORPORATION®
passbooks.com

PASSBOOK® SERIES

THE *PASSBOOK® SERIES* has been created to prepare applicants and candidates for the ultimate academic battlefield – the examination room.

At some time in our lives, each and every one of us may be required to take an examination – for validation, matriculation, admission, qualification, registration, certification, or licensure.

Based on the assumption that every applicant or candidate has met the basic formal educational standards, has taken the required number of courses, and read the necessary texts, the *PASSBOOK® SERIES* furnishes the one special preparation which may assure passing with confidence, instead of failing with insecurity. Examination questions – together with answers – are furnished as the basic vehicle for study so that the mysteries of the examination and its compounding difficulties may be eliminated or diminished by a sure method.

This book is meant to help you pass your examination provided that you qualify and are serious in your objective.

The entire field is reviewed through the huge store of content information which is succinctly presented through a provocative and challenging approach – the question-and-answer method.

A climate of success is established by furnishing the correct answers at the end of each test.

You soon learn to recognize types of questions, forms of questions, and patterns of questioning. You may even begin to anticipate expected outcomes.

You perceive that many questions are repeated or adapted so that you can gain acute insights, which may enable you to score many sure points.

You learn how to confront new questions, or types of questions, and to attack them confidently and work out the correct answers.

You note objectives and emphases, and recognize pitfalls and dangers, so that you may make positive educational adjustments.

Moreover, you are kept fully informed in relation to new concepts, methods, practices, and directions in the field.

You discover that you arre actually taking the examination all the time: you are preparing for the examination by "taking" an examination, not by reading extraneous and/or supererogatory textbooks.

In short, this PASSBOOK®, used directedly, should be an important factor in helping you to pass your test.

INFORMATION TECHNOLOGY SPECIALIST IV

DUTIES:

As an Information Technology Specialist IV, you would supervise computer systems analysis and design, application program development, systems testing, maintenance, and implementation.

SCOPE OF THE EXAMINATION:

The written test is designed to test for knowledge, skills, and/or abilities in such areas as:

1. **Preparing written material** - These questions test for the ability to present information clearly and accurately, and to organize paragraphs logically and comprehensibly. For some questions, you will be given information in two or three sentences followed by four restatements of the information. You must then choose the best version. For other questions, you will be given paragraphs with their sentences out of order. You must then choose, from four suggestions, the best order for the sentences.

2. **Supervising a project** - These questions test for the ability to conduct and supervise the activities necessary to achieve the goals and deadlines of a specific project. The questions cover such topics as setting up the project, developing the work plan for the project, assigning and reviewing work, evaluating performance and progress, coordinating phases of the project, handling problems as they arise, and meeting deadlines.

3. **Systems analysis** - These questions test for techniques and concepts of computer systems analysis. They cover such subjects as feasibility and applications studies, systems development tools and software, the systems life cycle, types of systems (e.g., client/server, web-based), controls, and systems documentation, testing, and implementation.

4. **Understanding and interpreting a manual** - These questions test for the ability to comprehend a set of directions and apply them. Candidates will be provided with a procedural manual excerpt to read. This information will be used to answer questions about procedures and the way operations should be carried out. All of the information needed to answer the questions is provided in the set of directions. Candidates will not be required to have any special knowledge about the content area covered.

5. **Understanding and interpreting tabular material** - These questions test your ability to understand, analyze, and use the internal logic of data presented in tabular form. You may be asked to perform tasks such as completing tables, drawing conclusions from them, analyzing data trends or interrelationships, and revising or combining data sets. The concepts of rate, ratio, and proportion are tested. Mathematical operations are simple, and computational speed is not a major factor in the test.

HOW TO TAKE A TEST

I. YOU MUST PASS AN EXAMINATION

A. WHAT EVERY CANDIDATE SHOULD KNOW

Examination applicants often ask us for help in preparing for the written test. What can I study in advance? What kinds of questions will be asked? How will the test be given? How will the papers be graded?

As an applicant for a civil service examination, you may be wondering about some of these things. Our purpose here is to suggest effective methods of advance study and to describe civil service examinations.

Your chances for success on this examination can be increased if you know how to prepare. Those "pre-examination jitters" can be reduced if you know what to expect. You can even experience an adventure in good citizenship if you know why civil service exams are given.

B. WHY ARE CIVIL SERVICE EXAMINATIONS GIVEN?

Civil service examinations are important to you in two ways. As a citizen, you want public jobs filled by employees who know how to do their work. As a job seeker, you want a fair chance to compete for that job on an equal footing with other candidates. The best-known means of accomplishing this two-fold goal is the competitive examination.

Exams are widely publicized throughout the nation. They may be administered for jobs in federal, state, city, municipal, town or village governments or agencies.

Any citizen may apply, with some limitations, such as the age or residence of applicants. Your experience and education may be reviewed to see whether you meet the requirements for the particular examination. When these requirements exist, they are reasonable and applied consistently to all applicants. Thus, a competitive examination may cause you some uneasiness now, but it is your privilege and safeguard.

C. HOW ARE CIVIL SERVICE EXAMS DEVELOPED?

Examinations are carefully written by trained technicians who are specialists in the field known as "psychological measurement," in consultation with recognized authorities in the field of work that the test will cover. These experts recommend the subject matter areas or skills to be tested; only those knowledges or skills important to your success on the job are included. The most reliable books and source materials available are used as references. Together, the experts and technicians judge the difficulty level of the questions.

Test technicians know how to phrase questions so that the problem is clearly stated. Their ethics do not permit "trick" or "catch" questions. Questions may have been tried out on sample groups, or subjected to statistical analysis, to determine their usefulness.

Written tests are often used in combination with performance tests, ratings of training and experience, and oral interviews. All of these measures combine to form the best-known means of finding the right person for the right job.

II. HOW TO PASS THE WRITTEN TEST

A. NATURE OF THE EXAMINATION

To prepare intelligently for civil service examinations, you should know how they differ from school examinations you have taken. In school you were assigned certain definite pages to read or subjects to cover. The examination questions were quite detailed and usually emphasized memory. Civil service exams, on the other hand, try to discover your present ability to perform the duties of a position, plus your potentiality to learn these duties. In other words, a civil service exam attempts to predict how successful you will be. Questions cover such a broad area that they cannot be as minute and detailed as school exam questions.

In the public service similar kinds of work, or positions, are grouped together in one "class." This process is known as *position-classification*. All the positions in a class are paid according to the salary range for that class. One class title covers all of these positions, and they are all tested by the same examination.

B. FOUR BASIC STEPS

1) Study the announcement

How, then, can you know what subjects to study? Our best answer is: "Learn as much as possible about the class of positions for which you've applied." The exam will test the knowledge, skills and abilities needed to do the work.

Your most valuable source of information about the position you want is the official exam announcement. This announcement lists the training and experience qualifications. Check these standards and apply only if you come reasonably close to meeting them.

The brief description of the position in the examination announcement offers some clues to the subjects which will be tested. Think about the job itself. Review the duties in your mind. Can you perform them, or are there some in which you are rusty? Fill in the blank spots in your preparation.

Many jurisdictions preview the written test in the exam announcement by including a section called "Knowledge and Abilities Required," "Scope of the Examination," or some similar heading. Here you will find out specifically what fields will be tested.

2) Review your own background

Once you learn in general what the position is all about, and what you need to know to do the work, ask yourself which subjects you already know fairly well and which need improvement. You may wonder whether to concentrate on improving your strong areas or on building some background in your fields of weakness. When the announcement has specified "some knowledge" or "considerable knowledge," or has used adjectives like "beginning principles of..." or "advanced ... methods," you can get a clue as to the number and difficulty of questions to be asked in any given field. More questions, and hence broader coverage, would be included for those subjects which are more important in the work. Now weigh your strengths and weaknesses against the job requirements and prepare accordingly.

3) Determine the level of the position

Another way to tell how intensively you should prepare is to understand the level of the job for which you are applying. Is it the entering level? In other words, is this the position in which beginners in a field of work are hired? Or is it an intermediate or advanced level? Sometimes this is indicated by such words as "Junior" or "Senior" in the class title. Other jurisdictions use Roman numerals to designate the level – Clerk I, Clerk II, for example. The word "Supervisor" sometimes appears in the title. If the level is not indicated by the title, check the description of duties. Will you be working under very close supervision, or will you have responsibility for independent decisions in this work?

4) Choose appropriate study materials

Now that you know the subjects to be examined and the relative amount of each subject to be covered, you can choose suitable study materials. For beginning level jobs, or even advanced ones, if you have a pronounced weakness in some aspect of your training, read a modern, standard textbook in that field. Be sure it is up to date and has general coverage. Such books are normally available at your library, and the librarian will be glad to help you locate one. For entry-level positions, questions of appropriate difficulty are chosen – neither highly advanced questions, nor those too simple. Such questions require careful thought but not advanced training.

If the position for which you are applying is technical or advanced, you will read more advanced, specialized material. If you are already familiar with the basic principles of your field, elementary textbooks would waste your time. Concentrate on advanced textbooks and technical periodicals. Think through the concepts and review difficult problems in your field.

These are all general sources. You can get more ideas on your own initiative, following these leads. For example, training manuals and publications of the government agency which employs workers in your field can be useful, particularly for technical and professional positions. A letter or visit to the government department involved may result in more specific study suggestions, and certainly will provide you with a more definite idea of the exact nature of the position you are seeking.

III. KINDS OF TESTS

Tests are used for purposes other than measuring knowledge and ability to perform specified duties. For some positions, it is equally important to test ability to make adjustments to new situations or to profit from training. In others, basic mental abilities not dependent on information are essential. Questions which test these things may not appear as pertinent to the duties of the position as those which test for knowledge and information. Yet they are often highly important parts of a fair examination. For very general questions, it is almost impossible to help you direct your study efforts. What we can do is to point out some of the more common of these general abilities needed in public service positions and describe some typical questions.

1) General information

Broad, general information has been found useful for predicting job success in some kinds of work. This is tested in a variety of ways, from vocabulary lists to questions about current events. Basic background in some field of work, such as

4

sociology or economics, may be sampled in a group of questions. Often these are principles which have become familiar to most persons through exposure rather than through formal training. It is difficult to advise you how to study for these questions; being alert to the world around you is our best suggestion.

2) Verbal ability

An example of an ability needed in many positions is verbal or language ability. Verbal ability is, in brief, the ability to use and understand words. Vocabulary and grammar tests are typical measures of this ability. Reading comprehension or paragraph interpretation questions are common in many kinds of civil service tests. You are given a paragraph of written material and asked to find its central meaning.

3) Numerical ability

Number skills can be tested by the familiar arithmetic problem, by checking paired lists of numbers to see which are alike and which are different, or by interpreting charts and graphs. In the latter test, a graph may be printed in the test booklet which you are asked to use as the basis for answering questions.

4) Observation

A popular test for law-enforcement positions is the observation test. A picture is shown to you for several minutes, then taken away. Questions about the picture test your ability to observe both details and larger elements.

5) Following directions

In many positions in the public service, the employee must be able to carry out written instructions dependably and accurately. You may be given a chart with several columns, each column listing a variety of information. The questions require you to carry out directions involving the information given in the chart.

6) Skills and aptitudes

Performance tests effectively measure some manual skills and aptitudes. When the skill is one in which you are trained, such as typing or shorthand, you can practice. These tests are often very much like those given in business school or high school courses. For many of the other skills and aptitudes, however, no short-time preparation can be made. Skills and abilities natural to you or that you have developed throughout your lifetime are being tested.

Many of the general questions just described provide all the data needed to answer the questions and ask you to use your reasoning ability to find the answers. Your best preparation for these tests, as well as for tests of facts and ideas, is to be at your physical and mental best. You, no doubt, have your own methods of getting into an exam-taking mood and keeping "in shape." The next section lists some ideas on this subject.

IV. KINDS OF QUESTIONS

Only rarely is the "essay" question, which you answer in narrative form, used in civil service tests. Civil service tests are usually of the short-answer type. Full instructions for answering these questions will be given to you at the examination. But in case this is your first experience with short-answer questions and separate answer sheets, here is what you need to know:

1) Multiple-choice Questions

Most popular of the short-answer questions is the "multiple choice" or "best answer" question. It can be used, for example, to test for factual knowledge, ability to solve problems or judgment in meeting situations found at work.

A multiple-choice question is normally one of three types—

- It can begin with an incomplete statement followed by several possible endings. You are to find the one ending which *best* completes the statement, although some of the others may not be entirely wrong.
- It can also be a complete statement in the form of a question which is answered by choosing one of the statements listed.
- It can be in the form of a problem – again you select the best answer.

Here is an example of a multiple-choice question with a discussion which should give you some clues as to the method for choosing the right answer:

When an employee has a complaint about his assignment, the action which will *best* help him overcome his difficulty is to
A. discuss his difficulty with his coworkers
B. take the problem to the head of the organization
C. take the problem to the person who gave him the assignment
D. say nothing to anyone about his complaint

In answering this question, you should study each of the choices to find which is best. Consider choice "A" – Certainly an employee may discuss his complaint with fellow employees, but no change or improvement can result, and the complaint remains unresolved. Choice "B" is a poor choice since the head of the organization probably does not know what assignment you have been given, and taking your problem to him is known as "going over the head" of the supervisor. The supervisor, or person who made the assignment, is the person who can clarify it or correct any injustice. Choice "C" is, therefore, correct. To say nothing, as in choice "D," is unwise. Supervisors have and interest in knowing the problems employees are facing, and the employee is seeking a solution to his problem.

2) True/False Questions

The "true/false" or "right/wrong" form of question is sometimes used. Here a complete statement is given. Your job is to decide whether the statement is right or wrong.

SAMPLE: A roaming cell-phone call to a nearby city costs less than a non-roaming call to a distant city.

This statement is wrong, or false, since roaming calls are more expensive.

This is not a complete list of all possible question forms, although most of the others are variations of these common types. You will always get complete directions for answering questions. Be sure you understand *how* to mark your answers – ask questions until you do.

V. RECORDING YOUR ANSWERS

Computer terminals are used more and more today for many different kinds of exams.

For an examination with very few applicants, you may be told to record your answers in the test booklet itself. Separate answer sheets are much more common. If this separate answer sheet is to be scored by machine – and this is often the case – it is highly important that you mark your answers correctly in order to get credit.

An electronic scoring machine is often used in civil service offices because of the speed with which papers can be scored. Machine-scored answer sheets must be marked with a pencil, which will be given to you. This pencil has a high graphite content which responds to the electronic scoring machine. As a matter of fact, stray dots may register as answers, so do not let your pencil rest on the answer sheet while you are pondering the correct answer. Also, if your pencil lead breaks or is otherwise defective, ask for another.

Since the answer sheet will be dropped in a slot in the scoring machine, be careful not to bend the corners or get the paper crumpled.

The answer sheet normally has five vertical columns of numbers, with 30 numbers to a column. These numbers correspond to the question numbers in your test booklet. After each number, going across the page are four or five pairs of dotted lines. These short dotted lines have small letters or numbers above them. The first two pairs may also have a "T" or "F" above the letters. This indicates that the first two pairs only are to be used if the questions are of the true-false type. If the questions are multiple choice, disregard the "T" and "F" and pay attention only to the small letters or numbers.

Answer your questions in the manner of the sample that follows:

32. The largest city in the United States is
    A. Washington, D.C.
    B. New York City
    C. Chicago
    D. Detroit
    E. San Francisco

1) Choose the answer you think is best. (New York City is the largest, so "B" is correct.)
2) Find the row of dotted lines numbered the same as the question you are answering. (Find row number 32)
3) Find the pair of dotted lines corresponding to the answer. (Find the pair of lines under the mark "B.")
4) Make a solid black mark between the dotted lines.

VI. BEFORE THE TEST

Common sense will help you find procedures to follow to get ready for an examination. Too many of us, however, overlook these sensible measures. Indeed, nervousness and fatigue have been found to be the most serious reasons why applicants fail to do their best on civil service tests. Here is a list of reminders:

- Begin your preparation early – Don't wait until the last minute to go scurrying around for books and materials or to find out what the position is all about.
- Prepare continuously – An hour a night for a week is better than an all-night cram session. This has been definitely established. What is more, a night a week for a month will return better dividends than crowding your study into a shorter period of time.
- Locate the place of the exam – You have been sent a notice telling you when and where to report for the examination. If the location is in a different town or otherwise unfamiliar to you, it would be well to inquire the best route and learn something about the building.
- Relax the night before the test – Allow your mind to rest. Do not study at all that night. Plan some mild recreation or diversion; then go to bed early and get a good night's sleep.
- Get up early enough to make a leisurely trip to the place for the test – This way unforeseen events, traffic snarls, unfamiliar buildings, etc. will not upset you.
- Dress comfortably – A written test is not a fashion show. You will be known by number and not by name, so wear something comfortable.
- Leave excess paraphernalia at home – Shopping bags and odd bundles will get in your way. You need bring only the items mentioned in the official notice you received; usually everything you need is provided. Do not bring reference books to the exam. They will only confuse those last minutes and be taken away from you when in the test room.
- Arrive somewhat ahead of time – If because of transportation schedules you must get there very early, bring a newspaper or magazine to take your mind off yourself while waiting.
- Locate the examination room – When you have found the proper room, you will be directed to the seat or part of the room where you will sit. Sometimes you are given a sheet of instructions to read while you are waiting. Do not fill out any forms until you are told to do so; just read them and be prepared.
- Relax and prepare to listen to the instructions
- If you have any physical problem that may keep you from doing your best, be sure to tell the test administrator. If you are sick or in poor health, you really cannot do your best on the exam. You can come back and take the test some other time.

VII. AT THE TEST

The day of the test is here and you have the test booklet in your hand. The temptation to get going is very strong. Caution! There is more to success than knowing the right answers. You must know how to identify your papers and understand variations in the type of short-answer question used in this particular examination. Follow these suggestions for maximum results from your efforts:

1) Cooperate with the monitor

The test administrator has a duty to create a situation in which you can be as much at ease as possible. He will give instructions, tell you when to begin, check to see that you are marking your answer sheet correctly, and so on. He is not there to guard you, although he will see that your competitors do not take unfair advantage. He wants to help you do your best.

2) Listen to all instructions

Don't jump the gun! Wait until you understand all directions. In most civil service tests you get more time than you need to answer the questions. So don't be in a hurry. Read each word of instructions until you clearly understand the meaning. Study the examples, listen to all announcements and follow directions. Ask questions if you do not understand what to do.

3) Identify your papers

Civil service exams are usually identified by number only. You will be assigned a number; you must not put your name on your test papers. Be sure to copy your number correctly. Since more than one exam may be given, copy your exact examination title.

4) Plan your time

Unless you are told that a test is a "speed" or "rate of work" test, speed itself is usually not important. Time enough to answer all the questions will be provided, but this does not mean that you have all day. An overall time limit has been set. Divide the total time (in minutes) by the number of questions to determine the approximate time you have for each question.

5) Do not linger over difficult questions

If you come across a difficult question, mark it with a paper clip (useful to have along) and come back to it when you have been through the booklet. One caution if you do this – be sure to skip a number on your answer sheet as well. Check often to be sure that you have not lost your place and that you are marking in the row numbered the same as the question you are answering.

6) Read the questions

Be sure you know what the question asks! Many capable people are unsuccessful because they failed to *read* the questions correctly.

7) Answer all questions

Unless you have been instructed that a penalty will be deducted for incorrect answers, it is better to guess than to omit a question.

8) Speed tests

It is often better NOT to guess on speed tests. It has been found that on timed tests people are tempted to spend the last few seconds before time is called in marking answers at random – without even reading them – in the hope of picking up a few extra points. To discourage this practice, the instructions may warn you that your score will be "corrected" for guessing. That is, a penalty will be applied. The incorrect answers will be deducted from the correct ones, or some other penalty formula will be used.

9) Review your answers

If you finish before time is called, go back to the questions you guessed or omitted to give them further thought. Review other answers if you have time.

10) Return your test materials

If you are ready to leave before others have finished or time is called, take ALL your materials to the monitor and leave quietly. Never take any test material with you. The monitor can discover whose papers are not complete, and taking a test booklet may be grounds for disqualification.

VIII. EXAMINATION TECHNIQUES

1) Read the general instructions carefully. These are usually printed on the first page of the exam booklet. As a rule, these instructions refer to the timing of the examination; the fact that you should not start work until the signal and must stop work at a signal, etc. If there are any *special* instructions, such as a choice of questions to be answered, make sure that you note this instruction carefully.

2) When you are ready to start work on the examination, that is as soon as the signal has been given, read the instructions to each question booklet, underline any key words or phrases, such as *least, best, outline, describe* and the like. In this way you will tend to answer as requested rather than discover on reviewing your paper that you *listed without describing*, that you selected the *worst* choice rather than the *best* choice, etc.

3) If the examination is of the objective or multiple-choice type – that is, each question will also give a series of possible answers: A, B, C or D, and you are called upon to select the best answer and write the letter next to that answer on your answer paper – it is advisable to start answering each question in turn. There may be anywhere from 50 to 100 such questions in the three or four hours allotted and you can see how much time would be taken if you read through all the questions before beginning to answer any. Furthermore, if you come across a question or group of questions which you know would be difficult to answer, it would undoubtedly affect your handling of all the other questions.

4) If the examination is of the essay type and contains but a few questions, it is a moot point as to whether you should read all the questions before starting to answer any one. Of course, if you are given a choice – say five out of seven and the like – then it is essential to read all the questions so you can eliminate the two that are most difficult. If, however, you are asked to answer all the questions, there may be danger in trying to answer the easiest one first because you may find that you will spend too much time on it. The best technique is to answer the first question, then proceed to the second, etc.

5) Time your answers. Before the exam begins, write down the time it started, then add the time allowed for the examination and write down the time it must be completed, then divide the time available somewhat as follows:

- If 3-1/2 hours are allowed, that would be 210 minutes. If you have 80 objective-type questions, that would be an average of 2-1/2 minutes per question. Allow yourself no more than 2 minutes per question, or a total of 160 minutes, which will permit about 50 minutes to review.
- If for the time allotment of 210 minutes there are 7 essay questions to answer, that would average about 30 minutes a question. Give yourself only 25 minutes per question so that you have about 35 minutes to review.

6) The most important instruction is to *read each question* and make sure you know what is wanted. The second most important instruction is to *time yourself properly* so that you answer every question. The third most important instruction is to *answer every question*. Guess if you have to but include something for each question. Remember that you will receive no credit for a blank and will probably receive some credit if you write something in answer to an essay question. If you guess a letter – say "B" for a multiple-choice question – you may have guessed right. If you leave a blank as an answer to a multiple-choice question, the examiners may respect your feelings but it will not add a point to your score. Some exams may penalize you for wrong answers, so in such cases *only*, you may not want to guess unless you have some basis for your answer.

7) Suggestions
   a. Objective-type questions
      1. Examine the question booklet for proper sequence of pages and questions
      2. Read all instructions carefully
      3. Skip any question which seems too difficult; return to it after all other questions have been answered
      4. Apportion your time properly; do not spend too much time on any single question or group of questions
      5. Note and underline key words – *all, most, fewest, least, best, worst, same, opposite,* etc.
      6. Pay particular attention to negatives
      7. Note unusual option, e.g., unduly long, short, complex, different or similar in content to the body of the question
      8. Observe the use of "hedging" words – *probably, may, most likely,* etc.
      9. Make sure that your answer is put next to the same number as the question
      10. Do not second-guess unless you have good reason to believe the second answer is definitely more correct
      11. Cross out original answer if you decide another answer is more accurate; do not erase until you are ready to hand your paper in
      12. Answer all questions; guess unless instructed otherwise
      13. Leave time for review

   b. Essay questions
      1. Read each question carefully
      2. Determine exactly what is wanted. Underline key words or phrases.
      3. Decide on outline or paragraph answer

4. Include many different points and elements unless asked to develop any one or two points or elements
5. Show impartiality by giving pros and cons unless directed to select one side only
6. Make and write down any assumptions you find necessary to answer the questions
7. Watch your English, grammar, punctuation and choice of words
8. Time your answers; don't crowd material

8) Answering the essay question

Most essay questions can be answered by framing the specific response around several key words or ideas. Here are a few such key words or ideas:

M's: manpower, materials, methods, money, management
P's: purpose, program, policy, plan, procedure, practice, problems, pitfalls, personnel, public relations
   a. Six basic steps in handling problems:
      1. Preliminary plan and background development
      2. Collect information, data and facts
      3. Analyze and interpret information, data and facts
      4. Analyze and develop solutions as well as make recommendations
      5. Prepare report and sell recommendations
      6. Install recommendations and follow up effectiveness

   b. Pitfalls to avoid
      1. *Taking things for granted* – A statement of the situation does not necessarily imply that each of the elements is necessarily true; for example, a complaint may be invalid and biased so that all that can be taken for granted is that a complaint has been registered
      2. *Considering only one side of a situation* – Wherever possible, indicate several alternatives and then point out the reasons you selected the best one
      3. *Failing to indicate follow up* – Whenever your answer indicates action on your part, make certain that you will take proper follow-up action to see how successful your recommendations, procedures or actions turn out to be
      4. *Taking too long in answering any single question* – Remember to time your answers properly

IX. AFTER THE TEST

Scoring procedures differ in detail among civil service jurisdictions although the general principles are the same. Whether the papers are hand-scored or graded by machine we have described, they are nearly always graded by number. That is, the person who marks the paper knows only the number – never the name – of the applicant. Not until all the papers have been graded will they be matched with names. If other tests, such as training and experience or oral interview ratings have been given, scores will be combined. Different parts of the examination usually have different weights. For example, the written test might count 60 percent of the final grade, and a rating of training and experience 40 percent. In many jurisdictions, veterans will have a certain number of points added to their grades.

After the final grade has been determined, the names are placed in grade order and an eligible list is established. There are various methods for resolving ties between those who get the same final grade – probably the most common is to place first the name of the person whose application was received first. Job offers are made from the eligible list in the order the names appear on it. You will be notified of your grade and your rank as soon as all these computations have been made. This will be done as rapidly as possible.

People who are found to meet the requirements in the announcement are called "eligibles." Their names are put on a list of eligible candidates. An eligible's chances of getting a job depend on how high he stands on this list and how fast agencies are filling jobs from the list.

When a job is to be filled from a list of eligibles, the agency asks for the names of people on the list of eligibles for that job. When the civil service commission receives this request, it sends to the agency the names of the three people highest on this list. Or, if the job to be filled has specialized requirements, the office sends the agency the names of the top three persons who meet these requirements from the general list.

The appointing officer makes a choice from among the three people whose names were sent to him. If the selected person accepts the appointment, the names of the others are put back on the list to be considered for future openings.

That is the rule in hiring from all kinds of eligible lists, whether they are for typist, carpenter, chemist, or something else. For every vacancy, the appointing officer has his choice of any one of the top three eligibles on the list. This explains why the person whose name is on top of the list sometimes does not get an appointment when some of the persons lower on the list do. If the appointing officer chooses the second or third eligible, the No. 1 eligible does not get a job at once, but stays on the list until he is appointed or the list is terminated.

X. HOW TO PASS THE INTERVIEW TEST

The examination for which you applied requires an oral interview test. You have already taken the written test and you are now being called for the interview test – the final part of the formal examination.

You may think that it is not possible to prepare for an interview test and that there are no procedures to follow during an interview. Our purpose is to point out some things you can do in advance that will help you and some good rules to follow and pitfalls to avoid while you are being interviewed.

What is an interview supposed to test?
The written examination is designed to test the technical knowledge and competence of the candidate; the oral is designed to evaluate intangible qualities, not readily measured otherwise, and to establish a list showing the relative fitness of each candidate – as measured against his competitors – for the position sought. Scoring is not on the basis of "right" and "wrong," but on a sliding scale of values ranging from "not passable" to "outstanding." As a matter of fact, it is possible to achieve a relatively low score without a single "incorrect" answer because of evident weakness in the qualities being measured.

Occasionally, an examination may consist entirely of an oral test – either an individual or a group oral. In such cases, information is sought concerning the technical knowledges and abilities of the candidate, since there has been no written examination for this purpose. More commonly, however, an oral test is used to supplement a written examination.

Who conducts interviews?

The composition of oral boards varies among different jurisdictions. In nearly all, a representative of the personnel department serves as chairman. One of the members of the board may be a representative of the department in which the candidate would work. In some cases, "outside experts" are used, and, frequently, a businessman or some other representative of the general public is asked to serve. Labor and management or other special groups may be represented. The aim is to secure the services of experts in the appropriate field.

However the board is composed, it is a good idea (and not at all improper or unethical) to ascertain in advance of the interview who the members are and what groups they represent. When you are introduced to them, you will have some idea of their backgrounds and interests, and at least you will not stutter and stammer over their names.

What should be done before the interview?

While knowledge about the board members is useful and takes some of the surprise element out of the interview, there is other preparation which is more substantive. It *is* possible to prepare for an oral interview – in several ways:

1) Keep a copy of your application and review it carefully before the interview

This may be the only document before the oral board, and the starting point of the interview. Know what education and experience you have listed there, and the sequence and dates of all of it. Sometimes the board will ask you to review the highlights of your experience for them; you should not have to hem and haw doing it.

2) Study the class specification and the examination announcement

Usually, the oral board has one or both of these to guide them. The qualities, characteristics or knowledges required by the position sought are stated in these documents. They offer valuable clues as to the nature of the oral interview. For example, if the job involves supervisory responsibilities, the announcement will usually indicate that knowledge of modern supervisory methods and the qualifications of the candidate as a supervisor will be tested. If so, you can expect such questions, frequently in the form of a hypothetical situation which you are expected to solve. NEVER go into an oral without knowledge of the duties and responsibilities of the job you seek.

3) Think through each qualification required

Try to visualize the kind of questions you would ask if you were a board member. How well could you answer them? Try especially to appraise your own knowledge and background in each area, *measured against the job sought*, and identify any areas in which you are weak. Be critical and realistic – do not flatter yourself.

4) Do some general reading in areas in which you feel you may be weak

For example, if the job involves supervision and your past experience has NOT, some general reading in supervisory methods and practices, particularly in the field of human relations, might be useful. Do NOT study agency procedures or detailed manuals. The oral board will be testing your understanding and capacity, not your memory.

5) Get a good night's sleep and watch your general health and mental attitude

You will want a clear head at the interview. Take care of a cold or any other minor ailment, and of course, no hangovers.

What should be done on the day of the interview?

Now comes the day of the interview itself. Give yourself plenty of time to get there. Plan to arrive somewhat ahead of the scheduled time, particularly if your appointment is in the fore part of the day. If a previous candidate fails to appear, the board might be ready for you a bit early. By early afternoon an oral board is almost invariably behind schedule if there are many candidates, and you may have to wait. Take along a book or magazine to read, or your application to review, but leave any extraneous material in the waiting room when you go in for your interview. In any event, relax and compose yourself.

The matter of dress is important. The board is forming impressions about you – from your experience, your manners, your attitude, and your appearance. Give your personal appearance careful attention. Dress your best, but not your flashiest. Choose conservative, appropriate clothing, and be sure it is immaculate. This is a business interview, and your appearance should indicate that you regard it as such. Besides, being well groomed and properly dressed will help boost your confidence.

Sooner or later, someone will call your name and escort you into the interview room. *This is it.* From here on you are on your own. It is too late for any more preparation. But remember, you asked for this opportunity to prove your fitness, and you are here because your request was granted.

What happens when you go in?

The usual sequence of events will be as follows: The clerk (who is often the board stenographer) will introduce you to the chairman of the oral board, who will introduce you to the other members of the board. Acknowledge the introductions before you sit down. Do not be surprised if you find a microphone facing you or a stenotypist sitting by. Oral interviews are usually recorded in the event of an appeal or other review.

Usually the chairman of the board will open the interview by reviewing the highlights of your education and work experience from your application – primarily for the benefit of the other members of the board, as well as to get the material into the record. Do not interrupt or comment unless there is an error or significant misinterpretation; if that is the case, do not hesitate. But do not quibble about insignificant matters. Also, he will usually ask you some question about your education, experience or your present job – partly to get you to start talking and to establish the interviewing "rapport." He may start the actual questioning, or turn it over to one of the other members. Frequently, each member undertakes the questioning on a particular area, one in which he is perhaps most competent, so you can expect each member to participate in the examination. Because time is limited, you may also expect some rather abrupt switches in the direction the questioning takes, so do not be upset by it. Normally, a board member will not pursue a single line of questioning unless he discovers a particular strength or weakness.

After each member has participated, the chairman will usually ask whether any member has any further questions, then will ask you if you have anything you wish to add. Unless you are expecting this question, it may floor you. Worse, it may start you off on an extended, extemporaneous speech. The board is not usually seeking more information. The question is principally to offer you a last opportunity to present further qualifications or to indicate that you have nothing to add. So, if you feel that a significant qualification or characteristic has been overlooked, it is proper to point it out in a sentence or so. Do not compliment the board on the thoroughness of their examination – they have been sketchy, and you know it. If you wish, merely say, "No thank you, I have nothing further to add." This is a point where you can "talk yourself out" of a good impression or fail to present an important bit of information. Remember, *you close the interview yourself.*

The chairman will then say, "That is all, Mr. _____, thank you." Do not be startled; the interview is over, and quicker than you think. Thank him, gather your belongings and take your leave. Save your sigh of relief for the other side of the door.

How to put your best foot forward

Throughout this entire process, you may feel that the board individually and collectively is trying to pierce your defenses, seek out your hidden weaknesses and embarrass and confuse you. Actually, this is not true. They are obliged to make an appraisal of your qualifications for the job you are seeking, and they want to see you in your best light. Remember, they must interview all candidates and a non-cooperative candidate may become a failure in spite of their best efforts to bring out his qualifications. Here are 15 suggestions that will help you:

1) Be natural – Keep your attitude confident, not cocky

If you are not confident that you can do the job, do not expect the board to be. Do not apologize for your weaknesses, try to bring out your strong points. The board is interested in a positive, not negative, presentation. Cockiness will antagonize any board member and make him wonder if you are covering up a weakness by a false show of strength.

2) Get comfortable, but don't lounge or sprawl

Sit erectly but not stiffly. A careless posture may lead the board to conclude that you are careless in other things, or at least that you are not impressed by the importance of the occasion. Either conclusion is natural, even if incorrect. Do not fuss with your clothing, a pencil or an ashtray. Your hands may occasionally be useful to emphasize a point; do not let them become a point of distraction.

3) Do not wisecrack or make small talk

This is a serious situation, and your attitude should show that you consider it as such. Further, the time of the board is limited – they do not want to waste it, and neither should you.

4) Do not exaggerate your experience or abilities

In the first place, from information in the application or other interviews and sources, the board may know more about you than you think. Secondly, you probably will not get away with it. An experienced board is rather adept at spotting such a situation, so do not take the chance.

5) If you know a board member, do not make a point of it, yet do not hide it

Certainly you are not fooling him, and probably not the other members of the board. Do not try to take advantage of your acquaintanceship – it will probably do you little good.

6) Do not dominate the interview

Let the board do that. They will give you the clues – do not assume that you have to do all the talking. Realize that the board has a number of questions to ask you, and do not try to take up all the interview time by showing off your extensive knowledge of the answer to the first one.

7) Be attentive

You only have 20 minutes or so, and you should keep your attention at its sharpest throughout. When a member is addressing a problem or question to you, give him your undivided attention. Address your reply principally to him, but do not exclude the other board members.

8) Do not interrupt

A board member may be stating a problem for you to analyze. He will ask you a question when the time comes. Let him state the problem, and wait for the question.

9) Make sure you understand the question

Do not try to answer until you are sure what the question is. If it is not clear, restate it in your own words or ask the board member to clarify it for you. However, do not haggle about minor elements.

10) Reply promptly but not hastily

A common entry on oral board rating sheets is "candidate responded readily," or "candidate hesitated in replies." Respond as promptly and quickly as you can, but do not jump to a hasty, ill-considered answer.

11) Do not be peremptory in your answers

A brief answer is proper – but do not fire your answer back. That is a losing game from your point of view. The board member can probably ask questions much faster than you can answer them.

12) Do not try to create the answer you think the board member wants

He is interested in what kind of mind you have and how it works – not in playing games. Furthermore, he can usually spot this practice and will actually grade you down on it.

13) Do not switch sides in your reply merely to agree with a board member

Frequently, a member will take a contrary position merely to draw you out and to see if you are willing and able to defend your point of view. Do not start a debate, yet do not surrender a good position. If a position is worth taking, it is worth defending.

14) Do not be afraid to admit an error in judgment if you are shown to be wrong

The board knows that you are forced to reply without any opportunity for careful consideration. Your answer may be demonstrably wrong. If so, admit it and get on with the interview.

15) Do not dwell at length on your present job

The opening question may relate to your present assignment. Answer the question but do not go into an extended discussion. You are being examined for a *new* job, not your present one. As a matter of fact, try to phrase ALL your answers in terms of the job for which you are being examined.

Basis of Rating

Probably you will forget most of these "do's" and "don'ts" when you walk into the oral interview room. Even remembering them all will not ensure you a passing grade. Perhaps you did not have the qualifications in the first place. But remembering them will help you to put your best foot forward, without treading on the toes of the board members.

Rumor and popular opinion to the contrary notwithstanding, an oral board wants you to make the best appearance possible. They know you are under pressure – but they also want to see how you respond to it as a guide to what your reaction would be under the pressures of the job you seek. They will be influenced by the degree of poise you display, the personal traits you show and the manner in which you respond.

ABOUT THIS BOOK

This book contains tests divided into Examination Sections. Go through each test, answering every question in the margin. At the end of each test look at the answer key and check your answers. On the ones you got wrong, look at the right answer choice and learn. Do not fill in the answers first. Do not memorize the questions and answers, but understand the answer and principles involved. On your test, the questions will likely be different from the samples. Questions are changed and new ones added. If you understand these past questions you should have success with any changes that arise. Tests may consist of several types of questions. We have additional books on each subject should more study be advisable or necessary for you. Finally, the more you study, the better prepared you will be. This book is intended to be the last thing you study before you walk into the examination room. Prior study of relevant texts is also recommended. NLC publishes some of these in our Fundamental Series. Knowledge and good sense are important factors in passing your exam. Good luck also helps. So now study this Passbook, absorb the material contained within and take that knowledge into the examination. Then do your best to pass that exam.

———

EXAMINATION SECTION

EXAMINATION SECTION
TEST 1

DIRECTIONS: Each question or incomplete statement is followed by several suggested answers or completions. Select the one that BEST answers the question or completes the statement. *PRINT THE LETTER OF THE CORRECT ANSWER IN THE SPACE AT THE RIGHT.*

1. Which is NOT an example of a system?   1._____

    A. Management   B. Organization   C. Document
    D. Computer   E. Education

2. The systems process has three components.   2._____
    Which is NOT one of the components?

    A. Programming   B. Development   C. Design
    D. Analysis   E. None of the above

3. Which of the following lists the three components of the systems process in the COR-   3._____
    RECT order?

    A. Development, analysis, and design
    B. Analysis, design, and development
    C. Design, analysis, and development
    D. Development, design, and analysis
    E. Analysis, development, and design

4. Which component of the systems process comes FIRST?   4._____

    A. Design   B. Development   C. Review
    D. Analysis   E. Audit

5. Which component of the systems process comes THIRD?   5._____

    A. Design   B. Development   C. Review
    D. Analysis   E. Audit

6. Which component of the systems process comes SECOND?   6._____

    A. Design   B. Development   C. Review
    D. Analysis   E. Audit

7. Which component of the systems process comes FIFTH?   7._____

    A. Design   B. Development   C. Review
    D. Analysis   E. Audit

8. Who USUALLY initiates the systems process?   8._____

    A. An outside vendor
    B. A user
    C. Management
    D. Computer services staff
    E. The Federal government

9. During which phase of the systems process are programs written?   9.____

    A. Analysis   B. Design   C. Development
    D. Review   E. None of the above

10. During which phase of the systems process are alternatives identified?   10.____

    A. Design
    B. Analysis
    C. Development
    D. Review
    E. None of the above

11. During which phase of the systems process are files defined?   11.____

    A. Design   B. Analysis
    C. Development   D. Programming
    E. During all phases

12. Which of the following is NOT a part of computer-based systems?   12.____

    A. Hardware   B. Software   C. People
    D. Procedures   E. None of the above

13. Which of the following is an example of data?   13.____
    The

    A. cost of a pair of running shoes
    B. average price of a pair of running shoes
    C. most popular style of running shoe
    D. average size shoe worn by men
    E. average size shoe worn by women

14. Which of the following is an example of information?   14.____

    A. The cost of a pair of running shoes
    B. The number of pairs of size 8D shoes on hand
    C. The average price of a pair of running shoes
    D. All of the above
    E. None of the above

15. The adjusting of a system is called   15.____

    A. hardware   B. feedback   C. procedures
    D. alternatives   E. programming

16. Which of the following is NOT a common accounting system?   16.____

    A. Payroll   B. Spreadsheet   C. Inventory
    D. Payables   E. Receivables

17. Studying the way an organization retrieves and processes data is systems   17.____

    A. development   B. design   C. feedback
    D. analysis   E. hardware

18. Deciding on the formats of reports, storage methods, and data collection methods is systems   18.____

    A. design   B. analysis   C. development
    D. feedback   E. procedures

19. Implementing, programming, testing, and training is systems   19.____

    A. design   B. development   C. analysis
    D. procedures   E. alternatives

20. An organization that converts raw materials into finished or semi-finished goods is classified as   20.____

    A. not-for-profit   B. service
    C. governmental   D. manufacturing
    E. none of the above

21. An organization that performs tasks for consumers is classified as   21.____

    A. service   B. not-for-profit
    C. governmental   D. manufacturing
    E. none of the above

22. Line structure has overall responsibility and authority assigned to the   22.____

    A. bottom level workers   B. top level managers
    C. middle level workers   D. bottom level managers
    E. union representatives

23. An example of a department typically serving in a staff relationship is   23.____

    A. sales   B. manufacturing   C. finance
    D. personnel   E. marketing

24. Depicts the lines of authority between individuals and departments in a business   24.____

    A. flowchart   B. data flow diagram
    C. Warnier Orr chart   D. organization chart
    E. Gantt chart

25. The person responsible for performing the systems study is the   25.____

    A. systems analyst
    B. user
    C. manager of computing services
    D. vice-president of business services
    E. director of information services

———

KEY (CORRECT ANSWERS)

1.	C		11.	A
2.	A		12.	E
3.	B		13.	A
4.	D		14.	C
5.	B		15.	B
6.	A		16.	B
7.	E		17.	D
8.	B		18.	A
9.	C		19.	B
10.	B		20.	D

21. A
22. B
23. D
24. D
25. A

———

TEST 2

DIRECTIONS: Each question or incomplete statement is followed by several suggested answers or completions. Select the one that BEST answers the question or completes the statement. *PRINT THE LETTER OF THE CORRECT ANSWER IN THE SPACE AT THE RIGHT.*

1. The MOST important aspect of an analyst's relationship with a user is   1.____

   A. friendship   B. respect   C. comraderie
   D. knowledge   E. rapport

2. The device used MOST often to enter data into the computer is the   2.____

   A. keypunch   B. card reader   C. terminal
   D. printer   E. disk drive

3. The MOST rapidly growing segment of the computer marketplace is   3.____

   A. personal computers   B. terminals
   C. mainframes   D. mini-computers
   E. keypunch machines

4. The set of rules, guidelines, and tools that facilitate effective system analysis, design,   4.____
   and development is known as

   A. Warnier Orr methodology
   B. structured methodology
   C. Gantt chart
   D. PERT charts
   E. critical path methodology

5. Which is a DISADVANTAGE of the structured methodology?   5.____

   A. Lower maintenance costs
   B. Lower long-term costs
   C. Improved system reliability
   D. Higher design costs
   E. More flexible systems

6. Which is NOT an advantage of the structured methodology?   6.____

   A. Lower long-term costs
   B. Lower maintenance costs
   C. Wider user involvement
   D. Improved system reliability
   E. None of the above

7. Which is NOT an advantage of the structured methodology?   7.____

   A. More easily enhanced systems
   B. Fewer system failures
   C. Reduced likelihood of errors
   D. More understandable programs
   E. None of the above

8. This person was NOT a developer of the structured programming methodology.   8.____

    A. Bohm   B. Hollerith   C. Jacopini
    D. Dijkstra   E. Stevens

9. A(n) _____ is used in a data flow diagram to depict a process.   9.____

    A. square   B. line   C. circle
    D. rectangle   E. arrow

10. A(n) _____ is used to show a flow of data in a data flow diagram.   10.____

    A. square   B. parallelogram   C. trapezoid
    D. arrow   E. circle

11. The report resulting from detailed analysis is called the   11.____

    A. feasibility study   B. implementation study
    C. analysis study   D. systems study
    E. narrative analysis

12. The report resulting from the design stage is called the   12.____

    A. feasibility study   B. system specifications
    C. system audit   D. implementation plan
    E. system study

13. The final review of a completed system is called the   13.____

    A. feasibility study   B. system specifications
    C. systems study   D. system audit
    E. implementation plan

14. Ordering of any new hardware for a system would take place during   14.____

    A. analysis   B. design   C. development
    D. training   E. conversion

15. Developing operational procedures of the computer center staff would take place during   15.____

    A. analysis   B. design   C. development
    D. training   E. conversion

16. Defining the data requirements would take place during   16.____

    A. analysis   B. design   C. development
    D. training   E. conversion

17. Writing program specifications would take place during   17.____

    A. analysis   B. design   C. development
    D. training   E. conversion

18. Drawing a model of the new systems data flow would take place during   18.____

    A. analysis   B. design   C. development
    D. training   E. conversion

19. Listing costs and benefits of a new system would take place during   19.____

   A.   analysis   B.   design   C.   development
   D.   training   E.   conversion

20. MOST business applications programs are written in   20.____

   A.   FORTRAN   B.   BASIC   C.   COBOL   D.   PASCAL   E.   ADA

KEY (CORRECT ANSWERS)

1.	E	11.	A
2.	C	12.	B
3.	A	13.	D
4.	B	14.	B
5.	D	15.	C
6.	E	16.	B
7.	E	17.	B
8.	B	18.	B
9.	C	19.	A
10.	D	20.	C

EXAMINATION SECTION
TEST 1

DIRECTIONS: Each question or incomplete statement is followed by several suggested answers or completions. Select the one that BEST answers the question or completes the statement. *PRINT THE LETTER OF THE CORRECT ANSWER IN THE SPACE AT THE RIGHT.*

1. A square in a data flow diagram symbolizes   1.____

   A. a file
   B. a terminal
   C. a printer
   D. destination of data
   E. conversion of input data to output data

2. A three-sided rectangle in a data flow diagram symbolizes   2.____

   A. a file
   B. a terminal
   C. a printer
   D. destination of data
   E. conversion of input data to output data

3. A circle in a data flow diagram symbolizes   3.____

   A. a file
   B. a terminal
   C. a printer
   D. destination of data
   E. conversion of input data to output data

4. An arrow in a data flow diagram symbolizes   4.____

   A. a file
   B. a terminal
   C. the direction of data flow between processes
   D. destination of data
   E. conversion of input data to output data

5. Inputs to analysis include   5.____

   A. user needs
   B. budget
   C. schedule
   D. amount of time to complete the system
   E. all of the above

6. Outputs from analysis include   6.____

   A. budget   B. schedule
   C. documentation   D. feasibility study
   E. all of the above

7. Inputs to analysis do NOT include   7.___

    A. management funding
    B. user objectives
    C. expected costs
    D. computer services staff expertise
    E. none of the above

8. The feasibility study is output from which phase of the systems process?   8.___

    A. Development   B. Analysis   C. Design
    D. Programming   E. Database design

9. Decomposition or levelling refers to   9.___

    A. the feasibility study
    B. analysis documentation
    C. the systems study
    D. expansion of data flow diagrams to more detail levels
    E. expansion of hardware and software to solve user needs

10. The system's cycle begins with a request from   10.___

    A. a governmental body
    B. a user
    C. a trade union
    D. the custodian
    E. all of the above could initiate a system's cycle

11. Which of the following is NOT a part of preliminary analysis?   11.___

    A. Evaluation of a user request
    B. Drawing the logical system
    C. Analysis of a user request
    D. Management action
    E. All of the above are a part of preliminary analysis

12. When evaluating a user request, the analyst should NOT collect   12.___

    A. the user's name
    B. the description of the problem
    C. the problems solution
    D. the date of the request
    E. additional comments as necessary

13. In evaluating a user request, the goal is to isolate the   13.___

    A. problem   B. solution
    C. people involved   D. time to be expended
    E. cost savings

14. In evaluating the user request, the analyst will want to   14.___

    A. review the organizations sales   B. review the organizations profits
    C. review the organizations costs   D. interview the user
    E. all of the above

15. The period of time in an interview where the analyst establishes rapport is called   15.____

    A. closure   B. questioning   C. warm-up
    D. fact-finding   E. recording

16. The period of time in an interview where the analyst terminates discussion is called   16.____

    A. closure   B. questioning   C. warm-up
    D. fact-finding   E. recording

17. The period of time in an interview where the analyst states the problem and solicits responses is called   17.____

    A. closure   B. questioning   C. warm-up
    D. program review   E. initialization

18. Which of the following is NOT a part of the preliminary report?   18.____

    A. Findings
    B. Recommendations
    C. Solution to the problem
    D. Costs and schedules
    E. All of the above are a part of the preliminary report

19. An analyst must   19.____

    A. adapt to evolving technology
    B. remember that systems support people
    C. analyze an organization's needs
    D. determine the firm's requirements
    E. all of the above

20. In conducting a meeting, the analyst should   20.____

    A. prepare an agenda
    B. schedule a conference room
    C. set a time and date for the meeting
    D. invite appropriate personnel
    E. all of the above

KEY (CORRECT ANSWERS)

1.	C	11.	B
2.	A	12.	C
3.	E	13.	A
4.	C	14.	D
5.	A	15.	C
6.	E	16.	A
7.	C	17.	B
8.	B	18.	D
9.	D	19.	E
10.	E	20.	E

———

TEST 2

DIRECTIONS: Each question or incomplete statement is followed by several suggested answers or completions. Select the one that BEST answers the question or completes the statement. *PRINT THE LETTER OF THE CORRECT ANSWER IN THE SPACE AT THE RIGHT.*

1.   In conducting a meeting, the analyst should   1.____

   A.   set time limits
   B.   circulate an agenda before the meeting
   C.   avoid unnecessary meetings
   D.   see that the issues are stated
   E.   all of the above

2.   When evaluating a user request, the analyst should consider   2.____

   A.   the corporate logo
   B.   the effect of the meeting on fellow analysts
   C.   the organization's goals and objectives
   D.   the expertise of the user
   E.   all of the above

3.   Analysis can be levelled into   3.____

   A.   preliminary and future analysis
   B.   preliminary and detailed analysis
   C.   detailed and future analysis
   D.   needs assessment
   E.   hardware requirements

4.   Who approves the preliminary report?   4.____

   A.   Management   B.   The user   C.   The analyst
   D.   The government   E.   The union

5.   Who approves funding for preliminary and detailed analysis?   5.____

   A.   The user
   B.   The manager of the computer services department
   C.   Management
   D.   The analyst
   E.   None of the above

6.   Analysis documentation details   6.____

   A.   questions the analyst must ask
   B.   background information pertinent to the system
   C.   answers to interview questions
   D.   solutions that are unworkable
   E.   all of the above

7. The feasibility study details   7.____

    A. questions the analyst must ask
    B. background information pertinent to the system
    C. answers to interview questions
    D. system objectives
    E. all of the above

8. Systems developed during the 1950's were   8.____

    A. statistically or scientifically oriented
    B. mini-computer oriented
    C. micro-computer oriented
    D. user oriented
    E. all of the above

9. Systems developed during the 1980's must be   9.____

    A. network oriented
    B. user oriented
    C. user friendly
    D. micro-computer oriented
    E. all of the above

10. Once a decision to continue onto detailed analysis is made by management, all parties concerned should be notified by   10.____

    A. memorandum   B. telephone
    C. word of mouth   D. rumor
    E. a Christmas letter

11. After an interview, the analyst sends a follow-up memorandum.
Which of the following should the memorandum NOT include?   11.____

    A. Information gained
    B. Date and time of the interview
    C. Value judgments made by the analyst
    D. Names and titles of personnel interviewed
    E. None of the above

12. Follow-up memoranda help establish   12.____

    A. accuracy   B. rapport
    C. personal relationships   D. documentation
    E. all of the above

13. A preliminary report to management includes   13.____

    A. problem review and software solutions
    B. problem review and recommendations
    C. recommendations and software solutions
    D. software and hardware solution
    E. personnel change recommendations

14. A preliminary report should include 14.____

    A. transcripts of interviews
    B. all working papers collected during analysis
    C. lists of telephone calls made
    D. list of alternatives
    E. all of the above

15. After reviewing the preliminary report, management may decide to 15.____

    A. continue to detailed analysis
    B. terminate the study
    C. delay any further study for a short time
    D. choose an alternative other than the one recommended by the analyst
    E. all of the above

16. The preliminary report should be 16.____

    A. delivered verbally to management
    B. filled with computer jargon
    C. written and distributed in advance
    D. given to users for a decision
    E. given to computer services staff for decision

17. In MOST cases, management will 17.____

    A. terminate the systems process at their first opportunity
    B. choose an alternative not recommended by the analyst
    C. delay a decision for six to eight months
    D. decide to continue to detailed analysis
    E. none of the above

18. During the interview, the analyst should 18.____

    A. be a listener
    B. do all the talking
    C. make value judgments
    D. ask personal questions
    E. have a pre-determined solution in mind

19. In selecting the appropriate people to interview, the analyst should consult a(n) 19.____

    A. data flow diagram   B. entity diagram
    C. organization chart   D. organized specification chart
    E. any of the above

20. Before doing anything, the analyst should 20.____

    A. review old programs pertinent to the request
    B. review the user's request
    C. examine the user work area
    D. test the system software for proper operation
    E. talk with other analysts about the user

———

KEY (CORRECT ANSWERS)

1.	E	11.	C
2.	C	12.	E
3.	B	13.	B
4.	A	14.	D
5.	C	15.	E
6.	B	16.	C
7.	D	17.	D
8.	A	18.	A
9.	E	19.	C
10.	A	20.	B

———

EXAMINATION SECTION

TEST 1

DIRECTIONS: Each question or incomplete statement is followed by several suggested answers or completions. Select the one that BEST answers the question or completes the statement. *PRINT THE LETTER OF THE CORRECT ANSWER IN THE SPACE AT THE RIGHT.*

1.   Analysis of a system deals with   1.____
     A. study of an existing system   B. documenting an existing system
     C. only new systems   D. both A and B

2.   The primary tool that is used in structured design is known as a   2.____
     A. data flow diagram   B. module
     C. flow chart   D. structure chart

3.   Documentation is required at the _____ stage.   3.____
     A. system analysis   B. system design
     C. system development   D. every stage

4.   Which one of the following is NOT a factor in the failure of systems   4.____
     development projects?
     A. Size of the company   B. Inadequate user involvement
     C. Failure of integration   D. Both A and B

5.   Which one of the following is considered in system maintenance?   5.____
     A. System requirements   B. Analysis
     C. Testing   D. Remove faults after delivery

6.   Which one of the following cannot be used to capture a user's requirements?   6.____
     A. Interviews   B. Questionnaire
     C. Third-party inquiry   D. Observation

7.   Cost-Benefit Analysis is performed during the   7.____
     A. analysis phase   B. feasibility study
     C. design phase   D. maintenance phase

8.   System development life cycle is divided into _____ stages.   8.____
     A. five   B. four   C. six   D. seven

9.   _____ is the first stage in system development life cycle.   9.____
     A. Analysis   B. Design
     C. Problem identification   D. Development

10. The _____ determines whether a project should go forward or not.   10.____
     A. feasibility assessment   B. system evaluation
     C. program specification   D. both A and B

11. The _____ manages the system development, assigns staff, manages the budget and reporting, and ensures that deadlines are met.
    A. system analyst
    B. project manager
    C. network engineer
    D. graphic designer

11._____

12. The structure chart that is developed by studying the flow through a system assists the activities of _____ design.
    A. internal control   B. database   C. output   D. file

12._____

13. Which one of the following is an INCORRECT statement for the definition of a use case diagram?
    A. It is used to understand requirements
    B. It is an interaction between user and the system
    C. It demonstrates flow of activities
    D. It is used for requirement analysis

13._____

14. Which one of the following is NOT a relationship type in use case diagrams?
    A. Include   B. Extend   C. Aggregation   D. Association

14._____

15. A(n) _____ diagram is NOT an interaction diagram of the UML.
    A. activity   B. sequence   C. class   D. both A and B

15._____

16. Physical components of the system are modeled through a(n) _____ diagram.
    A. component   B. class   C. activity   D. use case

16._____

17. In UML, a built-in extensibility mechanism is obtained through
    A. association   B. stereotypes   C. notations   D. comments

17._____

18. Software testing that does not require knowledge of the internal code is known as _____ testing.
    A. black box   B. gray box   C. white box   D. regression

18._____

19. Total life cycle cost of a software in terms of largest percentage is called _____ cost.
    A. analysis   B. coding   C. testing   D. maintenance

19._____

20. Which one of the following is NOT a characteristic of waterfall process model?
    A. Rigid approach
    B. Sequence of activities
    C. Back-and-forth movement
    D. Less use these days

20._____

21. _____ feasibility determines the availability of support staff and team.
    A. Resource   B. Cultural   C. Economic   D. Schedule

21._____

22. Which one of the following is used to represent the schedule of a project?
    A. DFD   B. ERD   C. GANTT   D. CPM

22._____

23. _____ is not used in a context level diagram.
    A. Data store   B. Data flow   C. Process   D. Destination

23._____

24. In dynamic system development, business requirements are gathered through
    A. JAD   B. a flip chart
    C. an overhead projector   D. a board

24._____

25. A systems analyst determines the use of the system by analyzing the _____ diagram.
    A. use case   B. class   C. activity   D. sequence

25._____

KEY (CORRECT ANSWERS)

1.	D		11.	B
2.	D		12.	A
3.	D		13.	C
4.	A		14.	C
5.	D		15.	C
6.	C		16.	A
7.	B		17.	B
8.	C		18.	A
9.	C		19.	D
10.	A		20.	C

21. A
22. C
23. A
24. A
25. A

TEST 2

DIRECTIONS: Each question or incomplete statement is followed by several suggested answers or completions. Select the one that BEST answers the question or completes the statement. *PRINT THE LETTER OF THE CORRECT ANSWER IN THE SPACE AT THE RIGHT.*

1.   Data store in DFD represents
     A. disk store   B. data repository
     C. data   D. sequential file

1._____

2.   Programs, data files and documentation are an essential part of the _____ system.
     A. conceptual   B. logical   C. physical   D. data

2._____

3.   The _____ phase is very time consuming and crucial.
     A. design   B. analysis   C. development   D. testing

3._____

4.   The _____ phase of the SDLC (Software Development Life Cycle) identifies all of the required information.
     A. system analysis   B. system design
     C. testing   D. preliminary investigation

4._____

5.   The _____ provides the documentation of the new system.
     A. system analyst   B. technical writer
     C. programmer   D. requirement engineer

5._____

6.   Which one of the following implementation approaches has the LOWEST risk?
     A. Direct   B. Parallel   C. Pilot   D. Phased

6._____

7.   In the system analysis phase, _____ is/are defined.
     A. requirements   B. program specification
     C. goals   D. flow of events

7._____

8.   In UML, an optional behavior is specified when _____ relationship is used.
     A. extend   B. include   C. association   D. aggregation

8._____

9.   The _____ is NOT a participant in the requirement definition.
     A. developer   B. end user
     C. client manager   D. client engineer

9._____

10. _____ is an ongoing phase in which the system is evaluated and updated periodically.
     A. Analysis   B. Testing   C. Maintenance   D. Implementation

10._____

11. _____ is the last step in the system analysis phase.
     A. Collecting data   B. Proposing changes
     C. Analyzing data   D. System analysis report

11._____

12. Which one of the following is a fact-finding technique?   12.____
    A. Quality assurance   B. Sampling of existing documents
    C. Prototyping   D. Requirement specification

13. Data dictionary in SDLC includes description of   13.____
    A. DFD elements   B. class diagram
    C. ERD   D. component diagram

14. _____ is the graphical notation that is used in UML.   14.____
    A. Stereotype   B. Meta model   C. Model   D. Multiplicity

15. Which one of the following is used in analysis?   15.____
    A. Grid table   B. Check list
    C. Sheet   D. Interview guidelines

16. DDS is an abbreviation of   16.____
    A. Data Digital System   B. Data Dictionary System
    C. Digital Data Service   D. Data Defense System

17. Which one of the following is NOT included in DFD?   17.____
    A. Processes   B. Entities
    C. File   D. Offline storage

18. CASE stands for Computer _____ Engineering.   18.____
    A. Aided Software   B. Analysis and System
    C. Aided System   D. Analyzed System

19. The first step in application prototyping is   19.____
    A. to develop a working model   B. to identify known requirements
    C. to review prototype   D. the use of prototype

20. Which one of the following skills is NOT required for the system analyst?   20.____
    A. Management   B. Communication
    C. Technical   D. Programming

21. In SDLC, a system proposal is developed during the _____ phase.   21.____
    A. planning   B. analysis   C. design   D. development

22. Which one of the following provides fast delivery?   22.____
    A. Prototyping   B. RAD   C. Spiral   D. Iterative

23. The _____ diagram is a time-oriented diagram.   23.____
    A. sequence   B. activity   C. class   D. use case

24. The _____ diagram shows complete or partial view of the structure of a   24.____
    modeled system at a specific time.
    A. class   B. object   C. activity   D. sequence

25. Which one of the following UML diagrams shows static view of the system?   25.____
     A. Use case   B. Collaboration   C. State chart   D. Activity

_____

KEY (CORRECT ANSWERS)

1.	B		11.	D
2.	C		12.	B
3.	B		13.	A
4.	D		14.	B
5.	B		15.	B
6.	D		16.	B
7.	B		17.	D
8.	A		18.	A
9.	A		19.	B
10.	C		20.	D

21.	B
22.	B
23.	A
24.	B
25.	A

_____

TEST 3

DIRECTIONS: Each question or incomplete statement is followed by several suggested answers or completions. Select the one that BEST answers the question or completes the statement. *PRINT THE LETTER OF THE CORRECT ANSWER IN THE SPACE AT THE RIGHT.*

1. Functionality of the system is known as _____ of the system. 1.____
   A. requirement   B. business need
   C. sponsors   D. fact

2. The systems analyst determines the system usage through 2.____
   A. actors   B. use case   C. package   D. component

3. _____ occurs in use case to trigger the system. 3.____
   A. Data flow   B. Process   C. Event   D. Data store

4. The _____ system is only an idea that has yet to progress to later stages. 4.____
   A. logical   B. physical   C. conceptual   D. legacy

5. Software testing aims to 5.____
   A. uncover errors
   B. eliminate errors
   C. eliminate need of maintenance
   D. determine productivity of programmers

6. Another name used for black box testing is 6.____
   A. verification   B. validation
   C. specification-based testing   D. gray box testing

7. Which of the following diagrams is NOT a UML diagram? 7.____
   A. Broadcast   B. Component   C. State chart   D. Deployment

8. Another term for encapsulation is 8.____
   A. generalization   B. polymorphism
   C. information hiding   D. association

9. _____ is not a characteristic of an object. 9.____
   A. Identity   B. Behavior   C. Action   D. State

10. In feasibility study, the _____ feasibility always focuses on the existing computer hardware and software. 10.____
   A. logical   B. behavior   C. economic   D. technical

11. In SDLC, the last step in the development phase is 11.____
   A. documentation   B. testing the system
   C. acquiring hardware   D. acquiring software

12. In a DFD, external entities are represented by a(n)   12.____
    A. eclipse   B. circle   C. rectangle   D. diamond

13. _____ means using an old system and new system simultaneously to   13.____
    compare the result.
    A. File conversion   B. Parallel operation
    C. Procedure writing   D. Simultaneous processing

14. _____ specification is prepared after the design phase.   14.____
    A. System   B. Performance   C. Design   D. Code

15. System _____ is the MOST comprehensive and recent technique to solve   15.____
    computer problems.
    A. analysis   B. data   C. procedure   D. record

16. A data flow diagram is a basic component of the _____ system.   16.____
    A. physical   B. logical   C. conceptual   D. real

17. Enhancements, upgrades and bug fixes are done at the _____ phase of   17.____
    SDLC.
    A. development   B. identification
    C. design   D. maintenance and evaluation

18. In a system analyst's job, identification of requirement specifications is similar   18.____
    to _____ a building.
    A. an architect designing   B. a structural engineer designing
    C. a contractor constructing   D. the workers who construct

19. It is essential to consult with _____ when drawing requirement specifications.   19.____
    A. only managers
    B. only top and middle management
    C. operational managers
    D. top, middle and operational managers and also all who will use the
       system

20. A feasibility study is carried out by the   20.____
    A. system analyst
    B. manager
    C. technical writer
    D. system analyst in consultation with managers of the organization

21. A class is a description of a set of objects that share the same   21.____
    A. attributes, behavior and operations
    B. identity, behavior and state
    C. attributes, operations and relationships
    D. relationship, operation and multiplicity

22. A(n) _____ diagram is an interaction diagram that involves time ordering   22._____
    messages.
    A. sequence   B. collaboration C. activity   D. state

23. _____ measures the strength of association among objects.   23._____
    A. Cohesion   B. Coupling
    C. Interaction   D. Collaboration

24. _____ is a combination of data and logic that represents some real-world   24._____
    entities.
    A. Class   B. Attribute   C. Object   D. Relationship

25. A _____ diagram represents the hierarchal relationship between the modules   25._____
    of a computer program.
    A. state chart   B. data flow   C. class   D. activity

KEY (CORRECT ANSWERS)

1.	A		11.	B
2.	B		12.	C
3.	C		13.	B
4.	C		14.	C
5.	A		15.	A
6.	C		16.	B
7.	A		17.	D
8.	C		18.	A
9.	C		19.	D
10.	D		20.	D

21.	C
22.	A
23.	B
24.	C
25.	A

TEST 4

DIRECTIONS: Each question or incomplete statement is followed by several suggested answers or completions. Select the one that BEST answers the question or completes the statement. *PRINT THE LETTER OF THE CORRECT ANSWER IN THE SPACE AT THE RIGHT.*

1. System approval criteria is specified
   A. during the feasibility study
   B. when the final specifications are drawn up
   C. during system study stage
   D. during requirement specification stage

   1.____

2. The PRIMARY objective of system design is to
   A. implement the system
   B. design user interface
   C. find functionality
   D. design the program, database and test plan

   2.____

3. Whenever _____ are changed, the system must be modified.
   A. user requirements   B. test plans
   C. software   D. companies

   3.____

4. What is MOST important when modifying an existing system?
   A. Software tools   B. Hardware
   C. Programming   D. System design at low cost

   4.____

5. Managers cannot design their own system because
   A. this is not their job
   B. they are busy
   C. they don't have required skills for system analysis
   D. the system is novel

   5.____

6. System components can be represented through
   A. DFD   B. PERT   C. GANTT   D. ERD

   6.____

7. Which one of the following cannot be included in phase four of SDLC?
   A. User training   B. Testing
   C. Conducting interviews   D. Acquiring hardware/software

   7.____

8. Programmers use _____ to summarize and organize results of problem analysis.
   A. a flow chart   B. an input chart
   C. an output chart   D. HIPO

   8.____

9. Coding and testing are done in a(n) _____ manner.
   A. top-down   B. bottom-up   C. ad hoc   D. cross-sectional

   9.____

10. _____ is the FIRST step in the problem-solving process.
    A. Algorithm planning   B. Problem analysis
    C. Evaluation   D. Modification

10.____

11. Any mistake in system analysis will be exposed during
    A. implementation   B. design   C. development   D. maintenance

11.____

12. Which one of the following does NOT belong to the implementation phase?
    A. User training   B. File conversion
    C. Program testing   D. Designing

12.____

13. File conversion is related to system
    A. design   B. development C. analysis   D. implementation

13.____

14. _____ is NOT used in the design phase of the system.
    A. Data flow   B. Decision table
    C. Flow chart   D. Pie chart

14.____

15. Which one of the following is NOT used for system analysis?
    A. Decision table   B. Flow charts
    C. Data flow diagrams   D. System-test data

15.____

16. Initial requirement specification is
    A. not changed until the end of the project
    B. is subject to change continuously
    C. only a rough indication of the requirements
    D. finalized after the feasibility study

16.____

17. System test plan is specified when
    A. final specifications are done   B. a feasibility study is completed
    C. analysis is done   D. design is done

17.____

18. The organization chart is a type of _____ chart.
    A. basic   B. state   C. flow   D. hieratical

18.____

19. Structure of an organization could be shown through a(n)
    A. state chart   B. HIPO
    C. data flow   D. organization chart

19.____

20. A(n) _____ diagram represents static behavior of the system.
    A. class   B. object   C. flow chart   D. both A and B

20.____

21. Which one of the following diagrams is similar to a flow chart?
    A. Sequence   B. Use case   C. Activity   D. Class

21.____

22. A(n) _____ diagram is not a structural diagram in UML.
    A. class   B. component   C. object   D. use case

22.____

23. A _____ diagram is an example of a behavior diagram. 23.____
    A. collaboration   B. class   C. component   D. deployment

24. The purpose of a(n) _____ diagram is to visualize the organization of 24.____
    objects and their interaction.
    A. collaboration   B. object   C. class   D. activity

25. _____ is used in a class diagram to represent the concurrency of the system. 25.____
    A. Class   B. Activity class
    C. Super class   D. Object

KEY (CORRECT ANSWERS)

1.	B		11.	A
2.	D		12.	C
3.	A		13.	D
4.	D		14.	D
5.	C		15.	D
6.	A		16.	C
7.	C		17.	A
8.	D		18.	D
9.	A		19.	D
10.	B		20.	A

21.	C
22.	D
23.	A
24.	A
25.	B

EXAMINATION SECTION
TEST 1

DIRECTIONS: Each question or incomplete statement is followed by several suggested answers or completions. Select the one the BEST answers the question or completes the statement. *PRINT THE LETTER OF THE CORRECT ANSWER IN THE SPACE AT THE RIGHT.*

1. Object-oriented programming languages include each of the following, EXCEPT   1.____

    A. Java
    B. Ada
    C. Smalltalk
    D. C++

2. _____ is a programming language that is good for processing numerical data, but does   2.____
not lend itself very well to organizing large programs.

    A. Pascal
    B. Java
    C. FORTRAN
    D. COBOL

3. Which of the following is a method for insuring that a transmitted message has not been   3.____
tampered with?

    A. Indexing
    B. Hashing
    C. Stringing
    D. Spoofing

4. Many expert systems use _____ programming, which is characterized by programs that   4.____
are self-learning.

    A. algorithmic
    B. natural-language
    C. heuristic
    D. neural

5. Data transfer rates for devices such as hard disks are typically measured in   5.____

    A. Kbps
    B. KBps
    C. Mbps
    D. MBps

6. The most powerful way of requesting information from a database is through the use of   6.____
a(n)

    A. query language
    B. menu parameter(s)
    C. query by example (QBE)
    D. query string

7. A network of computers located within a limited geographic area usually, a single building or group of buildingsis known as a(n)

    A. Server farm
    B. LAN
    C. MAN
    D. token ring

    7.___

8. Viewing video presentations on the Web sometimes requires the use of an additional software program that adds functionality to a browser. This program is called a(n)

    A. plug-in
    B. grain
    C. applet
    D. script

    8.___

9. In a _____ attack, a criminal exploits limits in the TCP/IP protocol to flood a network with useless traffic and bring it to a standstill.

    A. spoofing
    B. denial-of-service
    C. wire closet
    D. logic bomb

    9.___

10. What is the term used for the technique used by some Web sites to deliver one page to a search engine for indexing while serving an entirely different page to everyone else?

    A. Diddling
    B. Port scanning
    C. Spamming
    D. Cloaking

    10.___

11. _____ is a method for checking data transmission errors in which bits are added to the message and then compared against a bit that says whether the sum should be odd or even.

    A. Cyclic redundancy checking
    B. Parity checking
    C. Checksum
    D. MNP

    11.___

12. A storage device's most important performance attribute is measured as

    A. latency
    B. access time
    C. permanence
    D. density

    12.___

13. Most contemporary personal computers contain a CPU with a register that is _____ bits wide.

    A. 8   B. 16   C. 32   D. 64

    13.___

14. A Web user wants to use a search engine for a particular color or pattern. What type of search should be used?   14.____

   A. Image content
   B. Raster-pixel
   C. Keyword
   D. Picot

15. An important difference between a router and a switcher is that a router   15.____

   A. does not perform error correction
   B. operates in software
   C. often suffers from interference
   D. is selective about the type of data it handles

16. Which of the following terms differs from the others in meaning?   16.____

   A. Software interrupt
   B. Exception
   C. Burst
   D. Trap

17. Which of the following is a database, used by the Windows operating system, that contains information about installed peripherals and software?   17.____

   A. Configuration
   B. Registry
   C. Finder
   D. Directory

18. A network server typically uses its own _____ to manage the flow of network data.   18.____

   A. RAM cache
   B. database management system
   C. virtual memory
   D. operating system

19. Which of the following types of firewall techniques applies security mechanisms whenever a TCP or UDP connection is made?   19.____

   A. Packet filter
   B. Proxy server
   C. Application gateway
   D. Circuit-level gateway

20. The frequent creation, deletion, and modification of files on a computer hard drive often leads to the condition known as   20.____

   A. clustering
   B. optimization
   C. partitioning
   D. fragmentation

21. Engineers or architects often use an output device known as a _____ to create large drawings.
    21.___

    A. banner
    B. LED printer
    C. plotter
    D. thermal printer

22. In most application software, utilities such as the spell checker are usually included in the _____ menu.
    22.___

    A. file
    B. edit
    C. help
    D. tools

23. The primary factor driving the use of telephone networks for the provision of Internet services throughout its first two decades was
    23.___

    A. collusion between ISPs and telephone companies
    B. a lack of more suitable technologies
    C. the widespread availability of hardware and protocols
    D. the existence of analog coding for data

24. CPU clock speeds are expressed in
    24.___

    A. nanoseconds
    B. MHz
    C. seconds
    D. Mbps

25. If a filename includes an extension, a(n) _____ separates the extension from the rest of the filename.
    25.___

    A. period
    B. backslash
    C. parentheses
    D. space

26. Database software that uncovers previously unknown relationships among data—for example, that would reveal customers with common interests—is described as _____ software.
    26.___

    A. drilldown
    B. warehousing
    C. on-line analytical processing (OLAP)
    D. data mining

27. Which of the following is a technology that combines the guaranteed delivery of circuit-switched networks and the robustness and efficiency of packet-switching networks?
    27.___

    A. Frame relay
    B. DWDM
    C. SONET
    D. ATM

28. Advantages of vector graphics over bitmapped graphics include   28.____
    - I.   easier manipulation of images
    - II. smaller memory requirements
    - III. greater scalability
    - IV. more refined output

    A. I and II
    B. II only
    C. II and III
    D. I, II, III and IV

29. Which of the following types of translator programs works on one line of source code at a   29.____
    time before execution?

    A. modulator
    B. assembler
    C. compiler
    D. interpreter

30. The protocol developed by Netscape for transmitting private documents over the Internet   30.____
    is

    A. Secure HTTP
    B. IPsec
    C. Secure Sockets Layer (SSL)
    D. Layer 2 Tunneling Protocol (L2TP)

31. _____ specifies the format of URLs and the procedure clients and servers follow to   31.____
    communicate.

    A. TCP/IP
    B. FTP
    C. HTTP
    D. HTML

32. In the 1990s, significant advancements were made in each of the following portable com-   32.____
    puting technologies, EXCEPT

    A. graphics
    B. battery performance
    C. networking capabilities
    D. storage capacity

33. Each of the following is a multimedia input device, EXCEPT   33.____

    A. image scanner
    B. digital camera
    C. microphone
    D. video camcorder

34. In a _____ network, there is no file server.   34.___

    A. two-tier
    B. three-tier
    C. peer-to-peer
    D. thin client

35. When an operating system runs different parts of a program on different processors, it is   35.___
    performing

    A. multiprocessing
    B. multitasking
    C. multithreading
    D. task switching

36. Hard disks   36.___
    I.   generally allow for a high density of bits
    II. are much faster than floppy disks
    III. can improve their performance through caching
    IV. are the most economical form of storage

    A. I and II
    B. I, II and III
    C. II, III and IV
    D. I, II, III and IV

37. To represent a single color on a computer screen, at least _____ color values must be   37.___
    used.

    A. 2
    B. 3
    C. 4
    D. 5

38. The increasing popularity of the Linux operating system has been due to the fact that it is   38.___
    I.   available for free
    II. platform-independent
    III. more secure than other operating systems
    IV. more user-friendly than other operating systems

    A. I and II
    B. I, II and III
    C. II only
    D. I, II, III and IV

39. The total package of protocols that specifies how a specific network functions is known   39.___
    as the protocol

    A. suite
    B. train
    C. stack
    D. milieu

40. Another term for the autonumber field in a database management system is _____ field.

    40.____

    A. calculated
    B. key
    C. counter
    D. computational

41. Operating systems can be used to

    41.____

    I. communicate with a printer
    II. format disks
    III. control the mouse cursor
    IV. save files

    A. I and II
    B. II and III
    C. II, III and IV
    D. I, II, III and IV

42. XML is a development in networking technology whose most significant contribution is in the area of

    42.____

    A. functionality
    B. scalability
    C. economy
    D. interoperability

43. The most significant difference between computer viruses and Trojan horses is that

    43.____

    A. Trojan horses are not destructive
    B. Trojan horses do not replicate themselves
    C. most firewalls are not built to withstand Trojan horses
    D. viruses are not disguised as useful programs

44. Slide presentation applications such as PowerPoint allow users to resize a frame within a slide by means of dragging

    44.____

    A. text
    B. borders
    C. handles
    D. flaps

45. Each of the following serve to translate object code into machine language, EXCEPT

    45.____

    A. binders
    B. linkers
    C. assemblers
    D. compilers

46. The most important difference between the Macintosh operating system and MS-DOS is the   46.___

   A. memory requirements
   B. functionality of drivers
   C. interface
   D. multitasking capabilities

47. Which of the following is a looser, more basic way of organizing data in order to support management decision-making?   47.___

   A. Data mart
   B. Data mine
   C. Data vault
   D. Data warehouse

48. What is the term for the amount of data that can be transmitted over a network during a fixed period of time?   48.___

   A. Bandwidth
   B. Frequency
   C. Packet volume
   D. Amplitude

49. The OSI (Open System Interconnection) model defines a networking framework for implementing protocols in seven layers. The first layer of the OSI model consists of   49.___

   A. the network
   B. transport
   C. applications
   D. hardware/physical components

50. Many paint and draw programs organize complex drawings by means of tools known as   50.___

   A. vectors
   B. sectors
   C. layers
   D. models

KEY (CORRECT ANSWERS)

1.	B	11.	B	21.	C	31.	C	41.	D
2.	C	12.	B	22.	D	32.	B	42.	D
3.	B	13.	C	23.	C	33.	A	43.	B
4.	C	14.	A	24.	B	34.	C	44.	C
5.	D	15.	B	25.	A	35.	A	45.	D
6.	A	16.	C	26.	D	36.	B	46.	C
7.	B	17.	B	27.	D	37.	B	47.	D
8.	A	18.	D	28.	C	38.	A	48.	A
9.	B	19.	D	29.	D	39.	A	49.	D
10.	D	20.	D	30.	C	40.	C	50.	C

TEST 2

DIRECTIONS: Each question or incomplete statement is followed by several suggested answers or completions. Select the one the BEST answers the question or completes the statement. *PRINT THE LETTER OF THE CORRECT ANSWER IN THE SPACE AT THE RIGHT.*

1.   The "physical layer" of a network would include each of the following, EXCEPT   1.___

    A.   RAM
    B.   Error correction
    C.   Virtual memory
    D.   Data organization on disk

2.   Servers   2.___

    A.   are not designed to be used directly by the user
    B.   function solely to manage network traffic
    C.   often perform tasks other than their server tasks
    D.   are not "computers" in the strictest sense of the word

3.   Advantages of using RISC CPUs in personal computers include   3.___
        I.   fewer transistors required
      II.   rapid execution of instructions
     III.   smaller burden placed on software

    A.   I only
    B.   I and II
    C.   II and III
    D.   I, II and III

4.   Which of the following is NOT an example of middleware?   4.___

    A.   Object request broker (ORB)
    B.   Web server
    C.   TP monitor
    D.   Database access system

5.   The main disadvantage to the bus network topology is its   5.___

    A.   centralized point of failure
    B.   high data error frequency
    C.   tendency to bottleneck
    D.   extensive cabling

6.   Java, C++, and Perl are examples of   6.___

    A.   query languages
    B.   program languages
    C.   markup languages
    D.   application programs

7. The most significant obstacle organizations face when they try to implement ERP software is

   7.____

   A. training personnel
   B. data migration
   C. reshaping business practices to conform to the system
   D. managing the up-front hardware investment

8. A storage disk's concentric circles of information, or tracks, are divided into subsections known as

   8.____

   A. arcs   B. blocks   C. sectors   D. radii

9. In the client-server architecture, an ORB is sometimes necessary to

   9.____

   A. provide error-checking between client and server
   B. translate the languages and protocols of distributed elements
   C. patrol the firewalls surrounding network servers
   D. help the client locate a file on a particular server

10. An office worker is proofreading a speech transcribed by a colleague. The previous worker has repeatedly and consistently misspelled the word "fiscal" as "physical." In a word processing application, the tool for automatically changing each of the misspellings is the

   10.____

   A. undo command
   B. find and replace
   C. cut and paste
   D. spelling and grammar checker

11. The programs that enable a computer and its peripheral devices to function smoothly are known collectively as the

   11.____

   A. operating system
   B. BIOS
   C. system software
   D. driver set

12. The act of registering a popular Internet address—usually a company name-with the intent of selling it to its rightful owner is known as

   12.____

   A. spoofing
   B. steganography
   C. warchalking
   D. cybersquatting

13. A relational database management system (RDBMS) is BEST described as a database that

   13.____

   A. groups related fields together in a single table
   B. organized around groups of records that have a common field value
   C. stores data in a set of associated tables
   D. helps to analyze large clusters of records

14. In object-oriented programming, a class of objects sometimes uses portions of another class in order to extend its functionality. This is a process known as

   A. inheritance
   B. annexation
   C. overlay
   D. torque

14.__

15. In digital communications, the assurance that a transferred message has been sent and received by the parties claiming to have sent and received the message is known as

   A. nonrepudiation
   B. private key encryption
   C. packet sniffing
   D. certification

15.__

16. In the hexadecimal coding system, the sequence 01001000 would represent

   A. ABC
   B. 2AC
   C. 48
   D. 136

16.__

17. The most important impact of legacy applications on software developers is a(n)

   A. large amount of time spent rewriting old code
   B. complication of bundled sales
   C. necessity for sticking with an older programming language
   D. limit placed on the functionality of new software

17.__

18. Copyrighted software that is delivered/downloaded free of charge, but requires a registration free for those who decide to keep it and use it, is known as

   A. abandonware
   B. freeware
   C. public-domain software
   D. shareware

18.__

19. _____ is a programming language that embodies powerful object-oriented features, but is complex and difficult to learn.

   A. C++
   B. Java
   C. Pascal
   D. COBOL

19.__

20. A router detects network congestion in each of the following ways, EXCEPT

   A. average queue lengths
   B. choke packet totals
   C. percentage of buffers in use
   D. line utilization

20.__

21. A Web site or service that offers a broad array of resources and services, such as e-mail, forums, search engines, and on-line shopping mallsis often referred to as a(n)

    A. site map
    B. browser
    C. host
    D. portal

21.____

22. In most Web page design software,
    I. a WYSIWYG interface is used
    II. the user is required to answer all given questions before results can be viewed
    III. the software produces HTML code
    IV. hotspots are created

    A. I and III
    B. I, III and IV
    C. II, III and IV
    D. I, II, III and IV

22.____

23. The primary difference between XML and HTML is that XML

    A. is tied to a particular applications and hardware types
    B. specifies what each data tag means
    C. contains built-in security features
    D. uses tags only to delimit items of data, and leaves interpretation up to the application that created a file

23.____

24. In draw programs, each line in a drawing is defined as a

    A. voxel
    B. bitmap
    C. pixel
    D. vector

24.____

25. "Distributions" of the Linux operating system include each of the following, EXCEPT

    A. Corel
    B. Solaris
    C. Red Hat
    D. Debian

25.____

26. Depending on the operating system, filenames may
    I. include extensions that indicate the type of file
    II. be limited in length
    III. not be permitted to use certain characters
    IV. make use of "wildcard" characters for selecting multiple files with a single selection

    A. I only
    B. I, II and III
    C. II and III
    D. I, II, III and IV

26.____

27. The "fax revolution" came about by the gradual blending of telecommunications, optical scanning, and printing technologies into a single device. This is an example of the phenomenon known as   27.__

    A. synergy
    B. coincidence
    C. asymmetry
    D. convergence

28. The security protocol most widely deployed over virtual private networks is   28.__

    A. IPsec
    B. Layer 2 tunneling protocol (L2TP)
    C. Point-to-point tunneling protocol (PPTP)
    D. Secure sockets layer (SSL)

29. The SVGA display standard supports a resolution of   29.__

    A. 640 x 480
    B. 720 x 400
    C. 800 x 600
    D. 1024 x 768

30. The expansion problems of the bus network topology are most easily solved by introducing a hub and forming a _____ topology.   30.__

    A. star
    B. line
    C. ring
    D. tree

31. When an operating system runs different parts of a program on the same processor at different times, it is performing   31.__

    A. multithreading
    B. time-sharing
    C. task switching
    D. multiprocessing

32. For long distance links, the most suitable wireless technology is   32.__

    A. radio frequencies
    B. infrared
    C. microwaves
    D. optics

33. In packet-switching networks, packets contain each of the following, EXCEPT their   33.__

    A. route through the network
    B. address of origin
    C. destination address
    D. data

34. The unit of information that precedes a data object in packet transmission, and which   34._____
    contains transparent information about the file or transmission, is the

    A. payload   B. comptroller   C. hash   D. header

35. What is the general term for a message given to a Web browser by a Web server?   35._____

    A. Trojan horse
    B. Cookie
    C. Token
    D. Spyware

36. In the URL *http://www.technophobia.com/index.html,* the domain name is   36._____

    A. .com
    B. technophobia.com
    C. http://www.technophobia.com
    D. technophobia

37. The purpose of a driver is to   37._____

    A. keep the CPU running at a minimum clock speed
    B. keep the bus free of interference
    C. enable the operating system to communicate with a device
    D. manage memory

38. Data on the Internet can often be manipulated dishonestly to further the agenda of the   38._____
    people using the data. Such methods of data manipulation include
         I. standard deviation
         II. false relevance
         III. skewed sample
         IV. deduction

    A. I and II
    B. II and III
    C. II, III and IV
    D. I, II, III and IV

39. Any circuit board in a computer that is attached directly to another board is known as a(n)   39._____

    A. controller board
    B. expansion board
    C. adapter
    D. daughtercard

40. Which of the following types of viruses propagates by means of an infected program and   40._____
    installs itself on the first sector of the hard disk?

    A. Trojan horse
    B. Worm
    C. MBR virus
    D. Macro virus

41. Currently, the greatest advances in the field of artificial intelligence have occurred in the field of   41.___

    A.   games playing
    B.   neural networks
    C.   robotics
    D.   expert systems

42. Most laser printers require about _____ MB of RAM to print a full-page graphic at 300 dpi.   42.___

    A.   1
    B.   2
    C.   3
    D.   5

43. In a database application, a _____ check validation would ensure that a worker's benefit eligibility status was entered into a field, rather than his/her salary or other information.   43.___

    A.   consistency
    B.   format
    C.   range
    D.   sequence

44. Heuristic programs   44.___

    A.   are based on mathematically provable procedures
    B.   don't usually improve over time
    C.   don't always reach the very best result, but usually produce a good result
    D.   are most widely used in scientific modeling

45. Which of the following types of computer programs are most susceptible to virus attacks?   45.___

    A.   Operating systems
    B.   Database applications
    C.   Compilers
    D.   Web design applications

46. The main problem with having a "fragmented" hard disk is that   46.___

    A.   retrieving data can be much slower
    B.   the magnetic charge on the disk is weakened
    C.   the disk cache is inhibited by interference
    D.   it becomes impossible to move data from one location to another

47. The OSI (Open System Interconnection) model defines a networking framework for implementing protocols in seven layers. The _____ layer, or layer 5, establishes, manages and terminates connections between applications.   47.___

    A.   Transport
    B.   Data link
    C.   Session
    D.   Network

48. Management information systems are typically written in

    A. FORTRAN
    B. C
    C. COBOL
    D. BASIC

49. Because each command is executed independently, without any knowledge of the commands that came before it, HTTP is described as a(n) _____ protocol.

    A. shallow
    B. isolate
    C. stateless
    D. marooned

50. Advantages of fiber optic communications over traditional metal lines include

    I. greater bandwidth
    II. more lightweight
    III. less interference
    IV. sturdier and more durable

    A. I only
    B. I, II, III
    C. II and III
    D. I, II, III and IV

———

KEY (CORRECT ANSWERS)

1. C	11. C	21. D	31. B	41. A
2. A	12. D	22. B	32. C	42. A
3. B	13. C	23. D	33. A	43. B
4. B	14. A	24. D	34. D	44. C
5. A	15. A	25. B	35. B	45. A
6. B	16. C	26. D	36. B	46. A
7. C	17. D	27. D	37. C	47. C
8. C	18. D	28. A	38. B	48. C
9. B	19. A	29. C	39. D	49. C
10. B	20. B	30. A	40. C	50. B

———

EXAMINATION SECTION
TEST 1

DIRECTIONS: Each question or incomplete statement is followed by several suggested answers or completions. Select the one that BEST answers the question or completes the statement. *PRINT THE LETTER OF THE CORRECT ANSWER IN THE SPACE AT THE RIGHT.*

1. A microprocessor includes media for each of the following EXCEPT   1.____

   A. secondary storage   B. control
   C. logic   D. memory

2. Which of the following protocols is LEAST likely to be used in a wide–area network   2.____
   (WAN)?

   A. SNA   B. Token passing
   C. TCP/IP   D. DEC DNA

3. In an expert system, the rule base is sometimes searched using a strategy that begins   3.____
   with a hypothesis and seeks out more information until the hypothesis is either proved or
   disproved. This strategy is known as

   A. backward chaining
   B. key fielding
   C. indexed sequential access
   D. process specification

4. The meaning of signs, symbols, messages or systems are involved in a body of inquiry   4.____
   known as

   A. linguistics   B. semantics
   C. communications   D. syntactics

5. Which of the following is a query language?   5.____

   A. Nomad   B. Ideal   C. Systat   D. RPG–III

6. Which of the following is the typical unit of measurement used by systems designers to   6.____
   estimate the length of time needed to complete a project?

   A. Data–week   B. Man–hour
   C. File–hour   D. Man–month

7. Which of the following is the oldest professional computer society in the United States?   7.____

   A. Data Processing Management Association (DPMA)
   B. Institute for Certification of Computer Professionals (ICP)
   C. Association of Computing Machinery (ACM)
   D. Information Technology Association of America (ITAA)

8. Which of the following terms is commonly used to describe the interaction of people and   8.____
   machines in the work environment, especially in terms of job design and health issues?

   A. Connectivity   B. Ergonomics
   C. Feasibility   D. Interface

9. Which of the following is a likely application of the sensitivity analysis models of a decision–support system?   9.___

    A. Forecasting sales
    B. Determining the proper product mix within a given market
    C. Predicting the actions of competitors
    D. Goal seeking

10. What is the term for the temporary storage location in a control unit where small amounts of data or instructions reside for thousandths of a second just before use?   10.___

    A. Cache   B. Register   C. Sector   D. Buffer

11. Systems whose behavior includes options without specification of probabilities within the system are described as   11.___

    A. runaway   B. possibilistic
    C. stochastic   D. probabilistic

12. The physical devices and software that link various hardware components and transfer data from one physical location to another are known collectively as   12.___

    A. cyberspace
    B. wide–area networks
    C. telecommunications technology
    D. semantic networks

13. Which of the following is a tangible benefit associated with organizational information systems?   13.___

    A. Streamlined operations   B. Higher asset utilization
    C. Inventory reduction   D. Improved planning

14. Which of the following is NOT generally considered to be a physical component of an MIS?   14.___

    A. Personnel   B. Information
    C. Procedures   D. Software

15. Any undesired information in a communication channel which is not part of the intended message is typically referred to as   15.___

    A. resistance   B. noise
    C. data error   D. cross–talk

16. Which of the following is the ASCII 8–bit binary code for the number 1?   16.___

    A. 0001 0001   B. 0101 0001
    C. 0000 1000   D. 1001 0001

17. Which of the following is a method of organizing expert system knowledge into chunks in which relationships are based on shared characteristics determined by the user?   17.___

    A. Indexing   B. GUI
    C. Batch processing   D. Frames

18. Which of the following is a telecommunications requirement that is particular to the task   18.____
    of on–line data entry?

    A.   High–capacity video and data capabilities
    B.   Infrequent, high–volume bursts of information
    C.   Instant response
    D.   Direct response

19. What is the term for the technology which breaks blocks of text into small fixed bundles of   19.____
    data and routes them in an economical way through an available communications chan-
    nel?

    A.   Optical character recognition
    B.   Frame relay
    C.   Packet switching
    D.   Branch exchange

20. A transaction processing system rejects a transaction on the basis that it includes a   20.____
    Social Security number which contains an alphabetic character. This is an example of
    a(n) _____ check.

    A.   reasonableness   B.   format
    C.   dependency   D.   existence

21. The smallest unit of data for defining an image in a computer is the   21.____

    A.   byte   B.   pixel   C.   quark   D.   bit

22. In a microcomputer, which of the following transmits signals specifying whether to read or   22.____
    write data from a given primary storage address, input device, or output device?

    A.   Control bus   B.   Address bus
    C.   Data bus   D.   CPU

23. Which of the following stages occurs the LATEST in the traditional systems life cycle   23.____
    model?

    A.   Systems study   B.   Programming
    C.   Design   D.   Project definition

24. The fastest and most expensive memory used in a microcomputer is located in the   24.____

    A.   cache   B.   register   C.   hard disk   D.   RAM

25. Which of the following is an optical disk system that allows users to record data only   25.____
    once, but to read the data indefinitely?

    A.   WORM   B.   EPROM   C.   RAM   D.   TQM

4(#1)

KEY (CORRECT ANSWERS)

1.	A	11.	B
2.	B	12.	C
3.	A	13.	C
4.	B	14.	B
5.	D	15.	B
6.	D	16.	B
7.	C	17.	D
8.	B	18.	D
9.	D	19.	C
10.	B	20.	B

21.	B
22.	A
23.	B
24.	B
25.	A

———

50

TEST 2

DIRECTIONS: Each question or incomplete statement is followed by several suggested answers or completions. Select the one that BEST answers the question or completes the statement. *PRINT THE LETTER OF THE CORRECT ANSWER IN THE SPACE AT THE RIGHT.*

1. Which of the following styles of systems development is most often used for information systems at the individual level?

    1.____

    A. End–user computing
    B. Commercial software packages
    C. Prototyping
    D. Traditional life cycle

2. Which of the following is a programming language that was developed in 1956 for scientific and mathematical applications?

    2.____

    A. COBOL   B. BASIC   C. Pascal   D. FORTRAN

3. Which of the following personnel would be considered a *technical specialist* in an MIS department?

    3.____

    A. Education specialist   B. Database administrator
    C. Applications programmer   D. Systems analyst

4. Which of the following is NOT a characteristic of a fault–tolerant system?

    4.____

    A. The use of special software routines to detect hardware failures
    B. Extra memory chips, processors, and disk storage
    C. Continuous detection of bugs or program defects
    D. Hardware parts that can be removed without system disruption

5. Defining a system program in such a way that it may call itself is an example of

    5.____

    A. eudemony   B. recursion
    C. redundancy   D. artificial intelligence

6. What is the term used to enumerate the number of bits that can be processed at one time by a computer?

    6.____

    A. Data bus width   B. Word length
    C. RAM capacity   D. Bandwidth

7. Which of the following is another term for a field, or a grouping of characters into a word, group of words, or complete number?

    7.____

    A. Code   B. Byte
    C. Data element   D. File

8. A person in a multi–user system sends a message using the OSI model to another user at a different location. At the messenger's end of the system, after passing through the *session* layer of the model, the message will then enter the _____ layer.

    8.____

    A. transport   B. network
    C. presentation   D. data link

9. Which of the following is NOT a disadvantage associated with the traditional life cycle model of systems development?

    A. Time consumption   B. Oversimplification
    C. Cost   D. Inflexibility

9.___

10. Transmission speeds that would fall within the expected range of coaxial cable are _____ per second.

    A. 400 bits   B. 50 megabits
    C. 300 megabits   D. 7 gigabits

10.___

11. Which of the following is a telecommunications computer that collects and temporarily stores messages from terminals for batch transmission to the host computer?

    A. Assembler   B. Concentrator
    C. Buffer   D. Compiler

11.___

12. Which of the following is an advantage associated with the centralized or teleprocessing model of multi–user systems?

    A. Local computing   B. Scaleability
    C. Low start–up costs   D. Low technical risk

12.___

13. Software systems that can operate on different hardware platforms are referred to as _____ systems.

    A. open   B. interoperable
    C. branched   D. transmigrational

13.___

14. What is the term for the process by which the properties of a collection (i.e., of data) are described in terms of the sums of the properties of the units contained in the collection?

    A. Unity   B. Autarky
    C. Chunking   D. Aggregation

14.___

15. In systems terminology, what is the term for output that is returned to the appropriate members of an organization to help them evaluate or correct input?

    A. Exit data   B. Feedback
    C. Assessor   D. Valuation

15.___

16. The years 1957 to 1963 are generally considered to have been the _____ generation in the evolution of computer hardware technology.

    A. first   B. second   C. third   D. fourth

16.___

17. A conversion approach in which the new system completely replaces the old one on an appointed day is known as

    A. focused differentiation   B. direct cutover
    C. allied distribution   D. batch processing

17.___

18. Of the following types of business network redesign, the one that can be said to be most highly coupled is/are   18.____

    A. interenterprise system access
    B. knowledge networks
    C. EDI
    D. interenterprise process integration

19. Which of the following terms is used to describe the shape or configuration of a telecommunications network?   19.____

    A. Duplex   B. Topology
    C. Protocol   D. Transmissivity

20. Which of the following is/are recognized differences between microcomputers and workstations?   20.____
    I.   Microcomputers have more powerful mathematical processing capabilities.
    II. Microcomputers are more useful for computer–aided design (CAD).
    III. Workstations are more widely used by knowledge workers.
    IV. Workstations can more easily perform multiple tasks simultaneously.
    The CORRECT answer is:

    A. I, II   B. II, III   C. III, IV   D. II, IV

21. Which of the following signifies a tool for retrieving and transferring files from a remote computer?   21.____

    A. EDI   B. CPU   C. TCP/IP   D. FTP

22. Which of the following is a federal privacy law that applies to private institutions?   22.____

    A. Freedom of Information Act of 1968 (as amended)
    B. Privacy Act of 1974 (as amended)
    C. Privacy Protection Act of 1980
    D. Computer Matching and Privacy Protection Act of 1988

23. The main contribution of end–user systems development typically occurs in the area of   23.____

    A. productivity enhancement
    B. improved updating functions
    C. increased technical complexity
    D. improved efficiency in transaction processing

24. In cooperative processing, a mainframe and a microcomputer generally share tasks. The mainframe, however, is generally best at performing   24.____

    A. screen presentation   B. error processing
    C. data field editing   D. file input and output

25. In a systems development process, users are made active members of development
25.___
project teams, and some users are placed in charge of system training and installation.
In this case, management has made use of _____ tools.

    A. external integration   B. internal integration
    C. formal planning   D. formal control

_____

KEY (CORRECT ANSWERS)

1.	C		11.	B
2.	D		12.	D
3.	B		13.	A
4.	C		14.	D
5.	B		15.	B
6.	B		16.	B
7.	C		17.	B
8.	A		18.	B
9.	B		19.	B
10.	B		20.	C

21.	D
22.	C
23.	A
24.	D
25.	A

_____

TEST 3

DIRECTIONS: Each question or incomplete statement is followed by several suggested answers or completions. Select the one that BEST answers the question or completes the statement. *PRINT THE LETTER OF THE CORRECT ANSWER IN THE SPACE AT THE RIGHT.*

1. As a general rule, the development of a system that will be used by others can be expected to take_____ as long as the development of an individual system that will be used only by the developer.

   A. half   B. twice
   C. three times   D. five times

   1.____

2. In LANs, the token ring configuration is most useful for

   A. broadcasting messages to the entire network through a single circuit
   B. multidirectional transmissions between microcomputers or between micros and a larger computer
   C. transmissions between microcomputers and a larger computer that require a degree of traffic control
   D. transmitting large volumes of data between microcomputers

   2.____

3. Which of the following statements about expert systems is generally TRUE? They

   A. function best in lower–level clerical functions
   B. require minimal development resources
   C. are highly adaptable over time
   D. are capable of representing a wide range of causal models

   3.____

4. A middle–range machine with a RAM capacity that measures from about 10 megabytes to over 1 gigabyte is known as a

   A. microcomputer   B. minicomputer
   C. desktop computer   D. mainframe

   4.____

5. Which of the following media uses the sector method for storing data?

   A. Cache   B. Floppy disk
   C. Hard disk   D. CD–ROM

   5.____

6. When mechanisms of functional subsystems are connected causally to influence each other, they are said to be

   A. aggregated   B. coupled
   C. synchronous   D. constrained

   6.____

7. Which of the following storage media generally has the largest capacity?

   A. Cache   B. Magnetic disk
   C. Optical disk D. Magnetic tape

   7.____

8. In terms of information ethics, the mechanisms for assessing responsibility for decisions and actions are referred to as

   A. liability   B. capacity
   C. creditability D. accountability

   8.____

9. Which of the following signifies the central switching system that handles a firm's voice and digital communications?   9.___

   A. OSI   B. DSS   C. PBX   D. LAN

10. What is the term for the LAN channel technology that provides a single path for transmitting text, graphics, voice, or video data at one time?   10.___

   A. Bus   B. Baseband
   C. Firewall   D. Broadband

11. The stage in a system's life cycle in which testing, training, and conversion occur is termed   11.___

   A. evaluation   B. design
   C. installation   D. documentation

12. Which of the following is NOT a type of processor used in telecommunications systems?   12.___

   A. Coaxial cable   B. Controller
   C. Modem   D. Multiplexer

13. A database that is stored in more than one physical location is described as   13.___

   A. sequential   B. wide–area
   C. distributed   D. indexed

14. An organization decides to redesign its information system using only the components that are already available to it. In the language of systems theory, the resulting system would be described as a(n)   14.___

   A. ensemble   B. creod   C. kluge   D. cyborg

15. What is the term for an integrated circuit made by printing thousands or millions of transistors on a small silicon chip?   15.___

   A. Cache   B. Semiconductor
   C. Control unit   D. Microprocessor

16. Computer programming includes a logic pattern that allows for the repetition of certain actions while a specified condition occurs or until a certain conditions exists. This pattern is known as the   16.___

   A. object linkage   B. selection construct
   C. key field   D. iteration construct

17. Which of the following is the standard or reference model for allowing e–mail systems operating on different hardware to communicate?   17.___

   A. X.400   B. X.25   C. X.12   D. FDDI

18. Which of the following terms is used to denote circular tracks on the same vertical line within a disk pack?   18.___

   A. Track   B. Spindle   C. Sector   D. Cylinder

19. A system that is capable of listing the descriptions of each of a certain set of alternatives is described as   19.____

    A. generative   B. contingency–based
    C. smart   D. stochastic

20. Which of the following is an operating cost associated with an information system?   20.____

    A. Database establishment   B. Facilities
    C. Personnel training   D. Hardware acquisition

21. As a collaboration tool, the World Wide Web involves   21.____

    A. data that undergoes frequent updating
    B. documents predominantly authored by a single user
    C. applications with data at multiple sites
    D. applications with high security requirements

22. A mathematical formula used to translate a record's key field directly into its storage location is known as a(n) _____ algorithm.   22.____

    A. synchronous   B. genetic
    C. asynchronous   D. transform

23. Which of the following is a common DISADVANTAGE associated with outsourcing the systems development process?   23.____

    A. Loss of control over system function
    B. Increased costs
    C. Generally slow progress
    D. Increased paperwork requirements

24. Which of the following is a network topology in which all computers and other devices are connected to a central host computer?   24.____

    A. LAN   B. Star   C. Ring   D. Bus

25. In terms of information systems, *processing* means the   25.____

    A. assignment of data to certain categories for later use
    B. calculation or computation of data to arrive at a solution or conclusion
    C. conversion, manipulation, and analysis of raw input into a meaningful form
    D. collection or capture of raw data for use in an information system

---

KEY (CORRECT ANSWERS)

1.	C		11.	C
2.	D		12.	A
3.	A		13.	C
4.	B		14.	C
5.	B		15.	B
6.	B		16.	D
7.	C		17.	A
8.	D		18.	D
9.	C		19.	A
10.	B		20.	B

21.	B
22.	D
23.	A
24.	B
25.	C

———

EXAMINATION SECTION
TEST 1

DIRECTIONS: Each question or incomplete statement is followed by several suggested answers or completions. Select the one that BEST answers the question or completes the statement. *PRINT THE LETTER OF THE CORRECT ANSWER IN THE SPACE AT THE RIGHT.*

1. Representations of human knowledge used in expert systems generally include each of the following EXCEPT

    A. frames   B. semantic nets
    C. fuzzy logic   D. rules

1.____

2. Routines performed to verify input data and correct errors prior to processing are known as

    A. edit checks   B. pilots
    C. control aids   D. data audits

2.____

3. Which of the following statements about database management systems is generally FALSE?
They

    A. are able to separate logical and physical views of data
    B. eliminate data confusion by providing central control of data creation and definitions
    C. reduce data redundancy
    D. involve slight increases in program development and maintenance costs

3.____

4. In systems theory, there is a *what-if* method of treating uncertainty that explores the effect on the alternatives of environmental change. This method is generally referred to as _____ analysis.

    A. sensitivity   B. contingency
    C. a fortiori   D. systems

4.____

5. One of the core capabilities of a decision support system (DSS) is the logical and mathematical manipulation of data_____ a capability referred to as

    A. control aids   B. representations
    C. memory aids   D. operations

5.____

6. What is the term for the ability to move software from one generation of hardware to another more powerful generation?

    A. Adaptability   B. Interoperability
    C. Multitasking   D. Migration

6.____

7. In an enterprise information system, which of the following is considered to be an input control?

    A. Documentation of operating procedures
    B. Reviews of processing logs
    C. Verification of control totals
    D. Program testing

7.____

8. Low-speed transmission of data that occurs one character at a time is described as   8.___

    A. asynchronous   B. unchained
    C. phased   D. unstructured

9. Which of the following is a disadvantage associated with the use of relational databases?   9.___

    A. Limited ability to combine information from different sources
    B. Simplicity in maintenance
    C. Relatively slower speed of operation
    D. Limited flexibility regarding ad hoc queries

10. When all the elements in a system are in the same category, _____ is said to be at a minimum.   10.___

    A. uncertainty   B. synergy
    C. inefficiency   D. entropy

11. Which of the following is most likely to rely on parallel processing?   11.___

    A. Minicomputer   B. Workstation
    C. Microcomputer   D. Supercomputer

12. In imaging systems, what is the term for the device that allows a user to identify and retrieve a specific document?   12.___

    A. Forward chain   B. Index server
    C. Knowledge base   D. Search engine

13. Which of the following systems exists at the strategic level of an organization?   13.___

    A. Decision support system (DSS)
    B. Executive support system (ESS)
    C. Knowledge work system (KWS)
    D. Management information system (MIS)

14. What is the term for the secondary storage device on which a complete operating system is stored?   14.___

    A. Central Processing Unit   B. Microprocessor
    C. Optical code recognizer   D. System residence drive

15. Which of the following is NOT a type of knowledge work system (KWS)?   15.___

    A. Investment workstations
    B. Virtual reality systems
    C. Computer-aided design (CAD)
    D. Decision support system (DSS)

16. A transmission over a telecommunications network in which data can flow two ways, but in only one direction at a time, is described as   16.___

    A. simplex   B. half duplex
    C. full duplex   D. multiplex

17. The functions of knowledge workers in an organization generally include each of the following EXCEPT   17._____

    A. updating knowledge
    B. managing documentation of knowledge
    C. serving as internal consultants
    D. acting as change agents

18. The predominant programming language for business was   18._____

    A. Perl   B. COBOL   C. FORTRAN   D. SGML

19. In general, the technology associated with reduced instruction set (RISC) computers is most appropriate for   19._____

    A. decision support systems (DSS)
    B. network communications
    C. scientific and workstation computing
    D. desktop publishing

20. Which of the following signifies the international reference model for linking different types of computers and networks?   20._____

    A. WAN   B. ISDN   C. TCP/IP   D. OSI

21. The main difference between neural networks and expert systems is that neural networks   21._____

    A. seek a generalized capability to learn
    B. program solutions
    C. are aimed at solving one specific problem at a time
    D. seek to emulate or model a person's way of solving a set of problems

22. Which of the following is not a management benefit associated with end-user development of information systems?   22._____

    A. Reduced application backlog
    B. Increased user satisfaction
    C. Simplified testing and documentation procedures
    D. Improved requirements determination

23. Which of the following is NOT an example of an output control associated with information systems?   23._____

    A. Balancing output totals with input and processing totals
    B. formal procedures and documentation specifying recipients of reports and checks
    C. Error handling
    D. Review of computer processing logs

24. Of the following statements about the evolutionary planning method of strategic information systems design, which is FALSE?   24.____
    It is

    A. a top-down method
    B. high adaptive
    C. best for use in a dynamic environment
    D. susceptible to domination by a few users

25. In a relational database, a row or record is referred to as a(n)   25.____

    A. applet   B. key field
    C. tuple   D. bitmap

KEY (CORRECT ANSWERS)

1.	C		11.	D
2.	A		12.	B
3.	D		13.	B
4.	B		14.	D
5.	D		15.	D
6.	D		16.	B
7.	C		17.	B
8.	A		18.	B
9.	C		19.	C
10.	A		20.	D

21.	A
22.	C
23.	C
24.	A
25.	C

TEST 2

DIRECTIONS: Each question or incomplete statement is followed by several suggested answers or completions. Select the one that BEST answers the question or completes the statement. *PRINT THE LETTER OF THE CORRECT ANSWER IN THE SPACE AT THE RIGHT.*

1. The technical staff of an organization are most likely to be users of a(n)   1.____

   A. transaction processing system (TPS)
   B. management information system (MIS)
   C. decision support system (DSS)
   D. knowledge work system (KWS)

2. The predefined packet of data in some LANs, which includes data indicating the sender,   2.____
   receiver, and whether the packet is in use, is known as a

   A. bus   B. check   C. token   D. parity

3. Which of the following is NOT a typical characteristic of hypertext and hypermedia appli-   3.____
   cations?

   A. Users given commands to delete frames
   B. Independence from GUI environment
   C. Frames displayed in windows
   D. In shared systems, concurrent access to hypermedia data

4. Which of the following is a commercial digital information service that exists to provide   4.____
   business information?

   A. Prodigy   B. Dialog   C. Quotron   D. Lexis

5. Which of the following is NOT a characteristic of an enterprise MIS?   5.____

   A. Standardization
   B. Requires systems managers
   C. Homogeneous data
   D. Supports multiple applications

6. In workgroup information systems, the simplest type of group conferencing is referred to   6.____
   as a(n)

   A. videoconference   B. group meeting
   C. asynchronous meeting   D. electronic bulletin board

7. Which of the following is an advantage associated with the LAN model of multi-user sys-   7.____
   tems?

   A. Reliability of many computers
   B. Unlimited performance
   C. Centralized control
   D. Relative independence from technology

8. The main advantage of digital private branch exchanges over other local networking   8.____
   options is that they

A. make use of existing phone lines
B. have a greater geographical range
C. perform important traffic control functions
D. can generally transmit larger volumes of data

9. In a typical organization, tactical and operational planning of an MIS would be the responsibility of the

9.___

A. steering committee and MIS managers
B. project teams
C. operations personnel and end users
D. chief information officer

10. _____ code is the term for program instructions written in a high-level language before translation into machine language.

10.___

A. Spaghetti   B. Source   C. Macro   D. Pseudo

11. In its current form, the technology of electronic data interchange (EDI) is appropriate for transmitting all of the following EXCEPT

11.___

A. purchase orders   B. bills of lading
C. solicitations   D. invoices

12. Which of the following types of applications is generally most dependent on the graphical user interface (GUI) environment?

12.___

A. Electronic communication
B. Desktop publishing
C. Word processing
D. Spreadsheet

13. Which of the following is a logical design element of an information system?

13.___

A. Hardware specifications   B. Output media
C. Data models   D. Software

14. A processing system rejects an order transaction for 10,000 units, on the basis that no order larger than 70 units had been placed previously. This is an example of a

14.___

A. check digit   B. format check
C. reasonableness check   D. dependency check

15. The concentric circle on the surface area of a disk, on which data are stored as magnetized spots, is known as a

15.___

A. cylinder   B. track   C. register   D. sector

16. Which of the following storage media generally has the slowest access speed?

16.___

A. Optical disk   B. RAM
C. Magnetic disk   D. Cache

17. The most time-consuming element of system conversion plans is

17.___

A. hardware upgrading   B. personnel training
C. documentation   D. data conversion

18. In most organizations, the chief information officer is given a rank equivalent to   18.____

    A. project manager   B. data administrator
    C. team leader   D. vice president

19. Which of the following statements about the prototyping approach to systems develop-   19.____
    ment is FALSE?
    It is

    A. especially valuable for designing an end-user interface
    B. generally better suited for larger applications
    C. most useful when there is some uncertainty about requirements or design solu-
       tions
    D. as iterative process

20. What is the term for the final step in system reengineering, when the revised specifica-   20.____
    tions are used to generate new, structure program code for a structured and maintain-
    able system?

    A. Direct cutover   B. Reverse engineering
    C. Workflow engineering   D. Forward engineering

21. Which of the following are included in an MIS audit?   21.____
           I.   Physical facilities
           II. Telecommunications
           III. Control systems
           IV. Manual procedures
    The CORRECT answer is:

    A. I, IV   B. II, III
    C. I, II, III   D. I, II, III, IV

22. In the traditional systems life cycle model, which of the following stages occurs EARLI-   22.____
    EST?

    A. Programming   B. Design
    C. Installation   D. Systems study

23. Which of the following concerns is addressed by front-end CASE (Computer-Assisted   23.____
    Software Engineering) tools?

    A. Testing   B. Analysis
    C. Maintenance   D. Coding

24. In an individual MIS, the most commonly used analytical application is a   24.____

    A. statistical program   B. gateway
    C. spreadsheet   D. utility

25. Certain kinds of expert systems use the property of inheritance to organize and classify   25.____
    knowledge when the knowledge base is composed of easily identifiable chunks or
    objects of interrelated characteristics. These systems are known specifically as

    A. political models   B. rule bases
    C. formal control tools   D. semantic nets

KEY (CORRECT ANSWERS)

1.	D	11.	C
2.	C	12.	B
3.	B	13.	C
4.	B	14.	C
5.	C	15.	B
6.	D	16.	C
7.	A	17.	D
8.	A	18.	D
9.	A	19.	B
10.	B	20.	D

21.	D
22.	D
23.	B
24.	C
25.	D

TEST 3

Each question or incomplete statement is followed by several suggested answers or completions. Select the one that BEST answers the question or completes the statement. *PRINT THE LETTER OF THE CORRECT ANSWER IN THE SPACE AT THE RIGHT.*

1. Of an organization's total MIS budget, the majority can be expected to be spent on   1.____

   A. training
   C. operations
   B. programming
   D. administration

2. Each of the following is an element of the installation stage in the traditional model of a systems life cycle EXCEPT   2.____

   A. testing
   C. conversion
   B. programming
   D. training

3. For network applications in which some processing must be centralized and some can be performed locally, which of the following configurations is most appropriate?   3.____

   A. Bus   B. Ring   C. Star   D. Token ring

4. In systems development, the main difference between strategic analysis and enterprise analysis is that   4.____

   A. enterprise analysis makes use of the personal interview
   B. enterprise analysis produces a smaller data set
   C. strategic analysis is used exclusively in profit concerns
   D. strategic analysis tends to have a broader focus

5. Each of the following is a type of source data automation technology EXCEPT   5.____

   A. magnetic ink character recognition (MICR)
   B. touch screen
   C. bar code
   D. optical character recognition (OCR)

6. The main DISADVANTAGE associated with the parallel strategy of information system conversion is that   6.____

   A. run and personnel costs are extremely high
   B. it presents many difficulties in the area of documentation
   C. it provides no fallback in case of trouble
   D. it does not provide a clear picture of how the system will eventually operate throughout the entire organization

7. Which of the following types of systems is most appropriate for solving unstructured problems?   7.____

   A. Expert system
   B. Executive support system (ESS)
   C. Management information system (MIS)
   D. Decision support system (DSS)

8. In terms of information ethics, what is the term for the existence of laws that permit indi-   8.___
viduals to recover damages done to them by actors, systems, or organizations?

    A. Liability   B. Subrogation
    C. Accountability   D. Due process

9. Descriptions that focus on the dynamic aspects of a system's structure, or on change,   9.___
evolution, and processes in general, are described as

    A. charismatic   B. synchronic
    C. motile   D. diachronic

10. One of the features of object-oriented programming is that all objects in a certain group   10.___
have all the characteristics of that group. This feature is defined as

    A. base   B. legitimacy
    C. class   D. multiplexing

11. The most prominent data manipulation language in use today is   11.___

    A. Intellect   B. Easytrieve
    C. APL   D. SQL

12. Feasibility studies involved in systems analysis tend to focus on three specific   12.___
areas._____ feasibility is NOT one of these.

    A. Technical   B. Operational
    C. Cultural   D. Economic

13. A computer may sometimes handle programs more efficiently by dividing them into small   13.___
fixed-or variable-length portions, with only a small portion stored in primary memory at
one time. This is known as

    A. multitasking   B. caching
    C. allocation   D. virtual storage

14. Of the following applications, end-user computing is MOST appropriate for the develop-   14.___
ment of

    A. scheduling systems for optimal production
    B. tracking daily trades of securities
    C. systems for handling air traffic
    D. systems for the development of three-dimensional graphics

15. In a hierarchical database, what is the term for the specialized data element attached to   15.___
a record that shows the absolute or relative address of another record?

    A. Tickler   B. Index   C. Register   D. Pointer

16. For which of the following types of databases is the direct file access method most   16.___
appropriate?

    A. Bank statements
    B. Payroll
    C. On-line hotel reservations
    D. Government benefits program

17. A _____ structured project with_____ technology requirements would most likely   17._____
involve the lowest degree of risk to an organization.

    A. small, highly; low   B. small, flexibly; high
    C. large, flexibly; high   D. large, highly; low

18. Historically, under federal law creators of intellectual property were protected against   18._____
copying by others for a period of

    A. 10 years
    B. 17 years
    C. 28 years
    D. the creator's natural life

19. Most modern secondary storage devices operate at speeds measured in   19._____

    A. nanoseconds   B. milliseconds
    C. microseconds   D. seconds

20. Which of the following signifies the international standard for transmitting voice, video,   20._____
and data to support a wide range of service over the public telephone lines?

    A. HTML   B. ISDN   C. TCP/IP   D. ASCII

21. An important limitation associated with executive support systems today is that they   21._____

    A. use data from different systems designed for very different purposes
    B. have a narrow range of easy-to-use desktop analytical tools
    C. are used almost exclusively by executives
    D. do an inadequate job of filtering data

22. Each of the following is an element of the systems study stage in the traditional model of   22._____
a systems life cycle EXCEPT

    A. identifying objectives to be attained by a solution
    B. determining whether the organization has a problem that can be solved with a system
    C. analyzing problems with existing systems
    D. describing alternative solutions

23. The commercial software product *Lotus Notes* is an example of   23._____

    A. intelligent agent software
    B. groupware
    C. a star network
    D. electronic data interchange (EDI)

24. Weaknesses in a system's _____ controls may create errors or failures in new or modi-   24._____
fied systems.

    A. data file security   B. implementation
    C. physical hardware   D. software

25. Which of the following is a term used to describe the ability to move from summary data   25.___
   to more specific levels of detail?

    A. Drill down   B. Forward chaining
    C. Downsizing   D. Semantic networking

KEY (CORRECT ANSWERS)

1.	C		11.	D
2.	B		12.	C
3.	C		13.	D
4.	D		14.	D
5.	B		15.	D
6.	A		16.	C
7.	B		17.	A
8.	A		18.	C
9.	D		19.	B
10.	C		20.	B

21.	A
22.	B
23.	B
24.	B
25.	A

EXAMINATION SECTION
TEST 1

DIRECTIONS: Each question or incomplete statement is followed by several suggested answers of completions. Select the one that best answers the question or Complete the statement. *PRINT THE LETTER OF THE CORRECT ANSWER IN THE SPACE AT THE RIGHT.*

1. In the OSI model, a hub is defined in which of the following layers?

    A. Session
    B. Application
    C. Data link
    D. Physical

1._____

2. A simple definition of bandwidth is the

    A. number of computers in a network
    B. transmission capacity
    C. classification of network IPs
    D. none of the above

2._____

3. _____ topology makes use of terminators.

    A. Star
    B. Ring
    C. Bus
    D. Token ring

3._____

4. Which of the following is an advantage of the use of multimedia in the learning process?

    A. Students can express their abilities in many different ways
    B. It is useful for the students to develop their career in media sciences
    C. It enhances students' motivation for learning
    D. None of the above

4._____

5. For the purpose of transfer of technology, companies/organizations must

    A. allocate much better budget for research and development
    B. have a good networking structure
    C. have willingness to spend on technology to gain long-term benefits
    D. all of the above

5._____

6. The focus of teacher education must be on the development of

    A. professional identity
    B. personal identity
    C. academic identity
    D. none of the above

6._____

7. System Study is a study that

    A. studies an existing system
    B. performs the documentation of the existing system
    C. highlights existing deficiencies and establishes new goals
    D. all of the above

7._____

8. Which of these is the starting point for the establishment of an MIS?   8._____

    A. Development of physical hardware and networking structure
    B. Development of a DBMS
    C. Understanding and identification of business processes
    D. None of the above

9. A new system is designed by the system analyst by   9._____

    A. identifying the subsystems and then creating links among these subsystems
    B. customizing an existing system to the new system
    C. creating a one unit larger system
    D. proposing new system alternatives

10. Process mapping may be defined by which of the following?   10._____

    A. Activities are related to the different functional units of the organization
    B. It is developed by the placement of different activities with the help of symbols in a logical order
    A. It is used to present different activities of a process in a hierarchical form
    B. Process efficiency is measured with the help of process mapping

11. Which of the following is an example of a payment system?   11._____

    A. E-commerce shopping
    B. Travel reimbursement
    C. Accounts payable
    D. All of the above

12. _____ phase performs problem analysis.   12._____

    A. Systems Analysis
    B. System Design
    C. System Implementation
    D. None of the above

13. Top management is most concerned with   13._____

    A. daily transactions
    B. strategic decisions
    C. tactical decisions
    D. both (B) and (C)

14. Most companies and organizations have their _____ MIS plans.   14._____

    A. master
    B. broad
    C. prototype
    D. control

15. Data integrity refers to   15._____

    A. simplicity
    B. security
    C. validity
    D. none of the above

16. The desired outcome for project integration is   16._____

    A. better focus on the organization
    B. ideal usage of resources of the organization
    C. better communication among projects and their teams
    D. all of the above

17. If you are working on more than one project and you frequently need to put work on   17._____
    one project on hold and move to another project, then return later to the original
    project, this is known as

    A. excessive burden
    B. flexible Processing
    C. multitasking
    D. burnout

18. Which of the following may be defined as a project aim?   18._____

    A. Meeting the specific quality requirements
    B. On-time delivery
    C. Working within budget constraints
    D. All of the above

19. The progressive phases of management over large projects are best described as   19._____

    A. planning, evaluating and scheduling
    B. planning, scheduling and operating
    C. scheduling, planning and operating
    D. planning, scheduling and controlling

20. Variance of the total project completion time is computed in the PERT analysis as   20._____

    A. project final activity variance
    B. the aggregation of variances of the project activities
    C. the aggregation of all the activities variance on the critical path
    D. the aggregation of all the activities variance not on the critical path

21. What will be critical path standard deviation if there are three activities -- X, Y and Z -- in   21._____
    the path? X has a deviation of 2, Y has a deviation of 1 and there is a deviation of 2 for Z.
    In this case, what is the standard deviation of critical path?

    A. 20
    B. 3
    C. 12
    D. 5

22. Linear regression is much similar to

    A. simple moving average forecasting approach
    B. trend project forecasting approach
    C. weighted moving average forecasting approach
    D. naïve forecasting approach

22._____

23. The purpose of risk tolerance is to

    A. observe that how much risk can be tolerated by the project
    B. rank project risks
    C. help the project manager in project estimation
    D. help in project scheduling

23._____

24. The process group for project management is ordered

    A. initiating, planning, executing, controlling, and closeout
    B. starting, planning, accelerating, and control
    C. planning, establishing, developing, and control
    D. none of the above

24._____

25. Which risk management process identifies the workaround?

    A. Risk identification
    B. Risk monitoring
    C. Risk measurement
    D. Risk monitoring and control

25._____

———

KEY (CORRECT ANSWERS)

1. D		11. D	
2. B		12. A	
3. C		13. B	
4. C		14. A	
5. D		15. C	
6. A		16. C	
7. D		17. C	
8. C		18. D	
9. A		19. D	
10. A		20. C	

21. B
22. B
23. B
24. A
25. D

———

TEST 2

1. What is a computer network?   1._____

   A. Information and resource sharing
   B. A combination of computer systems and other hardware elements
   C. A network of communication channels
   D. All of above

2. A network bridge _____.   2.____

   A. monitors network traffic
   B. distinguishes LANs
   C. is a source of connection among LANs
   D. none of the above

3. Which topology is best for the larger networks?   3._____

   A. Ring token
   B. Star
   C. Ring
   D. Bus

4. Interactive books are used in the form of   4._____

   A. educational games
   B. interactive storybooks
   C. interactive texts
   D. both B and C

5. Which of the following are used for GSM technology?   5._____

   A. OFDMA
   B. FDMA/TDMA
   C. CDMA
   D. None of the above

6. What is the main objective of a MIS department?   6._____

   A. To aid the other business areas in performing their tasks
   B. Information processing for the better utilization of data
   C. To be useful for chief executives
   D. To generate useful information

7. Documentation is prepared at   7._____

   A. every phase
   B. the system analysis phase
   C. the system design phase
   D. the system implementation phase

8. System prototyping is useful for the 　　　　　　　　　　　　　　　8._____

    A. programmer in regards to understanding the whole system
    B. purpose of communication with the users, telling them how the
       system will look after development
    A. purpose of system demo to the higher project management
    B. Both A and B

9. Mistakes made during the requirements analysis phase normally show up in 　　9._____

    A. system design
    B. system testing
    C. system implementation
    D. none of the above

10. Use case analysis is best described by which of the following statements? 　　10._____

    A. It is used for interface design by highlighting the stages of user interaction with the
       system
    A. It minimizes the number of steps in order to access the content
    B. A consistent site design with the products and services
    C. It is used for the purpose of information categorization

11. Who is responsible for the analysis and design of the systems? 　　　　　11._____

    A. Developer
    B. System analyst
    C. System operator
    D. Project manager

12. _____ is an outline for the development of bugs-free information systems. 　　12._____

    A. System development life cycle
    B. System conversion
    C. Case tools
    D. System analysis

13. Top-down analysis and design is performed by 　　　　　　　　　　13._____

    A. the creation of system flow chart after design process
    B. identifying the top-level functions and development of subsequent lower-level
       components
    C. identifying the root elements and then moving gradually up to the top level
    D. none of the above

14. Which of the following is not the part of marketing mix? 　　　　　　14._____

    A. Place
    B. Product
    C. Part
    D. Promotion

15. A distributed MIS mainly deals with the   15._____

    A. local data processing
    B. multiprocessing
    C. sharing of workload
    D. all of the above

16. Project managers unaware of the importance of a project for the organization might tend to   16._____

    A. focus on less important things
    B. emphasize too much on the use of technology
    C. concentrate more on the customer in hand
    D. all of the above

17. Why is it necessary for the project managers to understand the organization's mission?   17._____

    A. To make better decisions and required adjustments
    B. To advocate for projects in a better way
    C. In order to perform their jobs more effectively
    D. Both (A) and (B) are correct

18. Common multi-criteria selection models include   18._____

    A. checklist
    B. NPV
    C. weighted criteria model
    D. both A and C

19. The project management process does not involve   19._____

    A. project scheduling
    B. project planning
    C. system analysis
    D. project estimation

20. Which of the following is the best tool for monitoring projects against the original plan?   20._____

    A. Network diagrams
    B. Gantt Charts
    C. Data Flow diagrams
    D. All of the above

21. A project can be treated as a failed project if   21._____

    A. project requirements are met on schedule
    B. the project is completed on time but with flaws that require additional work
    C. costs are in line with original projections
    D. all of the above

22. Which of the following is a basic assumption of PERT?   22._____

    A. There is no repetition of any activity within the network
    B. There is known time for the completion of each activity
    C. Only the activities in the critical path must be performed
    D. Project start to project end contains only one route

23. Sharing of confidential information with some bidders with the purpose of providing them some undue favor is considered as

    23._____

    A. bribery
    B. bid rigging
    C. bid fixing
    D. favoritism

24. The advantages of centralized contracting include

    24._____

    A. provision of easier access to contracting expertise
    B. enhanced organizational contracting expertise
    C. higher level of loyalty
    D. none of the above

25. All of the following are features and characteristics of a project EXCEPT

    25._____

    A. a defined start and end
    B. a network of related activities
    C. repeated at a regular interval
    D. temporary in nature

KEY (CORRECT ANSWERS)

1. D		11. B	
2. C		12. A	
3. B		13. B	
4. D		14. C	
5. B		15. C	
6. A		16. D	
7. A		17. D	
8. B		18. D	
9. C		19. C	
10. A		20. B	

21. B
22. A
23. B
24. B
25. C

TEST 3

DIRECTIONS: Each question or incomplete statement is followed by several suggested answers of completions. Select the one that best answers the question or Complete the statement. *PRINT THE LETTER OF THE CORRECT ANSWER IN THE SPACE AT THE RIGHT.*

1. The number of layers in the OSI Reference Model are

   A. 5
   B. 6
   C. 7
   D. 8

   1._____

2. Which of these is a source of connection oriented message communication?

   A. TCP
   B. UDP
   C. IP
   D. None of the above

   2._____

3. Which buffer is used by the print server for the holding of data before printing?

   A. Node
   B. Spool
   C. Queue
   D. None of above

   3._____

4. Criteria for evaluating commercial hypermedia products include

   A. instructional design
   B. low cost
   C. portability
   D. use of all media channels

   4._____

5. The domain of .net is used by

   A. universities
   B. internet service providers
   C. government organizations
   D. none of the above

   5._____

6. Which of the following is a technology used for the routing of phone calls over a network?

   A. Video-conferencing
   B. VOIP
   C. Teleconferencing
   D. None of the above

   6._____

7. The maintenance phase

   A. defines system requirements
   B. develops system design
   C. performs system testing
   D. none of the above

   7._____

8. Reconstruction of a system requires the consideration of

    A. system inputs and outputs
    B. control and processors
    C. comprehensive user feedback
    D. all of the above

8._____

9. Cost-Benefit analysis

    A. performs an estimation of the cost of hardware and software
    B. performs a comparison of costs with the benefits of development of new system
    C. considers both the tangible and non-tangible elements
    D. all of the above

9._____

10. Who is responsible for the sponsoring and funding of the project development and its maintenance?

    A. System manager
    B. Project manager
    C. Systems owner
    D. External system user

10._____

11. The system implementation approach used in the event you want to run both the old and new systems is called

    A. parallel
    B. pilot
    C. synchronized
    D. phased

11._____

12. DBMS advantages include

    A. data integrity
    B. minimization of storage space
    C. centralized access to the data
    D. all of the above

12._____

13. Which of the following is a well-known and popular forecasting approach?

    A. Chi Square
    B. Correlation
    C. Regression Analysis
    D. None of the above

13._____

14. Who is responsible for the tactical decisions of allocation of resources and establishment of control over project activities?

    A. Middle-level management
    B. Higher-level management
    C. Lower-level management
    D. All of the above

14._____

15. The mission statement of an organization answers which of the following questions?　　　　15.＿＿＿

    A. How do we utilize resources?
    B. What are our goals and intentions as an organization?
    C. What are our plans in the long run?
    D. What is the mode of operations in the current environment?

16. What is the benefit of network approach?　　　　16.＿＿＿

    A. Forecasts may be carried on
    B. Structured approach is avoided
    C. Project progress against the original plan can be monitored
    D. Requirement of management judgment is eliminated

17. A Gantt chart is composed of　　　　17.＿＿＿

    A. activities in a sequence
    B. mention of different project activities with the elapsed time
    C. overall project elapsed time
    D. all of the above

18. What does *slack* mean with reference to PERT and CPM?　　　　18.＿＿＿

    A. It is the latest time on which a project may be started without causing any delay for the project
    B. It is a task which must be completed
    C. This reflects the amount of time a specific task may be delayed without having a need to change the overall time of completion of the project
    D. It reflects the start and end time of a task

19. The direct responsibilities of the project manager include　　　　19.＿＿＿

    A. calculation of probability of the task's completion
    B. design of the network diagrams
    C. acting on all aspects of the project
    D. ensuring that all people assigned to a project carry out their required duties and utilize appropriate resources and information in order to perform their tasks

20. What is standard error in a regression forecast?　　　　20.＿＿＿

    A. The highest error level for the forecast
    B. The regression line variability
    C. Time to be consumed for the computation of regression forecast
    D. Forecast validity time

21. Which management process helps in risk identification?　　　　21.＿＿＿

    A. Risk identification, monitoring and control
    B. Qualitative risk analysis
    C. Quantitative risk analysis
    D. Risk detection

22. The cost reimbursable contracts are termed as _____ contracts.   22._____

   A. gradual payment
   B. cost plus
   C. back charge
   D. secure cost

23. The style of conflict resolution that typically has the best impact is   23._____

   A. empathy
   B. problem solving
   C. willingness
   D. mapping

24. Decomposition of deliverables into more manageable components is termed as   24._____

   A. scope segmentation
   B. scope certification
   C. scoping
   D. scope definition

25. What is quality?   25._____

   A. The level at which project requirements are met
   B. Providing output beyond customer demand
   C. Meeting the objectives of management
   D. Meeting customer demands

_____

KEY (CORRECT ANSWERS)

1. C		11. A	
2. A		12. D	
3. B		13. C	
4. A		14. A	
5. B		15. B	
6. B		16. C	
7. D		17. D	
8. D		18. C	
9. D		19. D	
10. C		20. B	

21. A
22. B
23. B
24. D
25. A

_____

TEST 4

DIRECTIONS: Each question or incomplete statement is followed by several suggested answers of completions. Select the one that best answers the question or Complete the statement. *PRINT THE LETTER OF THE CORRECT ANSWER IN THE SPACE AT THE RIGHT.*

1. A firewall is a   1._____

   A. tool for web browsing
   B. network boundary established physically
   C. system that blocks unauthorized access
   D. computer's network

2. For data transfer in both directions, which communication approach is utilized?   2._____

   A. Simplex
   B. Half duplex
   C. Full duplex
   D. None of the above

3. Which of the following is utilized for the purpose of modulation and demodulation?   3._____

   A. Satellite
   B. Fiber optics
   C. Modem
   D. Coaxial Cable

4. After looking at the header of the data packet, a _____ decides the destination of the packet.   4._____

   A. hub
   B. switch
   C. router
   D. firewall

5. Which of the following is software for video editing?   5._____

   A. iMovie
   B. ScanImage
   C. PhotoShop
   D. HyperStudio

6. The use of educational technology must be considered as a(n)   6._____

   A. alternative to less technological strategies
   B. necessity for learning
   C. supplement to other teaching tools
   D. none the above

7. Parallel Run refers to   7._____

   A. job processing of two different tasks at two different terminals to compare the outputs
   B. concurrent running of old and new systems in order to identify the likely mistakes of the new system and to perform the daily routine tasks
   C. a job run at two different systems for the purpose of speed comparison
   D. all of the above

8. The purpose of a context diagram is to   8._____

    A. establish system context
    B. present the flow of data of the system in order to provide a broader system overview
    C. provide a detailed system description
    D. none of the above

9. The number of steps in the systems development life cycle (SDLC) is   9._____

    A. 4
    B. 5
    C. 6
    D. 10

10. Who is the person responsible for ensuring that the project is completed on time with   10._____
    the defined quality and specified budget constraints?

    A. Systems designer
    B. Project manager
    C. Systems owner
    D. Systems manager

11. Which of the following is the deliverable at the system implementation phase?   11._____

    A. A solution meeting the specific business needs
    B. Defined business problem
    C. Clear identification of business requirements
    D. A blueprint and sketch of the desired system

12. What type of mail requires proof of delivery?   12._____

    A. Express post
    B. External post
    C. Licensed post
    D. Registered post

13. Which of these is a good quality measure?   13._____

    A. Authority
    B. Correctness
    C. Precision
    D. All of the above

14. A group of related projects combine to form a _____.   14._____

    A. projects classification
    B. product
    C. department
    D. program

15. _____ analysis performs an assessment of internal and external environment.   15._____

    A. SWOT
    B. Comprehensive
    C. Organizational
    D. Strategic

16. A dummy activity is required when there is/are   16._____

    A. different ending events for more than one activity
    B. one ending event for more than one activity
    C. one starting event for two or more activities
    D. one starting and ending event for more than one activity in the network

17. Limitations of PERT and CPM include   17._____

    A. only a limited type of projects can be applied to these
    B. too much consideration is given to the critical path
    C. these are only to monitor the schedules
    D. it is difficult to interpret because of the graphical nature of the network

18. If there is a negative tracking signal against a forecasting, it means   18._____

    A. this forecast approach regularly underpredicts
    B. MAPE, too, will be negative
    C. this forecast approach regularly overpredicts
    D. MSE, too, will be negative

19. Quality management is the responsibility of   19._____

    A. team Leader
    B. team member
    C. quality assurance coordinator
    D. project manager

20. Purchasing insurance is considered what type of risk?   20._____

    A. Recognition
    B. Prevention
    C. Mitigation
    D. Transfer

21. Project costs may be monitored with respect to different categories with the help of   21._____

    A. standard accounting practices
    B. chart of accounts
    C. WBS
    D. UAS

22. What is the output of an administrative closure?   22._____

    A. Project documentation
    B. Project archives
    C. Risk analysis
    D. None of the above

23. A detailed project budget is created in the _____ process.   23._____

   A. establishment
   B. execution
   C. planning
   D. control

24. The person who can gain or lose something from the result of a project activity is the   24._____

   A. team member
   B. team leader
   C. supporter
   D. project manager

25. When a project manager apologizes for failing to deal with some issue, this is considered   25._____
   which of the following conflict resolutions?

   A. Forcing
   B. Withdrawal
   C. Compromising
   D. Collaborating

KEY (CORRECT ANSWERS)

1. C	11. A
2. C	12. D
3. C	13. D
4. C	14. D
5. A	15. A
6. C	16. D
7. B	17. B
8. B	18. C
9. C	19. D
10. B	20. D

21. B
22. B
23. C
24. C
25. B

EXAMINATION SECTION
TEST 1

DIRECTIONS: Each question or incomplete statement is followed by several suggested answers or completions. Select the one that BEST answers the question or completes the statement. *PRINT THE LETTER OF THE CORRECT ANSWER IN THE SPACE AT THE RIGHT.*

1. The one of the following which is the CHIEF reason for the difference between the administration of justice agencies and that of other units in public administration is that   1.____

   A. correctional institutions are concerned with security
   B. some defendants are proven to be innocent after trial
   C. the administration of justice is much more complicated than other aspects of public administration
   D. correctional institutions produce services their *clients* or *customers* fail to understand or ask for

2. Of the following, the MOST important reason why employees resist change is that   2.____

   A. they have not received adequate training in preparation for the change
   B. experience has shown that when new ideas don't work, employees get blamed and not the individuals responsible for the new ideas
   C. new ideas and methods almost always represent a threat to the security of the individuals involved
   D. new ideas often are not practical and disrupt operations unnecessarily

3. Stress situations are ideal for building up a backlog of knowledge about an employee's behavior. Not only does it inform the supervisor of many aspects of a person's behavior patterns, but it is also vitally important to have foreknowledge of how people behave under stress.
   The one of the following which is NOT implied by this passage is that   3.____

   A. a person under stress may give some indication of his unsuitability for work in an institution
   B. putting people under stress is the best means of determining their usual patterns of behavior
   C. stress situations may give important clues about performance in the service
   D. there is a need to know about a person's reaction to situations *when the chips are down*

4. There are situations requiring a supervisor to give direct orders to subordinates assigned to work under the direct control of other supervisors.
   Under which of the following conditions would this shift of command responsibility be MOST appropriate?   4.____

   A. Emergency operations require the cooperative action of two or more organizational units.
   B. One of the other supervisors is not doing his job, thus defeating the goals of the organization.
   C. The subordinates are performing their assigned tasks in the absence of their own supervisor.
   D. The subordinates ask a superior officer who is not their own supervisor how to perform an assignment given them by their supervisor.

5. The one of the following which BEST differentiates staff supervision from line supervision is that   5.__

     A. staff supervision has the authority to immediately correct a line subordinate's action
     B. staff supervision is an advisory relationship
     C. line supervision goes beyond the normal boundaries of direct supervision within a *command*
     D. line supervision does not report findings and make recommendations

6. Decision-making is a rational process calling for a *suspended judgment* by the supervisor until all the facts have been ascertained and analyzed, and the consequences of alternative courses of action studied; *then* the decision maker   6.__

     A. acts as both judge and jury and selects what he believes to be the best of the alternative plans
     B. consults with those who will be most directly involved to obtain a recommendation as to the most appropriate course of action
     C. reviews the facts which he has already analyzed, reduces his thoughts to writing, and selects that course of action which can have the fewest negative consequences if his thinking contains an error
     D. stops, considers the matter for at least a 24-hour period, before referring it to a superior for evaluation

7. Decision-making can be defined as the   7.__

     A. delegation of authority and responsibility to persons capable of performing their assigned duties with moderate or little supervision
     B. imposition of a supervisor's decision upon a work group
     C. technique of selecting the course of action with the most desired consequences, and the least undesired or unexpected consequences
     D. process principally concerned with improvement of procedures

8. A supervisor who is not well-motivated and has no desire to accept basic responsibilities will   8.__

     A. compromise to the extent of permitting poor performance for lengthy periods without correction
     B. get good performance from his work group if the employees are satisfied with their pay and other working conditions
     C. not have marginal workers in his work group if the work is interesting
     D. perform adequately as long as the work of his group consists of routine operations

9. A supervisor is more than a bond or connecting link between two levels of employees. He has joint responsibility which must be shared with both management and with the work group.
Of the following, the item which BEST expresses the meaning of this statement is:

    9.____

    A. A supervisor works with both management and the work group and must reconcile the differences between them.
    B. In management, the supervisor is solely concerned with efforts directing the work of his subordinates.
    C. The supervisory role is basically that of a liaison man between management and the work force.
    D. What a supervisor says and does when confronted with day-to-day problems depends upon his level in the organization.

10. Operations research is the observation of operations in business or government, and it utilizes both hypotheses and controlled experiments to determine the outcome of decisions. In effect, it reproduces the future impact on the decision in a clinical environment suited to intensive study.
Operations research has

    10.____

    A. been more promising than applied research in the ascertaining of knowledge for the purpose of decision–making
    B. never been amenable to fact analysis on the grand scale
    C. not been used extensively in government
    D. proven to be the only rational and logical approach to decision–making on long–range problems

11. Assume that a civilian makes a complaint regarding the behavior of a certain worker to the supervisor of the worker. The supervisor regards the complaint as unjustified and unreasonable.
In these circumstances, the supervisor

    11.____

    A. must make a written note of the complaint and forward it through channels to the unit or individual responsible for complaint investigations
    B. should assure the complainant that disciplinary action will be appropriate to the seriousness of the alleged offense
    C. should immediately summon the worker if he is available so that the latter may attempt to straighten out the difficulty
    D. should inform the complainant that his complaint appears to be unjustified and unreasonable

12. Modern management usually establishes a personal history folder for an employee at the time of hiring. Disciplinary matters appear in such personal history folders. Employees do not like the idea of disciplinary actions appearing in their permanent personal folders.
Authorities believe that

    12.____

    A. after a few years have passed since the commission of the infraction, disciplinary actions should be removed from folders
    B. disciplinary actions should remain in folders; it is not the records but the use of records that requires detailed study
    C. most personnel have not had disciplinary action taken against them and would resent the removal of disciplinary actions from such folders
    D. there is no point in removing disciplinary actions from personal history folders since employees who have been guilty of infractions should not be allowed to forget their infractions

13. While supervisors should not fear the acceptance of responsibility, they   13.__

   A. generally seek out responsibility that subordinates should exercise, particularly when the supervisors do not have sufficient work to do

   B. must be on guard against the abuse of authority that often accompanies the acceptance of total responsibility

   C. should avoid responsibility that is customarily exercised by their superiors

   D. who are anxious for promotions accept responsibility but do not exercise the authority warranted by the responsibility

14. Planning is part of the decision-making process. By planning is meant the development   14.__
of details of alternative plans of action.
The key to *effective* planning is

   A. careful research to determine whether a tentative plan has been tried at some time in the past

   B. participation by employees in planning, preferably those employees who will be involved in putting the selected plan into action

   C. speed; poor plans can be discarded after they are put into effect while good plans usually are not put into effect because of delays

   D. writing the plan up in considerable detail and then forwarding the plan, through channels, to the executive officer having final approval of the plan

15. Equating strict discipline with punitive measures and lax discipline with rehabilitation creates a false dichotomy. The one of the statements given below that would BEST follow from the belief expressed in this statement is that discipline   15.__

   A. is important for treatment

   B. militates against treatment programs

   C. is not an important consideration in institutions where effective rehabilitation programs prevail

   D. minimizes the need for punitive measures if it is strict

16. If training starts at the lower level of command, it is like planting a seed in tilled ground but removing the sun and rain. Seeds cannot grow unless they have help from above. Of the following, the MOST appropriate conclusion to be drawn from this statement is that   16.__

   A. the head of an institution may not delegate authority for the planning of an institutional training program for staff

   B. on-the-job training is better than formalized training courses

   C. regularly scheduled training courses must be planned in advance

   D. staff training is the responsibility of higher levels of command

17. The one of the following that BEST describes the meaning of *in-service staff training* is: 17.__

   A. The training of personnel who are below average in performance

   B. The training given to each employee throughout his employment

   C. The training of staff only in their own specialized fields

   D. Classroom training where the instructor and employees develop a positive and productive relationship leading to improved efficiency on the job

18. All bureau personnel should be concerned about, and involved in, public relations. Of the following, the MOST important reason for this statement is that

    A. an institution is an agency of the government supported by public funds and responsible to the public
    B. institutions are places of public business and, therefore, the public is interested in them
    C. some personnel need publicity in order to advance
    D. personnel sometimes need publicity in order to ensure that their grievances are acted upon by higher authority

18.____

19. The MOST important factor in establishing a disciplinary policy in an organization is

    A. consistency of application
    B. strict supervisors
    C. strong enforcement
    D. the degree of toughness or laxity

19.____

20. The FIRST step in planning a program is to

    A. clearly define the objectives
    B. estimate the costs
    C. hire a program director
    D. solicit funds

20.____

21. The PRIMARY purpose of control in an organization is to

    A. punish those who do not do their job well
    B. get people to do what is necessary to achieve an objective
    C. develop clearly stated rules and regulations
    D. regulate expenditures

21.____

22. The UNDERLYING principle of *sound* administration is to

    A. base administration on investigation of facts
    B. have plenty of resources available
    C. hire a strong administrator
    D. establish a broad policy

22.____

23. An IMPORTANT aspect to keep in mind during the decision-making process is that

    A. all possible alternatives for attaining goals should be sought out and considered
    B. considering various alternatives only leads to confusion
    C. once a decision has been made, it cannot be retracted
    D. there is only one correct method to reach any goal

23.____

24. Implementation of accountability requires

    A. a leader who will not hesitate to take punitive action
    B. an established system of communication from the bottom to the top
    C. explicit directives from leaders
    D. too much expense to justify it

24.____

25. The CHIEF danger of a decentralized control system is that 25.___

    A. excessive reports and communications will be generated
    B. problem areas may not be detected readily
    C. the expense will become prohibitive
    D. this will result in too many *chiefs*

KEY (CORRECT ANSWERS)

1.	D	11.	D
2.	C	12.	A
3.	B	13.	B
4.	A	14.	B
5.	B	15.	A
6.	A	16.	D
7.	C	17.	B
8.	A	18.	A
9.	A	19.	A
10.	C	20.	A

21.	B
22.	A
23.	A
24.	B
25.	B

TEST 2

DIRECTIONS: Each question or incomplete statement is followed by several suggested answers or completions. Select the one that BEST answers the question or completes the statement. *PRINT THE LETTER OF THE CORRECT ANSWER IN THE SPACE AT THE RIGHT.*

1. When giving orders to his subordinates, a certain supervisor often includes information   1.____
    as to why the work is necessary.
    This approach by the supervisor is *generally*

    A. *inadvisable,* since it appears that he is avoiding responsibility and wishes to blame
        his superiors
    B. *inadvisable,* since it creates the impression that he is trying to impress the subordi-
        nates with his importance
    C. *advisable,* since it serves to motivate the subordinates by giving them a reason for
        wanting to do the work
    D. *advisable,* since it shows that he is knowledgeable and is in control of his assign-
        ments

2. Some supervisors often ask capable, professional subordinates to get some work done   2.____
    with questions such as: *Mary, would you try to complete that work today?*
    The use of such request orders *usually*

    A. gets results which are as good as or better than results from direct orders
    B. shows the supervisor to be weak and lowers the respect of his subordinates
    C. provokes resentment as compared to the use of direct orders
    D. leads to confusion as to the proper procedure to follow when carrying out orders

3. Assume that a supervisor, because of an emergency when time was essential, and in the   3.____
    absence of his immediate superior, went out of the chain of command to get a decision
    from a higher level.
    It would consequently be MOST appropriate for the immediate superior to

    A. reprimand him for his action, since the long-range consequences are far more det-
        rimental than the immediate gain
    B. encourage him to use this method, since the chain of command is an outmoded
        and discredited system which inhibits productive work
    C. order him to refrain from any repetition of this action in the future
    D. support him as long as he informed the superior of the action at the earliest oppor-
        tunity

4. A supervisor gave instructions which he knew were somewhat complex to a subordinate.   4.____
    He then asked the subordinate to repeat the instructions to him.
    The supervisor's decision to have the subordinate repeat the instructions was

    A. *good practice,* mainly because the subordinate would realize the importance of
        carefully following instructions
    B. *poor practice,* mainly because the supervisor should have given the employee time
        to ponder the instructions, and then, if necessary, to ask questions
    C. *good practice,* mainly because the supervisor could see whether the subordinate
        had any apparent problem in understanding the instructions
    D. *poor practice,* mainly because the subordinate should not be expected to have the
        same degree of knowledge as the supervisor

5. Supervisors and subordinates must successfully communicate with each other in order to work well together.
Which of the following statements concerning communication of this type is COR-RECT?

    A. When speaking to his subordinates, a supervisor should make every effort to appear knowledgeable about all aspects of their work.
    B. Written communications should be prepared by the supervisor at his own level of comprehension.
    C. The average employee tends to give meaning to communication according to his personal interpretation.
    D. The effective supervisor communicates as much information as he has available to anyone who is interested.

5.___

6. A supervisor should be aware of situations in which it is helpful to put his orders to his subordinates in writing.
Which of the following situations would MOST likely call for a WRITTEN order rather than an ORAL order? The order

    A. gives complicated instructions which vary from ordinary practice
    B. involves the performance of duties for which the subordinate is responsible
    C. directs subordinates to perform duties similar to those which they performed in the recent past
    D. concerns a matter that must be promptly completed or dealt with

6.___

7. Assume that a supervisor discovers that a false rumor about possible layoffs has spread among his subordinates through the grapevine.
Of the following, the BEST way for the supervisor to deal with this situation is to

    A. use the grapevine to leak accurate information
    B. call a meeting to provide information and to answer questions
    C. post a notice on the bulletin board denying the rumor
    D. institute procedures designed to eliminate the grapevine

7.___

8. Communications in an organization with many levels becomes subject to different inter-pretations at each level and have a tendency to become distorted. The more levels there are in an organization, the greater the likelihood that the final recipient of a communica-tion will get the wrong message.
The one of the following statements which BEST supports the foregoing viewpoint is:

    A. Substantial communications problems exist at high management levels in organi-zations.
    B. There is a relationship in an organization between the number of hierarchical levels and interference with communications.
    C. An opportunity should be given to subordinates at all levels to communicate their views with impunity.
    D. In larger organizations, there tends to be more interference with downward com-munications than with upward communications.

8.___

9. A subordinate comes to you, his supervisor, to ask a detailed question about a new   9._____
agency directive; however, you do not know the answer.
Of the following, the MOST helpful response to give the subordinate is to

   A. point out that since your own supervisor has failed to keep you informed of this
      matter, it is probably unimportant
   B. give the most logical interpretation you can, based on your best judgment
   C. ask him to raise the question with other supervisors until he finds one who knows
      the answer, then let you know also
   D. explain that you do not know and assure him that you will get the information for
      him

10. The traditional view of management theory is that communication in an organization   10._____
should follow the table of organization. A newer theory holds that timely communication
often requires bypassing certain steps in the hierarchical chain.
However, the MAIN advantage of using formal channels of communication within an
organization is that

   A. an employee is thereby restricted in his relationships to his immediate superior and
      his immediate subordinates
   B. information is thereby transmitted to everyone who should be informed
   C. the organization will have an appeal channel, or a mechanism by which subordi-
      nates can go over their superior's head
   D. employees are thereby encouraged to exercise individual initiative

11. It is unfair to hold subordinates responsible for the performance of duties for which they   11._____
do not have the requisite authority.
When this is done, it violates the principle that

   A. responsibility *cannot be greater* than that implied by delegated authority
   B. responsibility *should be greater* than that implied by delegated authority
   C. authority *cannot be greater* than that implied by delegated responsibility
   D. authority *should be greater* than that implied by delegated responsibility

12. Assume that a supervisor wishes to delegate some tasks to a capable subordinate.   12._____
It would be MOST in keeping with the principles of delegation for the supervisor to

   A. ask another supervisor who is experienced in the delegated tasks to evaluate the
      subordinate's work from time to time
   B. monitor continually the subordinate's performance by carefully reviewing his work
      at every step
   C. request experienced employees to submit peer ratings of the work of the subordi-
      nate
   D. tell the subordinates what problems are likely to be encountered and specify which
      problems to report on

13. There are *three* types of leadership: *autocratic,* in which the leader makes the decisions   13.__
and seeks compliance from his subordinates; *democratic,* in which the leader consults
with his subordinates and lets them help set policy; and *free rein,* in which the leader acts
as an information center and exercises minimum control over his subordinates.
A supervisor can be MOST effective if he decides to

   A. use democratic leadership techniques exclusively
   B. avoid the use of autocratic leadership techniques entirely
   C. employ the three types of leadership according to the situation
   D. rely mainly on autocratic leadership techniques

14. During a busy period of work, Employee A asked his supervisor for leave in order to take   14.__
an ordinary vacation. The supervisor denied the request. The following day, Employee B
asked for leave during the same period because his wife had just gone to the hospital for
an indeterminate stay and he had family matters to tend to.
Of the following, the BEST way for the supervisor to deal with Employee B's request is
to

   A. grant the request and give the reason to the other employee
   B. suggest that the employee make his request to higher management
   C. delay the request immediately since granting it would show favoritism
   D. defer any decision until the duration of the hospital stay is determined

15. Assume that you are a supervisor and that a subordinate tells you he has a grievance.   15.__
In general, you should FIRST

   A. move the grievance forward in order to get a prompt decision
   B. discourage this type of behavior on the part of subordinates
   C. attempt to settle the grievance
   D. refer the subordinate to the personnel office

16. A supervisor may have available a large variety of rewards he can use to motivate his   16.__
subordinates. However, some supervisors choose the wrong rewards.
A supervisor is *most likely* to make such a mistake if he

   A. appeals to a subordinate's desire to be well regarded by his co-workers
   B. assumes that the subordinate's goals and preferences are the same as his own
   C. conducts in-depth discussions with a subordinate in order to discover his prefer-
ence
   D. limits incentives to those rewards which he is authorized to provide or to recom-
mend

17. Employee performance appraisal is open to many kinds of errors.   17.__
When a supervisor is preparing such an appraisal, he is *most likely* to commit an error
if

   A. employees are indifferent to the consequences of their performance appraisals
   B. the entire period for which the evaluation is being made is taken into consideration
   C. standard measurement criteria are used as performance benchmarks
   D. personal characteristics of employees which are not job-related are given weight

18. Assume that a supervisor finds that a report prepared by an employee is unsatisfactory and should be done over. Which of the following should the supervisor do?

    A. Give the report to another employee who can complete it properly.
    B. Have the report done over by the same employee after successfully training him.
    C. Hold a meeting to train all the employees so as not to single out the employee who performed unsatisfactorily
    D. Accept the report so as not to discourage the employee and then make the corrections himself.

18.____

19. Employees sometimes wish to have personal advice and counseling, in confidence, about their job-related problems. These problems may include such concerns as health matters, family difficulties, alcoholism, debts, emotional disturbances, etc.
Such assistance is BEST provided through

    A. maintenance of an exit interview program to find reasons for, and solutions to, turn-over problems
    B. arrangements for employees to discuss individual problems informally outside normal administrative channels
    C. procedures which allow employees to submit anonymous inquiries to the personnel department
    D. special hearing committees consisting of top management in addition to immediate supervisors

19.____

20. An employee is always a member of some unit of the formal organization. He may also be a member of an informal work group.
With respect to employee productivity and job satisfaction, the informal work group can MOST accurately be said to

    A. have no influence of any kind on its members
    B. influence its members negatively only
    C. influence its members positively only
    D. influence its members negatively or positively

20.____

21. In order to encourage employees to make suggestions, many public agencies have employee suggestion programs.
What is the MAJOR benefit of such a program to the agency as a whole? It

    A. brings existing or future problems to management's attention
    B. reduces the number of minor accidents
    C. requires employees to share in decision-making responsibilities
    D. reveals employees who have inadequate job knowledge

21.____

22. Assume that you have been asked to interview a seemingly shy applicant for a temporary position in your department .
For you to ask the kinds of questions that begin with *What, Where, Why, When, Who, and How, is*

    A. *good practice ;* it informs the applicant that he must conform to the requirements of the department
    B. *poor practice;* it exceeds the extent and purpose of an initial interview
    C. *good practice;* it encourages the applicant to talk to a greater extent
    D. *poor practice;* it encourages the applicant to dominate the discussion

22.____

23. In recent years, job enlargement or job enrichment has tended to replace job simplifica-   23.__
tion.
Those who advocate job enrichment or enlargement consider it *desirable* CHIEFLY
because

    A. it allows supervisors to control closely the activities of subordinates
    B. it produces greater job satisfaction through reduction of responsibility
    C. most employees prefer to avoid work which is new and challenging
    D. positions with routinized duties are unlikely to provide job satisfaction

24. Job rotation is a training method in which an employee temporarily changes places with   24.__
another employee of equal rank.
What is usually the MAIN purpose of job rotation? To

    A. politely remove the person being rotated from an unsuitable assignment
    B. increase skills and provide broader experience
    C. prepare the person being rotated for a permanent change
    D. test the skills of the person being rotated

25. There are several principles that a supervisor needs to know if he is to deal adequately   25.__
with his training responsibilities.
Which of the following is usually NOT a principle of training?

    A. People should be trained according to their individual needs.
    B. People can learn by being told or shown how to do work, but best of all by doing
work under guidance.
    C. People can be easily trained even if they have no desire to learn.
    D. Training should be planned, scheduled, executed, and evaluated systematically.

KEY (CORRECT ANSWERS)

1.	C	11.	A
2.	A	12.	D
3.	D	13.	C
4.	C	14.	A
5.	C	15.	C
6.	A	16.	B
7.	B	17.	D
8.	B	18.	B
9.	D	19.	B
10.	B	20.	D

21.	A
22.	C
23.	D
24.	B
25.	C

EXAMINATION SECTION
TEST 1

DIRECTIONS: Each question or incomplete statement is followed by several suggested answers or completions. Select the one that BEST answers the question or completes the statement. *PRINT THE LETTER OF THE CORRECT ANSWER IN THE SPACE AT THE RIGHT.*

1. Professional staff members in large organizations are sometimes frustrated by a lack of vital work-related information because of the failure of some middle-management supervisors to pass along unrestricted information from top management.
   All of the following are considered to be reasons for such failure to pass along information EXCEPT the supervisors'

   A. belief that information affecting procedures will be ignored unless they are present to supervise their subordinates
   B. fear that specific information will require explanation or justification
   C. inclination to regard the possession of information as a symbol of higher status
   D. tendency to treat information as private property

   1.____

2. Increasingly in government, employees' records are being handled by automated data processing systems. However, employees frequently doubt a computer's ability to handle their records properly.
   Which of the following is the BEST way for management to overcome such doubts?

   A. Conduct a public relations campaign to explain the savings certain to result from the use of computers
   B. Use automated data processing equipment made by the firm which has the best repair facilities in the industry
   C. Maintain a clerical force to spot check on the accuracy of the computer's record-keeping
   D. Establish automated data processing systems that are objective, impartial, and take into account individual factors as far as possible

   2.____

3. Some management experts question the usefulness of offering cash to individual employees for their suggestions.
   Which of the following reasons for opposing cash awards is MOST valid?

   A. Emphasis on individual gain deters cooperative effort.
   B. Money spent on evaluating suggestions may outweigh the value of the suggestions.
   C. Awards encourage employees to think about unusual methods of doing work.
   D. Suggestions too technical for ordinary evaluation are usually presented.

   3.____

4. The use of outside consultants, rather than regular staff, in studying and recommending improvements in the operations of public agencies has been criticized.
   Of the following, the BEST argument in favor of using regular staff is that such staff can better perform the work because they

   A. are more knowledgeable about operations and problems
   B. can more easily be organized into teams consisting of technical specialists
   C. may wish to gain additional professional experience
   D. will provide reports which will be more interesting to the public since they are more experienced

   4.____

5. One approach to organizational problem-solving is to have all problem-solving authority   5.__
centralized at the top of the organization.
However, from the viewpoint of providing maximum service to the public, this practice
is UNWISE chiefly because it

    A. reduces the responsibility of the decision-makers
    B. produces delays
    C. reduces internal communications
    D. requires specialists

6. Research has shown that problem-solving efficiency is optimal when the motivation of   6.__
the problem-solver is at a moderate rather than an extreme level.
Of the following, probably the CHIEF reason for this is that the problem-solver

    A. will cause confusion among his subordinates when his motivation is too high
    B. must avoid alternate solutions that tend to lead him up blind alleys
    C. can devote his attention to both the immediate problem as well as to other relevant
       problems in the general area
    D. must feel the need to solve the problem but not so urgently as to direct all his atten-
       tion to the need and none to the means of solution

7. Don't be afraid to make mistakes. Many organizations are paralyzed from the fear of   7.__
making mistakes. As a result, they don't do the things they should; they don't try new and
different ideas.
For the effective supervisor, the MOST valid implication of this statement is that

    A. mistakes should not be encouraged, but there are some unavoidable risks in deci-
       sion-making
    B. mistakes which stem from trying new and different ideas are usually not serious
    C. the possibility of doing things wrong is limited by one's organizational position
    D. the fear of making mistakes will prevent future errors

8. The duties of an employee under your supervision may be either routine, problem-solv-   8.__
ing, innovative, or creative. Which of the following BEST describes duties which are both
innovative and creative?

    A. Checking to make sure that work is done properly
    B. Applying principles in a practical manner
    C. Developing new and better methods of meeting goals
    D. Working at two or more jobs at the same time

9. According to modern management theory, a supervisor who uses as little authority as   9.__
possible and as much as is necessary would be considered to be using a mode that is

    A. autocratic   B. inappropriate
    C. participative   D. directive

10. Delegation involves establishing and maintaining effective working arrangements between a supervisor and the persons who report to him.
Delegation is MOST likely to have taken place when the 10._____

    A. entire staff openly discusses common problems in order to reach solutions satisfactory to the supervisor
    B. performance of specified work is entrusted to a capable person, and the expected results are mutually understood
    C. persons assigned to properly accomplish work are carefully evaluated and given a chance to explain shortcomings
    D. supervisor provides specific written instructions in order to prevent anxiety on the part of inexperienced persons

11. Supervisors often are not aware of the effect that their behavior has on their subordinates.
The one of the following training methods which would be BEST for changing such supervisory behavior is 11._____

    A. essential skills training
    B. off-the-job training
    C. sensitivity training
    D. developmental training

12. A supervisor, in his role as a trainer, may have to decide on the length and frequency of training sessions.
When the material to be taught is new, difficult, and lengthy, the trainer should be guided by the principle that for BEST results in such circumstances, sessions should be 12._____

    A. longer, relatively fewer in number, and held on successive days
    B. shorter, relatively greater in number, and spaced at intervals of several days
    C. of average length, relatively fewer in number, and held at intermittent intervals
    D. of random length and frequency, but spaced at fixed intervals

13. Employee training which is based on realistic simulation, sometimes known as *game play* or *role play*, is sometimes preferable to learning from actual experience on the job. Which of the following is NOT a correct statement concerning the value of simulation to trainees? 13._____

    A. Simulation allows for practice in decision-making without any need for subsequent discussion.
    B. Simulation is intrinsically motivating because it offers a variety of challenges.
    C. Compared to other, more traditional training techniques, simulation is dynamic.
    D. The simulation environment is nonpunitive as compared to real life.

14. Programmed instruction as a method of training has all of the following advantages EXCEPT: 14._____

    A. Learning is accomplished in an optimum sequence of distinct steps
    B. Trainees have wide latitude in deciding what is to be learned within each program
    C. The trainee takes an active part in the learning process
    D. The trainee receives immediate knowledge of the results of his response

15. In a work-study program, trainees were required to submit weekly written performance   15.__
reports in order to insure that work assignments fulfilled the program objectives.
Such reports would also assist the administrator of the work-study program PRIMA-
RILY to

    A. eliminate personal counseling for the trainees
    B. identify problems requiring prompt resolution
    C. reduce the amount of clerical work for all concerned
    D. estimate the rate at which budgeted funds are being expended

16. Which of the following would be MOST useful in order to avoid misunderstanding when   16.__
preparing correspondence or reports?

    A. Use vocabulary which is at an elementary level
    B. Present each sentence as an individual paragraph
    C. Have someone other than the writer read the material for clarity
    D. Use general words which are open to interpretation

17. Which of the following supervisory methods would be MOST likely to train subordinates   17.__
to give a prompt response to memoranda in an organizational setting where most trans-
actions are informal?

    A. Issue a written directive setting forth a schedule of strict deadlines
    B. Let it be known, informally, that those who respond promptly will be rewarded
    C. Follow up each memorandum by a personal inquiry regarding the receiver's reac-
tion to it
    D. Direct subordinates to furnish a precise explanation for ignoring memos

18. Conferences may fail for a number of reasons. Still, a conference that is an apparent fail-   18.__
ure may have some benefit.
Which of the following would LEAST likely be such a benefit? It may

    A. increase for most participants their possessiveness about information they have
    B. produce a climate of good will and trust among many of the participants
    C. provide most participants with an opportunity to learn things about the others
    D. serve as a unifying force to keep most of the individuals functioning as a group

19. Assume that you have been assigned to study and suggest improvements in an operat-   19.__
ing unit of a delegate agency whose staff has become overwhelmed with problems, has
had inadequate resources, and has become accustomed to things getting worse. The
staff is indifferent to cooperating with you because they see no hope of improvement.
Which of the following steps would be LEAST useful in carrying out your assignment?

    A. Encourage the entire staff to make suggestions to you for change
    B. Inform the staff that management is somewhat dissatisfied with their performance
    C. Let staff know that you are fully aware of their problems and stresses
    D. Look for those problem areas where changes can be made quickly

20. Which of the following statements about employer-employee relations is NOT considered to be correct by leading managerial experts?

    A. An important factor in good employer-employee relations is treating workers respectfully.
    B. Employer-employee relations are profoundly influenced by the fundamentals of human nature.
    C. Good employer-employee relations must stem from top management and reach downward.
    D. Employee unions are usually a major obstacle to establishing good employer-employee relations.

20._____

21. In connection with labor relations, the term *management rights* GENERALLY refers to

    A. a managerial review level in a grievance system
    B. statutory prohibitions that bar monetary negotiations
    C. the impact of collective bargaining on government
    D. those subjects which management considers to be non-negotiable

21._____

22. Barriers may exist to the utilization of women in higher level positions. Some of these barriers are attitudinal in nature.
Which of the following is MOST clearly attitudinal in nature?

    A. Advancement opportunities which are vertical in nature and thus require seniority
    B. Experience which is inadequate or irrelevant to the needs of a dynamic and progressive organization
    C. Inadequate means of early identification of employees with talent and potential for advancement
    D. Lack of self-confidence on the part of some women concerning their ability to handle a higher position

22._____

23. Because a reader reacts to the meaning he associates with a word, we can never be sure what emotional impact a word may carry or how it may affect our readers.
The MOST logical implication of this statement for employees who correspond with members of the public is that

    A. a writer should try to select a neutral word that will not bias his writing by its hidden emotional meaning
    B. simple language should be used in writing letters denying requests so that readers are not upset by the denial
    C. every writer should adopt a writing style which he finds natural and easy
    D. whenever there is any doubt as to how a word is defined, the dictionary should be consulted

23._____

24. A public information program should be based on clear information about the nature of actual public knowledge and opinion. One way of learning about the views of the public is through the use of questionnaires.
Which of the following is of LEAST importance in designing a questionnaire?

    A. A respondent should be asked for his name and address.
    B. A respondent should be asked to choose from among several statements the one which expresses his views.
    C. Questions should ask for responses in a form suitable for processing.
    D. Questions should be stated in familiar language.

24._____

25. Assume that you have accepted an invitation to speak before an interested group about a problem. You have brought with you for distribution a number of booklets and other informational material.
Of the following, which would be the BEST way to use this material?

    A. Distribute it before you begin talking so that the audience may read it at their leisure.
    B. Distribute it during your talk to increase the likelihood that it will be read.
    C. Hold it until the end of your talk, then announce that those who wish may take or examine the material.
    D. Before starting the talk, leave it on a table in the back of the room so that people may pick it up as they enter.

25.__

KEY (CORRECT ANSWERS)

1.	A		11.	C
2.	D		12.	B
3.	A		13.	A
4.	A		14.	B
5.	B		15.	B
6.	D		16.	C
7.	A		17.	C
8.	C		18.	A
9.	C		19.	B
10.	B		20.	D

21.	D
22.	D
23.	A
24.	A
25.	C

TEST 2

DIRECTIONS: Each question or incomplete statement is followed by several suggested answers or completions. Select the one that BEST answers the question or completes the statement. *PRINT THE LETTER OF THE CORRECT ANSWER IN THE SPACE AT THE RIGHT.*

1. Of the following, the FIRST step in planning an operation is to   1.____

   A. obtain relevant information
   B. identify the goal to be achieved
   C. consider possible alternatives
   D. make necessary assignments

2. A supervisor who is extremely busy performing routine tasks is MOST likely making   2.____
   INCORRECT use of what basic principle of supervision?

   A. Homogeneous Assignment   B. Span of Control
   C. Work Distribution   D. Delegation of Authority

3. Controls help supervisors to obtain information from which they can determine whether   3.____
   their staffs are achieving planned goals.
   Which one of the following would be LEAST useful as a control device?

   A. Employee diaries   B. Organization charts
   C. Periodic inspections   D. Progress charts

4. A certain employee has difficulty in effectively performing a particular portion of his rou-   4.____
   tine assignments, but his overall productivity is average.
   As the direct supervisor of this individual, your BEST course of action would be to

   A. attempt to develop the man's capacity to execute the problematical facets of his
      assignments
   B. diversify the employee's work assignments in order to build up his confidence
   C. reassign the man to less difficult tasks
   D. request in a private conversation that the employee improve his work output

5. A supervisor who uses persuasion as a means of supervising a unit would GENERALLY   5.____
   also use which of the following practices to supervise his unit?

   A. Supervise and control the staff with an authoritative attitude to indicate that he is a
      take-charge individual
   B. Make significant changes in the organizational operations so as to improve job effi-
      ciency
   C. Remove major communication barriers between himself, subordinates, and man-
      agement
   D. Supervise everyday operations while being mindful of the problems of his subordi-
      nates

6. Whenever a supervisor in charge of a unit delegates a routine task to a capable subordi-   6.____
   nate, he tells him exactly how to do it.
   This practice is GENERALLY

   A. *desirable,* chiefly because good supervisors should be aware of the traits of their
      subordinates and delegate responsibilities to them accordingly
   B. *undesirable,* chiefly because only non-routine tasks should be delegated
   C. *desirable,* chiefly because a supervisor should frequently test the willingness of his
      subordinates to perform ordinary tasks
   D. *undesirable,* chiefly because a capable subordinate should usually be allowed to
      exercise his own discretion in doing a routine job

7. The one of the following activities through which a supervisor BEST demonstrates lead-   7.___
   ership ability is by

   A. arranging periodic staff meetings in order to keep his subordinates informed about
      professional developments in the field
   B. frequently issuing definite orders and directives which will lessen the need for sub-
      ordinates to make decisions in handling any tasks assigned to them
   C. devoting the major part of his time to supervising subordinates so as to stimulate
      continuous improvement
   D. setting aside time for self-development and research so as to improve the skills,
      techniques, and procedures of his unit

8. The following three statements relate to the supervision of employees: 8.___
   I.   The assignment of difficult tasks that offer a challenge is more conducive to
         good morale than the assignment of easy tasks
   II.   The same general principles of supervision that apply to men are equally
         applicable to women
   III. The best retraining program should cover all phases of an employee's work
         in a general manner
   Which of the following choices list ALL of the above statements that are generally cor-
   rect?

   A. II, III   B. I
   C. I, II   D. I, II, III

9. Which of the following examples BEST illustrates the application of the *exception princi-*   9.___
   ple as a supervisory technique?

   A. A complex job is divided among several employees who work simultaneously to
      complete the whole job in a shorter time.
   B. An employee is required to complete any task delegated to him to such an extent
      that nothing is left for the superior who delegated the task except to approve it.
   C. A superior delegates responsibility to a subordinate but retains authority to make
      the final decisions.
   D. A superior delegates all work possible to his subordinates and retains that which
      requires his personal attention or performance.

10. Assume that you are a supervisor. Your immediate superior frequently gives orders to   10.___
    your subordinates without your knowledge.
    Of the following, the MOST direct and effective way for you to handle this problem is to

    A. tell your subordinates to take orders only from you
    B. submit a report to higher authority in which you cite specific instances
    C. discuss it with your immediate superior
    D. find out to what extent your authority and prestige as a supervisor have been
       affected

11. In an agency which has as its primary purpose the protection of the public against fraud-   11.___
    ulent business practices, which of the following would GENERALLY be considered an
    auxiliary or *staff* rather than a *line* function?

    A. Interviewing victims of frauds and advising them about their legal remedies
    B. Daily activities directed toward prevention of fraudulent business practices
    C. Keeping records and statistics about business violations reported and corrected
    D. Follow-up inspections by investigators after corrective action has been taken

12. A supervisor can MOST effectively reduce the spread of false rumors through the *grapevine* by

    A. identifying and disciplining any subordinate responsible for initiating such rumors
    B. keeping his subordinates informed as much as possible about matters affecting them
    C. denying false rumors which might tend to lower staff morale and productivity
    D. making sure confidential matters are kept secure from access by unauthorized employees

12.____

13. A supervisor has tried to learn about the background, education, and family relationships of his subordinates through observation, personal contact, and inspection of their personnel records.
These supervisory actions are GENERALLY

    A. *inadvisable,* chiefly because they may lead to charges of favoritism
    B. *advisable,* chiefly because they may make him more popular with his subordinates
    C. *inadvisable,* chiefly because his efforts may be regarded as an invasion of privacy
    D. *advisable,* chiefly because the information may enable him to develop better understanding of each of his subordinates

13.____

14. In an emergency situation, when action must be taken immediately, it is BEST for the supervisor to give orders in the form of

    A. direct commands which are brief and precise
    B. requests, so that his subordinates will not become alarmed
    C. suggestions which offer alternative courses of action
    D. implied directives, so that his subordinates may use their judgment in carrying them out

14.____

15. When demonstrating a new and complex procedure to a group of subordinates, it is ESSENTIAL that a supervisor

    A. go slowly and repeat the steps involved at least once
    B. show the employees common errors and the consequences of such errors
    C. go through the process at the usual speed so that the employees can see the rate at which they should work
    D. distribute summaries of the procedure during the demonstration and instruct his subordinates to refer to them afterwards

15.____

16. After a procedures manual has been written and distributed,

    A. continuous maintenance work is necessary to keep the manual current
    B. it is best to issue new manuals rather than make changes in the original manual
    C. no changes should be necessary
    D. only major changes should be considered

16.____

17. Of the following, the MOST important criterion of effective report writing is   17.__

    A. eloquence of writing style
    B. the use of technical language
    C. to be brief and to the point
    D. to cover all details

18. The use of electronic data processing   18.__

    A. has proven unsuccessful in most organizations
    B. has unquestionable advantages for all organizations
    C. is unnecessary in most organizations
    D. should be decided upon only after careful feasibility studies by individual organizations

19. The PRIMARY purpose of work measurement is to   19.__

    A. design and install a wage incentive program
    B. determine who should be promoted
    C. establish a yardstick to determine extent of progress
    D. set up a spirit of competition among employees

20. The action which is MOST effective in gaining acceptance of a study by the agency which is being studied is   20.__

    A. a directive from the agency head to install a study based on recommendations included in a report
    B. a lecture-type presentation following approval of the procedures
    C. a written procedure in narrative form covering the proposed system with visual presentations and discussions
    D. procedural charts showing the *before* situation, forms, steps, etc., to the employees affected

21. Which organization principle is MOST closely related to procedural analysis and improvement?   21.__

    A. Duplication, overlapping, and conflict should be eliminated.
    B. Managerial authority should be clearly defined.
    C. The objectives of the organization should be clearly defined.
    D. Top management should be freed of burdensome detail.

22. Which one of the following is the MAJOR objective of operational audits?   22.__

    A. Detecting fraud
    B. Determining organization problems
    C. Determining the number of personnel needed
    D. Recommending opportunities for improving operating and management practices

23. Of the following, the formalization of organization structure is BEST achieved by   23.__

    A. a narrative description of the plan of organization
    B. functional charts
    C. job descriptions together with organization charts
    D. multi-flow charts

24. Budget planning is MOST useful when it achieves 24.____

    A. cost control   B. forecast of receipts
    C. performance review   D. personnel reduction

25. GENERALLY, in applying the principle of delegation in dealing with subordinates, a supervisor 25.____

    A. allows his subordinates to set up work goals and to fix the limits within which they can work
    B. allows his subordinates to set up work goals and then gives detailed orders as to how they are to be achieved
    C. makes relatively few decisions by himself and frames his orders in broad, general terms
    D. provides externalized motivation for his subordinates

KEY (CORRECT ANSWERS)

1. B		11. C
2. D		12. B
3. B		13. D
4. A		14. A
5. D		15. A
6. D		16. A
7. C		17. C
8. C		18. D
9. D		19. C
10. C		20. C

21. A
22. D
23. C
24. A
25. C

READING COMPREHENSION
UNDERSTANDING AND INTERPRETING WRITTEN MATERIAL
EXAMINATION SECTION
TEST 1

DIRECTIONS: Each question or incomplete statement is followed by several suggested answers or completions. Select the one that BEST answers the question or completes the statement. *PRINT THE LETTER OF THE CORRECT ANSWER IN THE SPACE AT THE RIGHT.*

Questions 1-3.

DIRECTIONS: Questions 1 through 3 are to be answered SOLELY on the basis of the following paragraph.

Every organization needs a systematic method of checking its operations as a means to increase efficiency and promote economy. Many successful private firms have instituted a system of audits or internal inspections to accomplish these ends. Law enforcement organizations, which have an extremely important service to *sell,* should be no less zealous in developing efficiency and economy in their operations. Periodic, organized, and systematic inspections are one means of promoting the achievement of these objectives. The necessity of an organized inspection system is perhaps greatest in those law enforcement groups which have grown to such a size that the principal officer can no longer personally supervise or be cognizant of every action taken. Smooth and effective operation demands that the head of the organization have at hand some tool with which he can study and enforce general policies and procedures and also direct compliance with day-to-day orders, most of which are put into execution outside his sight and hearing. A good inspection system can serve as that tool.

1.   The central thought of the above paragraph is that a system of inspections within a police department   1._____

    A.   is unnecessary for a department in which the principal officer can personally supervise all official actions taken
    B.   should be instituted at the first indication that there is any deterioration in job performance by the force
    C.   should be decentralized and administered by first-line supervisory officers
    D.   is an important aid to the police administrator in the accomplishment of law enforcement objectives

2.   The MOST accurate of the following statements concerning the need for an organized inspection system in a law enforcement organization is: It is   2._____

    A.   never needed in an organization of small size where the principal officer can give personal supervision
    B.   most needed where the size of the organization prevents direct supervision by the principal officer
    C.   more needed in law enforcement organizations than in private firms
    D.   especially needed in an organization about to embark upon a needed expansion of services

3. According to the above paragraph, the head of the police organization utilizes the internal inspection system   3.__

    A. as a tool which must be constantly re-examined in the light of changing demands for police service
    B. as an administrative technique to increase efficiency and promote economy
    C. by personally visiting those areas of police operation which are outside his sight and hearing
    D. to augment the control of local commanders over detailed field operations

Questions 4-10.

DIRECTIONS: Questions 4 through 10 are to be answered SOLELY on the basis of the following passage.

Job evaluation and job rating systems are intended to introduce scientific procedures. Any type of approach, when properly used, will give satisfactory results. The Point System, when properly validated by actual use, is more likely to be suitable for general use than the ranking system. In many aspects, the Factor Comparison Plan is a point system tied to money values. Of course, there may be another system that combines the ranking system with the point system, especially during the initial stages of the development of the program. After the program has been in use for some time, the tendency is to drop off the ranking phase and continue the use of the point system.

In the ranking system of rating of jobs, every job within the plant is arranged in some order, either from the one with the simplest qualifications to the one with maximum requirements, or in the reverse order. This system should be preceded by careful job analysis and the writing of accurate job descriptions before the rating process is undertaken. It is possible, of course, to take the jobs as they are found in the business enterprise and use the names as they are without any attempt at standardization, and merely rank them according to the general over-all impression of the raters. Such a procedure is certain to fall short of what may reasonably be expected of job rating. Another procedure that is in reality merely a modification of the simple rating described above is to establish a series of grades or zones and arrange all the jobs in the plant into groups within these grades and zones. The practice in most common use is to arrange all the jobs in the plant according to their requirements by rating them and then to establish the classifications or groups.

The actual ranking of jobs may be done by one individual, several individuals, or a committee. If several individuals are working independently on the task, it will usually be found that, in general, they agree but that their rankings vary in certain details. A conference between the individuals, with each person giving his reasons why he rated one way or another, usually produces agreement. The detailed job descriptions are particularly helpful when there is disagreement among raters as to the rating of certain jobs. It is not only possible but desirable to have workers participate in the construction of the job description and in rating the job.

4. The MAIN theme of this passage is   4.__

    A. the elimination of bias in job rating
    B. the rating of jobs by the ranking system

C. the need for accuracy in allocating points in the point system
D. pitfalls to avoid in selecting key jobs in the Factor Comparison Plan

5. The ranking system of rating jobs consists MAINLY of   5.____

    A. attaching a point value to each ratable factor of each job prior to establishing an equitable pay scale
    B. arranging every job in the organization in descending order and then following this up with a job analysis of the key jobs
    C. preparing accurate job descriptions after a job analysis and then arranging all jobs either in ascending or descending order based on job requirements
    D. arbitrarily establishing a hierarchy of job classes and grades and then fitting each job into a specific class and grade based on the opinions of unit supervisors

6. The above passage states that the system of classifying jobs MOST used in an organization is to   6.____

    A. organize all jobs in the organization in accordance with their requirements and then create categories or clusters of jobs
    B. classify all jobs in the organization according to the titles and rank by which they are currently known in the organization
    C. establish a pre-arranged series of grades or zones and then fit
    D. all jobs into one of the grades or zones
    E. determine the salary currently being paid for each job and then rank the jobs in order according to salary

7. According to the above passage, experience has shown that when a group of raters is assigned to the job evaluation task and each individual rates independently of the others, the raters GENERALLY   7.____

    A. agree with respect to all aspects of their rankings
    B. disagree with respect to all or nearly all aspects of the rankings
    C. disagree on overall ratings, but agree on specific rating factors
    D. agree on overall rankings, but have some variance in some details

8. The above passage states that the use of a detailed job description is of SPECIAL value when   8.____

    A. employees of an organization have participated in the preliminary step involved in actual preparation of the job description
    B. labor representatives are not participating in ranking of the jobs
    C. an individual rater who is unsure of himself is ranking the jobs
    D. a group of raters is having difficulty reaching unanimity with respect to ranking a certain job

9. A comparison of the various rating systems as described in the above passage shows that   9.____

    A. the ranking system is not as appropriate for general use as a properly validated point system
    B. the point system is the same as the Factor Comparison Plan except that it places greater emphasis on money

C. no system is capable of combining the point system and the Factor Comparison Plan
D. the point system will be discontinued last when used in combination with the Factor Comparison System

10. The above passage implies that the PRINCIPAL reason for creating job evaluation and rating systems was to help   10.___

A. overcome union opposition to existing salary plans
B. base wage determination on a more objective and orderly foundation
C. eliminate personal bias on the part of the trained scientific job evaluators
D. management determine if it was overpricing the various jobs in the organizational hierarchy

Questions 11-13.

DIRECTIONS: Questions 11 through 13 are to be answered SOLELY on the basis of the following paragraph.

The common sense character of the merit system seems so natural to most Americans that many people wonder why it should ever have been inoperative. After all, the American economic system, the most phenomenal the world has ever known, is also founded on a rugged selective process which emphasizes the personal qualities of capacity, industriousness, and productivity. The criteria may not have always been appropriate and competition has not always been fair, but competition there was, and the responsibilities and the rewards – with exceptions, of course – have gone to those who could measure up in terms of intelligence, knowledge, or perseverance. This has been true not only in the economic area, in the money-making process, but also in achievement in the professions and other walks of life.

11. According to the above paragraph, economic rewards in the United States have   11.___

A. always been based on appropriate, fair criteria
B. only recently been based on a competitive system
C. not gone to people who compete too ruggedly
D. usually gone to those people with intelligence, knowledge, and perseverance

12. According to the above passage, a merit system is   12.___

A. an unfair criterion on which to base rewards
B. unnatural to anyone who is not American
C. based only on common sense
D. based on the same principles as the American economic system

13. According to the above passage, it is MOST accurate to say that   13.___

A. the United States has always had a civil service merit system
B. civil service employees are very rugged
C. the American economic system has always been based on a merit objective
D. competition is unique to the American way of life

Questions 14-15.

DIRECTIONS: Questions 14 and 15 are to be answered SOLELY on the basis of the following paragraph.

In-basket tests are often used to assess managerial potential. The exercise consists of a set of papers that would be likely to be found in the in-basket of an administrator or manager at any given time, and requires the individuals participating in the examination to indicate how they would dispose of each item found in the in-basket. In order to handle the in-basket effectively, they must successfully manage their time, refer and assign some work to subordinates, juggle potentially conflicting appointments and meetings, and arrange for follow-up of problems generated by the items in the in-basket. In other words, the in-basket test is attempting to evaluate the participants' abilities to organize their work, set priorities, delegate, control, and make decisions.

14.   According to the above paragraph, to succeed in an in-basket test, an administrator must   14.____

      A.   be able to read very quickly
      B.   have a great deal of technical knowledge
      C.   know when to delegate work
      D.   arrange a lot of appointments and meetings

15.   According to the above paragraph, all of the following abilities are indications of manage-   15.____
      rial potential EXCEPT the ability to

      A.   organize and control   B.   manage time
      C.   write effective reports   D.   make appropriate decisions

Questions 16-19.

DIRECTIONS: Questions 16 through 19 are to be answered SOLELY on the basis of the following paragraph.

A personnel researcher has at his disposal various approaches for obtaining information, analyzing it, and arriving at conclusions that have value in predicting and affecting the behavior of people at work. The type of method to be used depends on such factors as the nature of the research problem, the available data, and the attitudes of those people being studied to the various kinds of approaches. While the experimental approach, with its use of control groups, is the most refined type of study, there are others that are often found useful in personnel research. Surveys, in which the researcher obtains facts on a problem from a variety of sources, are employed in research on wages, fringe benefits, and labor relations. Historical studies are used to trace the development of problems in order to understand them better and to isolate possible causative factors. Case studies are generally developed to explore all the details of a particular problem that is representative of other similar problems. A researcher chooses the most appropriate form of study for the problem he is investigating. He should recognize, however, that the experimental method, commonly referred to as the scientific method, if used validly and reliably, gives the most conclusive results.

16.   The above paragraph discusses several approaches used to obtain information on par-   16.____
      ticular problems. Which of the following may be MOST reasonably concluded from the paragraph?
      A(n)

A. historical study cannot determine causative factors
B. survey is often used in research on fringe benefits
C. case study is usually used to explore a problem that is unique and unrelated to other problems
D. experimental study is used when the scientific approach to a problem fails

17. According to the above paragraph, all of the following are factors that may determine the type of approach a researcher uses EXCEPT   17.___

    A. the attitudes of people toward being used in control groups
    B. the number of available sources
    C. his desire to isolate possible causative factors
    D. the degree of accuracy he requires

18. The words *scientific method*, as used in the last sentence of the above paragraph, refer to a type of study which, according to the above paragraph   18.___

    A. uses a variety of sources
    B. traces the development of problems
    C. uses control groups
    D. analyzes the details of a representative problem

19. Which of the following can be MOST reasonably concluded from the above paragraph? In obtaining and analyzing information on a particular problem, a researcher employs the method which is the   19.___

    A. most accurate   B. most suitable
    C. least expensive   D. least time-consuming

Questions 20-25.

DIRECTIONS: Questions 20 through 25 are to be answered SOLELY on the basis of the following passage.

The quality of the voice of a worker is an important factor in conveying to clients and co-workers his attitude and, to some degree, his character. The human voice, when not consciously disguised, may reflect a person's mood, temper, and personality. It has been shown in several experiments that certain character traits can be assessed with better than chance accuracy through listening to the voice of an unknown person who cannot be seen.

Since one of the objectives of the worker is to put clients at ease and to present an encouraging and comfortable atmosphere, a harsh, shrill, or loud voice could have a negative effect. A client who displays emotions of anger or resentment would probably be provoked even further by a caustic tone. In a face-to-face situation, an unpleasant voice may be compensated for, to some degree, by a concerned and kind facial expression. However, when one speaks on the telephone, the expression on one's face cannot be seen by the listener. A supervising clerk who wishes to represent himself effectively to clients should try to eliminate as many faults as possible in striving to develop desirable voice qualities.

20. If a worker uses a sarcastic tone while interviewing a resentful client, the client, according to the above passage, would MOST likely
    20.____

    A. avoid the face-to-face situation
    B. be ashamed of his behavior
    C. become more resentful
    D. be provoked to violence

21. According to the passage, experiments comparing voice and character traits have demonstrated that
    21.____

    A. prospects for improving an unpleasant voice through training are better than chance
    B. the voice can be altered to project many different psychological characteristics
    C. the quality of the human voice reveals more about the speaker than his words do
    D. the speaker's voice tells the hearer something about the speaker's personality

22. Which of the following, according to the above passage, is a person's voice MOST likely to reveal?
    His
    22.____

    A. prejudices   B. intelligence
    C. social awareness   D. temperament

23. It may be MOST reasonably concluded from the above passage that an interested and sympathetic expression on the face of a worker
    23.____

    A. may induce a client to feel certain he will receive welfare benefits
    B. will eliminate the need for pleasant vocal qualities in the interviewer
    C. may help to make up for an unpleasant voice in the interviewer
    D. is desirable as the interviewer speaks on the telephone to a client

24. Of the following, the MOST reasonable implication of the above paragraph is that a worker should, when speaking to a client, control and use his voice to
    24.____

    A. simulate a feeling of interest in the problems of the client
    B. express his emotions directly and adequately
    C. help produce in the client a sense of comfort and security
    D. reflect his own true personality

25. It may be concluded from the above passage that the PARTICULAR reason for a worker to pay special attention to modulating her voice when talking on the phone to a client is that, during a telephone conversation,
    25.____

    A. there is a necessity to compensate for the way in which a telephone distorts the voice
    B. the voice of the worker is a reflection of her mood and character
    C. the client can react only on the basis of the voice and words she hears
    D. the client may have difficulty getting a clear under-standing over the telephone

KEY (CORRECT ANSWERS)

1.	D	11.	D
2.	B	12.	D
3.	B	13.	C
4.	B	14.	C
5.	C	15.	C
6.	A	16.	B
7.	D	17.	D
8.	D	18.	C
9.	A	19.	B
10.	B	20.	C

21.	D
22.	D
23.	C
24.	C
25.	C

———

TEST 2

Questions 1-3.

DIRECTIONS: Questions 1 through 3 are to be answered SOLELY on the basis of the following paragraph.

Suppose you are given the job of printing, collating, and stapling 8,000 copies of a ten-page booklet as soon as possible. You have available one photo-offset machine, a collator with an automatic stapler, and the personnel to operate these machines. All will be available for however long the job takes to complete. The photo-offset machine prints 5,000 impressions an hour, and it takes about 15 minutes to set up a plate. The collator, including time for insertion of pages and stapling, can process about 2,000 booklets an hour. (Answers should be based on the assumption that there are no breakdowns or delays.)

1.   Assuming that all the printing is finished before the collating is started, if the job is given   1.____
     to you late Monday and your section can begin work the next day and is able to devote
     seven hours a day, Monday through Friday, to the job until it is finished, what is the BEST
     estimate of when the job will be finished?

     A.   Wednesday afternoon of the same week
     B.   Thursday morning of the same week
     C.   Friday morning of the same week
     D.   Monday morning of the next week

2.   An operator suggests to you that instead of completing all the printing and then begin-   2.____
     ning collating and stapling, you first print all the pages for 4,000 booklets, so that they
     can be collated and stapled while the last 4,000 booklets are being printed.
     If you accepted this suggestion, the job would be completed

     A.   sooner but would require more man-hours
     B.   at the same time using either method
     C.   later and would require more man-hours
     D.   sooner but there would be more wear and tear on the plates

3.   Assume that you have the same assignment and equipment as described above, but   3.____
     16,000 copies of the booklet are needed instead of 8,000.
     If you decided to print 8,000 complete booklets, then collate and staple them while you
     started printing the next 8,000 booklets, which of the following statements would
     MOST accurately describe the relationship between this new method and your original
     method of printing all the booklets at one time, and then collating and stapling them?
     The

     A.   job would be completed at the same time regardless of the method used
     B.   new method would result in the job's being completed 3 1/2 hours earlier
     C.   original method would result in the job's being completed an hour later
     D.   new method would result in the job's being completed 1 1/2 hours earlier.

Questions 4-6.

DIRECTIONS: Questions 4 through 6 are to be answered SOLELY on the basis of the following passage.

When using words like company, association, council, committee, and board in place of the full official name, the writer should not capitalize these short forms unless he intends them to invoke the full force of the institution's authority. In legal contracts, in minutes, or in formal correspondence where one is speaking formally and officially on behalf of the company, the term Company is usually capitalized, but in ordinary usage, where it is not essential to load the short form with this significance, capitalization would be excessive. (Example: The company will have many good openings for graduates this June.)

The treatment recommended for short forms of place names is essentially the same as that recommended for short forms of organizational names. In general, we capitalize the full form but not the short form. If Park Avenue is referred to in one sentence, then the *avenue* is sufficient in subsequent references. The same is true with words like building, hotel, station, and airport, which are capitalized when part of a proper name changed (Pan Am Building, Hotel Plaza, Union Station, O'Hare Airport), but are simply lower-cased when replacing these specific names.

4. The above passage states that USUALLY the short forms of names of organizations   4.____

   A. and places should not be capitalized
   B. and places should be capitalized
   C. should not be capitalized, but the short forms of names of places should be capitalized
   D. should be capitalized, but the short forms of names of places should not be capitalized

5. The above passage states that in legal contracts, in minutes, and in formal correspondence, the short forms of names of organizations should   5.____

   A. usually not be capitalized
   B. usually be capitalized
   C. usually not be used
   D. never be used

6. It can be INFERRED from the above passage that decisions regarding when to capitalize certain words   6.____

   A. should be left to the discretion of the writer
   B. should be based on generally accepted rules
   C. depend on the total number of words capitalized
   D. are of minor importance

Questions 7-10.

DIRECTIONS: Questions 7 through 10 are to be answered SOLELY on the basis of the following passage.

Use of the systems and procedures approach to office management is revolutionizing the supervision of office work. This approach views an enterprise as an entity which seeks to fulfill definite objectives. Systems and procedures help to organize repetitive work into a routine, thus reducing the amount of decision making required for its accomplishment. As a result, employees are guided in their efforts and perform only necessary work. Supervisors are relieved of any details of execution and are free to attend to more important work. Establishing work guides which require that identical tasks be performed the same way each time permits standardization of forms, machine operations, work methods, and controls. This approach also reduces the probability of errors. Any error committed is usually discovered quickly because the incorrect work does not meet the requirement of the work guides. Errors are also reduced through work specialization, which allows each employee to become thoroughly proficient in a particular type of work. Such proficiency also tends to improve the morale of the employees.

7. The above passage states that the accuracy of an employee's work is INCREASED by   7.____

    A. using the work specialization approach
    B. employing a probability sample
    C. requiring him to shift at one time into different types of tasks
    D. having his supervisor check each detail of work execution

8. Of the following, which one BEST expresses the main theme of the above passage? The   8.____

    A. advantages and disadvantages of the systems and procedures approach to office management
    B. effectiveness of the systems and procedures approach to office management in developing skills
    C. systems and procedures approach to office management as it relates to office costs
    D. advantages of the systems and procedures approach to office management for supervisors and office workers

9. Work guides are LEAST likely to be used when   9.____

    A. standardized forms are used
    B. a particular office task is distinct and different from all others
    C. identical tasks are to be performed in identical ways
    D. similar work methods are expected from each employee

10. According to the above passage, when an employee makes a work error, it USUALLY   10.____

    A. is quickly corrected by the supervisor
    B. necessitates a change in the work guides
    C. can be detected quickly if work guides are in use
    D. increases the probability of further errors by that employee

Questions 11-12.

DIRECTIONS: Questions 11 and 12 are to be answered SOLELY on the basis of the following passage.

    The coordination of the many activities of a large public agency is absolutely essential. Coordination, as an administrative principle, must be distinguished from and is independent of cooperation. Coordination can be of either the horizontal or the vertical type. In large organizations, the objectives of vertical coordination are achieved by the transmission of orders and statements of policy down through the various levels of authority. It is an accepted generalization that the more authoritarian the organization, the more easily may vertical coordination be accomplished. Horizontal coordination is arrived at through staff work, administrative management, and conferences of administrators of equal rank. It is obvious that of the two types of coordination, the vertical kind is more important, for at best horizontal coordination only supplements the coordination effected up and down the line.

11. According to the above passage, the ease with which vertical coordination is achieved in a large agency depends upon

    A. the extent to which control is firmly exercised from above
    B. the objectives that have been established for the agency
    C. the importance attached by employees to the orders and statements of policy transmitted through the agency
    D. the cooperation obtained at the various levels of authority

11.____

12. According to the above passage,

    A. vertical coordination is dependent for its success upon horizontal coordination
    B. one type of coordination may work in opposition to the other
    C. similar methods may be used to achieve both types of coordination
    D. horizontal coordination is at most an addition to vertical coordination

12.____

Questions 13-17.

DIRECTIONS: Questions 13 through 17 are to be answered SOLELY on the basis of the following situation.

Assume that you are a newly appointed supervisor in the same unit in which you have been acting as a provisional for some time. You have in your unit the following workers:

WORKER I - He has always been an efficient worker. In a number of his cases, the clients have recently begun to complain that they cannot manage on the departmental budget.

WORKER II - He has been under selective supervision for some time as an experienced, competent worker. He now begins to be late for his supervisory conferences and to stress how much work he has to do.

WORKER III - He has been making considerable improvement in his ability to handle the details of his job. He now tells you, during an individual conference, that he does not need such close supervision and that he wants to operate more independently. He says that Worker II is always available when he needs a little information or help but, in general, he can manage very well by himself.

WORKER IV - He brings you a complex case for decision as to eligibility. Discussion of the case brings out the fact that he has failed to consider all the available resources adequately but has stressed the family's needs to include every extra item in the budget. This is the third case of a similar nature that this worker has brought to you recently. This worker and Worker I work in adjacent territory and are rather friendly.

In the following questions, select the option that describes the method of dealing with these workers that illustrates BEST supervisory practice.

13. With respect to supervision of Worker I, the assistant supervisor should

13.____

   A. discuss with the worker, in an individual conference, any problems that he may be having due to the increase in the cost of living
   B. plan a group conference for the unit around budgeting, as both Workers I and IV seem to be having budgetary difficulties
   C. discuss with Workers I and IV together the meaning of money as acceptance or rejection to the clients
   D. discuss with Worker I the budgetary data in each case in relation to each client's situation

14. With respect to supervision of Worker II, the supervisor should

14.____

   A. move slowly with this worker and give him time to learn that the supervisor's official appointment has not changed his attitudes or methods of supervision
   B. discuss the worker's change of attitude and ask him to analyze the reasons for his change in behavior
   C. take time to show the worker how he is avoiding his responsibility in the supervisor-worker relationship and that he is resisting supervision
   D. hold an evaluatory conference with the worker and show him how he is taking over responsibilities that are not his by providing supervision for Worker III

15. With respect to supervision of Worker III, the supervisor should discuss with this worker

15.____

   A. why he would rather have supervision from Worker II than from the supervisor
   B. the necessity for further improvement before he can go on selective supervision
   C. an analysis of the improvement that has been made and the extent to which the worker is able to handle the total job for which he is responsible
   D. the responsibility of the supervisor to see that clients receive adequate service

16. With respect to supervision of Worker IV, the supervisor should

16.____

   A. show the worker that resources figures are incomplete but that even if they were complete, the family would probably be eligible for assistance
   B. ask the worker why he is so protective of these families since there are three cases so similar
   C. discuss with the worker all three cases at the same time so that the worker may see his own role in the three situations
   D. discuss with the worker the reasons for departmental policies and procedures around budgeting

17. With respect to supervision of Workers I and IV, since these two workers are friends and would seem to be influencing each other, the supervisor should

17.____

   A. hold a joint conference with them both, pointing out how they should clear with the supervisor and not make their own rules together
   B. handle the problems of each separately in individual conferences
   C. separate them by transferring one to another territory or another unit
   D. take up the problem of workers asking help of each other rather than from the supervisor in a group meeting

Questions 18-20.

DIRECTIONS: Questions 18 through 20 are to be answered SOLELY on the basis of the following passage.

One of the key supervisory problems in a large municipal recreation department is that many leaders are assigned to isolated playgrounds or small centers, where it is difficult to observe their work regularly. Often their facilities are extremely limited. In such settings, as well as in larger recreation centers, where many recreation leaders tend to have other jobs as well, there tends to be a low level of morale and incentive. Still, it is the supervisor's task to help recreation personnel to develop pride in their work and to maintain a high level of performance. With isolated leaders, the supervisor may give advice or assistance. Leaders may be assigned to different tasks or settings during the year to maximize their productivity and provide new challenges. When it is clear that leaders are not willing to make a real effort to contribute to the department, the possibility of penalties must be considered, within the scope of departmental policy and the union contract. However, the supervisor should be constructive, encourage and assist workers to take a greater interest in their work, be innovative, and try to raise morale and to improve performance in positive ways.

18.   The one of the following that would be the MOST appropriate title for the above passage is   18._____

A.   SMALL COMMUNITY CENTERS - PRO AND CON
B.   PLANNING BETTER RECREATION PROGRAMS
C.   THE SUPERVISOR'S TASK IN UPGRADING PERSONNEL PERFORMANCE
D.   THE SUPERVISOR AND THE MUNICIPAL UNION - RIGHTS AND OBLIGATIONS

19.   The above passage makes clear that recreation leadership performance in ALL recreation playgrounds and centers throughout a large city is   19._____

A.   generally above average, with good morale on the part of most recreation leaders
B.   beyond description since no one has ever observed or evaluated recreation leaders
C.   a key test of the personnel department's effort to develop more effective hiring standards
D.   of mixed quality, with many recreation leaders having poor morale and a low level of achievement

20.   According to the above passage, the supervisor's role is to   20._____

A.   use disciplinary action as his major tool in upgrading performance
B.   tolerate the lack of effort of individual employees since they are assigned to isolated playgrounds or small centers
C.   employ encouragement, advice, and, when appropriate, disciplinary action to improve performance
D.   inform the county supervisor whenever malfeasance or idleness is detected

Questions 21-25.

DIRECTIONS: Questions 21 through 25 are to be answered SOLELY on the basis of the following passage.

EMPLOYEE LEAVE REGULATIONS

Peter Smith, as a full-time permanent city employee under the Career and Salary Plan, earns an *annual leave allowance*. This consists of a certain number of days off a year with pay and may be used for vacation, personal business, and for observing religious holidays As a newly appointed employee, during his first 8 years of city service, he will earn an annual leave allowance of 20 days off a year (an average of 1 2/3 days off a month). After he has finished 8 full years of working for the city, he will begin earning an additional 5 days off a year. His *annual leave allowance*, therefore, will then be 25 days a year and will remain at this amount for seven full years. He will begin earning an additional two days off a year after he has completed a total of 15 years of city employment. Therefore, in his sixteenth year of working for the city, Mr. Smith will be earning 27 days off a year as his *annual leave allowance* (an average of 2 1/4 days off a month).

A *sick leave allowance* of one day a month is also given to Mr. Smith, but it can be used only in cases of actual illness. When Mr. Smith returns to work after *using sick leave allowance*, he must have a doctor's note if the absence is for a total of more than 3 days, but he may also be required to show a doctor's note for absences of 1, 2, or 3 days.

21. According to the above passage, Mr. Smith's *annual leave allowance* consists of a certain number of days off a year which he   21.____

   A.   does not get paid for
   B.   gets paid for at time and a half
   C.   may use for personal business
   D.   may not use for observing religious holidays

22. According to the above passage, after Mr. Smith has been working for the city for 9 years, his *annual leave allowance* will be _____ days a year.   22.____

   A.   20   B.   25   C.   27   D.   37

23. According to the above passage, Mr. Smith will begin earning an average of 2 days off a month as his *annual leave allowance* after he has worked for the city for full years.   23.____

   A.   7   B.   8   C.   15   D.   17

24. According to the above passage, Mr. Smith is given a *sick leave allowance* of   24.____

   A.   1 day every 2 months   B.   1 day per month
   C.   1 2/3 days per month   D.   2 1/4 days a month

25. According to the above passage, when he uses *sick leave allowance*, Mr. Smith may be required to show a doctor's note   25.____

   A.   even if his absence is for only 1 day
   B.   only if his absence is for more than 2 days
   C.   only if his absence is for more than 3 days
   D.   only if his absence is for 3 days or more

KEY (CORRECT ANSWERS)

1.	C		11.	A
2.	C		12.	D
3.	D		13.	D
4.	A		14.	A
5.	B		15.	C
6.	B		16.	C
7.	A		17.	B
8.	D		18.	C
9.	B		19.	D
10.	C		20.	C

21.	C
22.	B
23.	C
24.	B
25.	A

———

TEST 3

Questions 1-6.

DIRECTIONS: Questions 1 through 6 are to be answered SOLELY on the basis of the following passage.

A folder is made of a sheet of heavy paper (manila, kraft, pressboard, or red rope stock) that has been folded once so that the back is about one-half inch higher than the front. Folders are larger than the papers they contain in order to protect them. Two standard folder sizes are *letter size* for papers that are 8 1/2" x 11" and *legal cap* for papers that are 8 1/2" x 13".

Folders are cut across the top in two ways: so that the back is straight (straight-cut) or so that the back has a tab that projects above the top of the folder. Such tabs bear captions that identify the contents of each folder. Tabs vary in width and position. The tabs of a set of folders that are *one-half cut* are half the width of the folder and have only two positions.

One-third cut folders have three positions, each tab occupying a third of the width of the folder. Another standard tabbing is *one-fifth cut*, which has five positions. There are also folders with *two-fifths cut*, with the tabs in the third and fourth or fourth and fifth positions.

1. Of the following, the BEST title for the above passage is   1._____

   A. FILING FOLDERS   B. STANDARD FOLDER SIZES
   C. THE USES OF THE FOLDER   D. THE USE OF TABS

2. According to the above passage, one of the standard folder sizes is called   2._____

   A. Kraft cut   B. legal cap
   C. one-half cut   D. straight-cut

3. According to the above passage, tabs are GENERALLY placed along the _____ of the   3._____
   folder.

   A. back   B. front
   C. left side   D. right side

4. According to the above passage, a tab is GENERALLY used to   4._____

   A. distinguish between standard folder sizes
   B. identify the contents of a folder
   C. increase the size of the folder
   D. protect the papers within the folder

5. According to the above passage, a folder that is two-fifths cut has _____ tabs.   5._____

   A. no   B. two   C. three   D. five

6. According to the above passage, one reason for making folders larger than the papers   6._____
   they contain is that

   A. only a certain size folder can be made from heavy paper
   B. they will protect the papers
   C. they will aid in setting up a tab system
   D. the back of the folder must be higher than the front

Questions 7-15.

DIRECTIONS: Questions 7 through 15 are to be answered SOLELY on the basis of the following passage.

The City University of New York traces its origins to 1847, when the Free Academy, which later became City College, was founded as the first tuition-free municipal college. City and Hunter Colleges were placed under the direction of the Board of Higher Education in 1926, and Brooklyn and Queens Colleges were subsequently added to the system of municipal colleges. In 1955, Staten Island Community College, the first of the two-year colleges sponsored by the Board of Higher Education under the program of the State University of New York, joined the system.

In 1961, the four senior colleges and three community colleges then under the jurisdiction of the Board of Higher Education became the City University of New York, and a University Graduate Division was organized to offer programs leading to the Ph.D. Since then, the university has undergone even more rapid growth. Today, it consists of nine senior colleges, an upper division college which admits students at the junior level, eight community colleges, a graduate division, and an affiliated medical center.

In the summer of 1969, the Board of Higher Education resolved that the time had come to commit the resources of the university to meeting an urgent social need—unrestricted access to higher education for all youths of the City. Determined to prevent the waste of human potential represented by the thousands of high school graduates whose limited educational opportunities left them unable to meet existing admission standards, the Board moved to adopt a policy of Open Admissions. It was their judgment that the best way of determining whether a potential student can benefit from college work is to admit him to college, provide him with the learning assistance he needs, and then evaluate his performance.

Beginning with the class of June 1970, every New York City resident who received a high school diploma from a public or private high school was guaranteed a place in one of the colleges of City University.

7. Of the following, the BEST title for the above passage is   7.____

    A.   A BRIEF HISTORY OF THE CITY UNIVERSITY
    B.   HIGH SCHOOLS AND THE CITY UNIVERSITY
    C.   THE COMPONENTS OF THE UNIVERSITY
    D.   TUITION-FREE COLLEGES

8. According to the above passage, which one of the following colleges of the City University was ORIGINALLY called the Free Academy?   8.____

    A.   Brooklyn College   B.   City College
    C.   Hunter College   D.   Queens College

9. According to the above passage, the system of municipal colleges became the City University of New York in   9.____

    A.   1926   B.   1955   C.   1961   D.   1969

10. According to the above passage, Staten Island Community College came under the juris- 10.____
diction of the Board of Higher Education

    A. 6 years after a Graduate Division was organized
    B. 8 years before the adoption of the Open Admissions Policy
    C. 29 years after Brooklyn and Queens Colleges
    D. 29 years after City and Hunter Colleges

11. According to the above passage, the Staten Island Community College is 11.

    A. a graduate division center
    B. a senior college
    C. a two-year college
    D. an upper division college

12. According to the above passage, the TOTAL number of colleges, divisions, and affiliated 12.____
branches of the City University is

    A. 18   B. 19   C. 20   D. 21

13. According to the above passage, the Open Admissions Policy is designed to determine 13.____
whether a potential student will benefit from college by PRIMARILY

    A. discouraging competition for placement in the City University among high school
       students
    B. evaluating his performance after entry into college
    C. lowering admission standards
    D. providing learning assistance before entry into college

14. According to the above passage, the FIRST class to be affected by the Open Admissions 14.____
Policy was the

    A. high school class which graduated in January 1970
    B. City University class which graduated in June 1970
    C. high school class when graduated in June 1970
    D. City University class which graduated in June 1970

15. According to the above passage, one of the reasons that the Board of Higher Education 15.____
initiated the policy of Open Admissions was to

    A. enable high school graduates with a background of limited educational opportuni-
       ties to enter college
    B. expand the growth of the City University so as to increase the number and variety
       of degrees offered
    C. provide a social resource to the qualified youth of the City
    D. revise admission standards to meet the needs of the City

Questions 16-18.

DIRECTIONS: Questions 16 through 18 are to be answered SOLELY on the basis of the fol-
                lowing passage.

    Hereafter, all probationary students interested in transferring to community college
career programs (associate degrees) from liberal arts programs in senior colleges (bachelor

degrees) will be eligible for such transfers if they have completed no more than three semesters.

For students with averages of 1.5 or above, transfer will be automatic. Those with 1.0 to 1.5 averages can transfer provisionally and will be required to make substantial progress during the first semester in the career program. Once transfer has taken place, only those courses in which passing grades were received will be computed in the community college grade-point average.

No request for transfer will be accepted from probationary students wishing to enter the liberal arts programs at the community college.

16. According to this passage, the one of the following which is the BEST statement concerning the transfer of probationary students is that a probationary student   16.___

    A. may transfer to a career program at the end of one semester
    B. must complete three semester hours before he is eligible for transfer
    C. is not eligible to transfer to a career program
    D. is eligible to transfer to a liberal arts program

17. Which of the following is the BEST statement of academic evaluation for transfer purposes in the case of probationary students?   17.___

    A. No probationary student with an average under 1.5 may transfer.
    B. A probationary student with an average of 1.3 may not transfer.
    C. A probationary student with an average of 1.6 may transfer.
    D. A probationary student with an average of .8 may transfer on a provisional basis.

18. It is MOST likely that, of the following, the next degree sought by one who already holds the Associate in Science degree would be a(n)   18.___

    A. Assistantship in Science degree
    B. Associate in Applied Science degree
    C. Bachelor of Science degree
    D. Doctor of Philosophy degree

Questions 19-20.

DIRECTIONS: Questions 19 and 20 are to be answered SOLELY on the basis of the following passage.

Auto: Auto travel requires prior approval by the President and/or appropriate Dean and must be indicated in the *Request for Travel Authorization* form. Employees authorized to use personal autos on official College business will be reimbursed at the rate of 28¢ per mile for the first 500 miles driven and 18¢ per mile for mileage driven in excess of 500 miles. The Comptroller's Office may limit the amount of reimbursement to the expenditure that would have been made if a less expensive mode of transportation (railroad, airplane, bus, etc.) had been utilized. If this occurs, the traveler will have to pick up the excess expenditure as a personal expense.

Tolls, Parking Fees, and Parking Meter Fees are not reimbursable and may not be claimed.

19. Suppose that Professor T. gives the office assistant the following memorandum: 19.____
    Used car for official trip to Albany, New York, and return. Distance from New York to
    Albany is 148 miles. Tolls were $3.50 each way. Parking garage cost $3.00.
    When preparing the Travel Expense Voucher for Professor T., the figure which should
    be claimed for transportation is

    A. $120.88   B. $113.88   C. $82.88   D. $51.44

20. Suppose that Professor V. gives the office assistant the following memorandum: 20.____
    Used car for official trip to Pittsburgh, Pennsylvania, and return.
    Distance from New York to Pittsburgh is 350 miles. Tolls were $3.30, $11.40 going, and
    $3.30, $2.00 returning.
    When preparing the Travel Expense Voucher for Professor V., the figure which should
    be claimed for transportation is

    A. $225.40   B. $176.00   C. $127.40   D. $98.00

Questions 21-25.

DIRECTIONS: Questions 21 through 25 are to be answered SOLELY on the basis of the fol-
               lowing passage.

For a period of nearly fifteen years, beginning in the mid-1950's, higher education sus-
tained a phenomenal rate of growth. The factors principally responsible were continuing
improvement in the rate of college entrance by high school graduates, a 50 percent increase
in the size of the college-age (eighteen to twenty-one) group, and–until about 1967–a rapid
expansion of university research activity supported by the Federal government.

Today, as one looks ahead to the year 2010, it is apparent that each of these favorable
stimuli will either be abated or turn into a negative factor. The rate of growth of the college-
age group has already diminished; and from 2000 to 2005, the size of the college-age group
has shrunk annually almost as fast as it grew from 1965 to 1970. From 2005 to 2010, this
annual decrease will slow down so that by 2010 the age group will be about the same size as
it was in 2009. This substantial net decrease in the size of the college-age group (from 1995
to 2010) will dramatically affect college enrollments since, currently, 83 percent of undergraduates are twenty-one and under, and another 11 percent are twenty-two to twenty-four.

21. Which one of the following factors is NOT mentioned in the above passage as contribut-   21.____
    ing to the high rate of growth of higher education?

    A. A large increase in the size of the eighteen to twenty-one age group
    B. The equalization of educational opportunities among socio-economic groups
    C. The Federal budget impact on research and development spending in the higher
        education sector
    D. The increasing rate at which high school graduates enter college

22. Based on the information in the above passage, the size of the college-age group in   22.____
    2010 will be

    A. larger than it was in 2009
    B. larger than it was in 1995
    C. smaller than it was in 2005
    D. about the same as it was in 2000

23. According to the above passage, the tremendous rate of growth of higher education started around   23.___

   A.   1950   B.   1955   C.   1960   D.   1965

24. The percentage of undergraduates who are over age 24 is MOST NEARLY   24.___

   A.   6%   B.   8%   C.   11%   D.   17%

25. Which one of the following conclusions can be substantiated by the information given in the above passage?   25.___

   A.   The college-age group was about the same size in 2000 as it was in 1965.
   B.   The annual decrease in the size of the college-age group from 2000 to 2005 is about the same as the annual increase from 1965 to 1970.
   C.   The overall decrease in the size of the college-age group from 2000 to 2005 will be followed by an overall increase in its size from 2005 to 2010.
   D.   The size of the college-age group is decreasing at a fairly constant rate from 1995 to 2010.

KEY (CORRECT ANSWERS)

1.	A		11.	C
2.	B		12.	C
3.	A		13.	B
4.	B		14.	C
5.	B		15.	A
6.	B		16.	A
7.	A		17.	C
8.	B		18.	C
9.	C		19.	C
10.	D		20.	B

21.	B
22.	C
23.	B
24.	A
25.	B

INTERPRETING STATISTICAL DATA GRAPHS, CHARTS AND TABLES

TEST 1

DIRECTIONS:　Each question or incomplete statement is followed by several suggested answers or completions. Select the one that BEST answers the question or completes the statement. *PRINT THE LETTER OF THE CORRECT ANSWER IN THE SPACE AT THE RIGHT.*

Questions 1-5.

DIRECTIONS:　Questions 1 through 5 are to be answered SOLELY on the basis of the following chart.

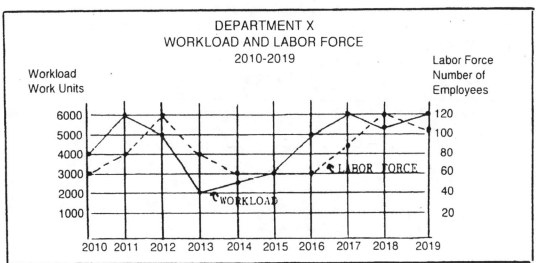

1. The one of the following years for which average employee production was LOWEST was

   A. 2011　　　B. 2013　　　C. 2015　　　D. 2017

2. The average annual employee production for the ten-year period was, in terms of work units, MOST NEARLY

   A. 30　　　B. 50　　　C. 70　　　D. 80

3. On the basis of the chart, it can be deduced that personnel needs for the coming year are budgeted on the basis of

   A. workload for the current year
   B. expected workload for the coming year
   C. no set plan
   D. average workload over the five years immediately preceding the period

1.＿＿＿

2.＿＿＿

3.＿＿＿

4. The chart indicates that the operation is carefully programmed and that the labor force
has been used properly. This opinion is

4.____

   A. *supported* by the chart; the organization has been able to meet emergency situa-
   tions requiring more additional work without commensurate increases in staff
   B. *not supported* by the chart; the irregular workload shows a complete absence of
   planning
   C. *supported* by the chart; the similar shapes of the WORKLOAD and LABOR
   FORCE curves show that these important factors are closely related
   D. *not supported* by the chart; poor planning with respect to labor requirements is
   obvious from the chart

5. The chart indicates that the department may be organized in such a way as to require a
permanent minimum staff which is too large for the type of operation indicated. This opinion is

5.____

   A. *supported* by the chart; there is indication that the operation calls for an irreducible
   minimum number of employees and application of the most favorable work production records show this to be too high for normal operation
   B. *not supported* by the chart; the absence of any sort of regularity makes it impossible to express any opinion with any degree of certainty
   C. *supported* by the chart; the expected close relationship between workload and
   labor force is displaced somewhat, a phenomenon which usually occurs as a result
   of a fixed minimum requirement
   D. *not supported* by the chart; the violent movement of the LABOR FORCE curve
   makes it evident that no minimum requirements are in effect

---

KEY (CORRECT ANSWERS)

1. B
2. B
3. A
4. D
5. A

TEST 2

Questions 1-4.

DIRECTIONS: Questions 1 through 4 are to be answered SOLELY on the basis of the chart below, which shows the annual average number of administrative actions completed for the four divisions of a bureau. Assume that the figures remain stable from year to year.

Administrative Actions	DIVISIONS				TOTALS
	W	X	Y	Z	
Telephone Inquiries Answered	8,000	6,800	7,500	4,800	27,100
Interviews Conducted	500	630	550	500	2,180
Applications Processed	15,000	18,000	14,500	9,500	57,000
Letters Typed	2,500	4,400	4,350	3,250	14,500
Reports Completed	200	250	100	50	600
Totals	26,200	30,080	27,000	18,100	101,380

1. In which division is the number of Applications Processed the GREATEST percentage of the total Administrative Actions for that division?

    A. W   B. X   C. Y   D. Z

1.____

2. The bureau chief is considering a plan that would consolidate the typing of letters in a separate unit. This unit would be responsible for the typing of letters for all divisions in which the number of letters typed exceeds 15% of the total number of administrative actions. Under this plan, which of the following divisions would CONTINUE to type its own letters?

    A. W and X   B. W, X, and Y
    C. X and Y   D. X and Z

2.____

3. The setting up of a central information service that would be capable of answering 25% of the whole bureau's telephone inquiries is under consideration. Under such a plan, the divisions would gain for other activities that time previously spent on telephone inquiries. Approximately how much total time would such a service gain for all four divisions if it requires 5 minutes to answer the average telephone inquiry?
_____ hours.

    A. 500   B. 515   C. 565   D. 585

3.____

4. Assume that the rate of production shown in the table can be projected as accurate for the coming year and that monthly output is constant for each type of administrative action within a division. Division Y is scheduled to work exclusively on a four-month long special project during that year. During the period of the project, Division Y's regular workload will be divided evenly among the remaining divisions.
Using the figures in the table, what would be MOST NEARLY the percentage increase in the total Administrative Actions completed by Division Z for the year?

    A. 8%   B. 16%   C. 25%   D. 50%

4.____

KEY (CORRECT ANSWERS)

1. B
2. A
3. C
4. B

———

TEST 3

Questions 1-3.

DIRECTIONS: The management study of employee absence due to sickness is an effective tool in planning. Questions 1 through 3 are to be answered SOLELY on the basis of the data below.

Number of days absent per worker (sickness)	1	2	3	4	5	6	7	8 or over
Number of workers	76	23	6	3	1	0	1	0

Total Number of Workers: 400
Period Covered: Jan. 1 - Dec. 31

1. The TOTAL number of man days lost due to illness was   1.____

    A. 110   B. 137   C. 144   D. 164

2. What percent of the workers had 4 or more days absence due to sickness?   2.____

    A. .25%   B. 2.5%   C. 1.25%   D. 12.5%

3. Of the 400 workers studied, the number who lost no days due to sickness was   3.____

    A. 190   B. 236   C. 290   D. 346

———

KEY (CORRECT ANSWERS)

1. D
2. C
3. C

———

TEST 4

Questions 1-3.

DIRECTIONS: In the graph below, the lines labeled A and B represent the cumulative progress in the work of two file clerks, each of whom was given 500 consecutively numbered applications to file in the proper cabinets over a five-day work week. Questions 1 through 3 are to be answered SOLELY on the basis of the data provided in the graph.

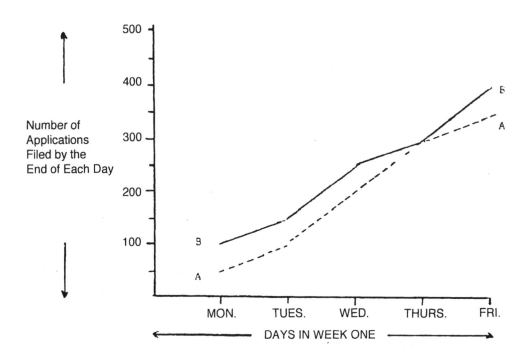

1. The day during which the LARGEST number of applications was filed by both clerks was   1.____

   A. Monday   B. Tuesday   C. Wednesday   D. Friday

2. At the end of the second day, the percentage of applications still to be filed was   2.____

   A. 25%   B. 50%   C. 66%   D. 75%

3. Assuming that the production pattern is the same the following week as the week shown   3.____
   in the chart, the day on which the file clerks will finish this assignment will be

   A. Monday   B. Tuesday   C. Wednesday   D. Friday

KEY (CORRECT ANSWERS)

1. C
2. D
3. B

TEST 5

Questions 1-3.

DIRECTIONS: Questions 1 through 3 are to be answered SOLELY on the basis of the information given in the chart below.

Number of Employees Producing Work-Units Within Range in 2006	Number of Work-Units Produced	Number of Employees Producing Work-Units Within Range in 2016
7	500-1000	4
14	1001-1500	11
26	1501-2000	28
22	2001-2500	36
17	2501-3000	39
10	3001-3500	23
4	3501-4000	9

1. Assuming that within each range of work-units produced, the average production was at the mid-point at that range (e.g., category 500-1000 = 750), then the AVERAGE number of work-units produced per employee in 2016 fell into the range

   A.   1001 - 1500   B.   1501 - 2000
   C.   2001 - 2500   D.   2501 - 3000

1.____

2. The ratio of the number of employees producing more than 2000 work-units in 2006 to the number of employees producing more than 2000 work-units in 2016 is MOST NEARLY

   A.   1:2   B.   2:3   C.   3:4   D.   4:5

2.____

3. In Department D, which of the following were GREATER in 2016 than in 2006?
       I.   Total number of employees
       II.   Total number of work-units produced
       III. Number of employees producing 2000 or fewer work-units
   The CORRECT answer is:

   A.   I, II, and III   B.   I and II, but not III
   C.   I and III, but not II   D.   II and III, but not I

3.____

KEY (CORRECT ANSWERS)

1.   C
2.   A
3.   B

TEST 6

Questions 1-9.

DIRECTIONS: Questions 1 through 9 are to be answered SOLELY on the basis of the information contained in the following four charts which relate to a municipal department. These charts show for the fiscal year the total departmental expenditures for salaries for all its employees; the distribution of expenditures for salaries for permanent employees by title; the distribution of all employees, both permanent and temporary by title; and the distribution of temporary employees by title.

For Departmental Expenditures
For Salaries For Fiscal Year.
Total: $129,000,000

Distribution of Expenditures
For Salaries For Permanent
Employees, By Title.

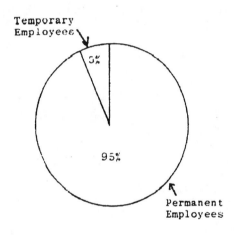

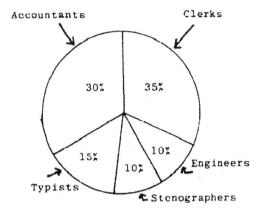

Distribution of All Employees, Both Permanent and Temporary, By Title.
Total Number of Employees: 3,200

Distribution of Temporary Employees, By Title.
Total Number of Temporary Employees: 150

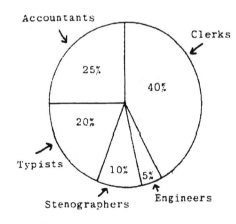

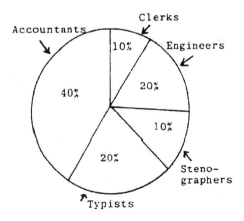

SAMPLE COMPUTATION

The total amount of money expended for the salaries of all the permanent typists can be computed as follows:

By taking 95% of $129,000,000, the total amount of money expended for the salaries of all permanent employees can be obtained. The total amount of money expended for the salaries of all the permanent typists can then be obtained by taking 15% of the money expended for the salaries of all permanent employees.

The answer is $18,382,500.

Candidates may find it useful to arrange their computations on their scratch paper in an orderly manner since the correct computations for one question may also be helpful in answering another question.

1. The TOTAL number of permanent typists is

    A. 640   B. 670   C. 608   D. 610

2. Of the total departmental expenditures for salaries for both permanent and temporary employees, the percentage allotted to permanent clerks is MOST NEARLY

    A. 25%   B. 31%   C. 33%   D. 35%

3. The number of permanent employees who are NOT engineers is

    A. 2,890   B. 3,070   C. 3,040   D. 2,920

4. Assume that the average annual salary of the temporary accountants is $40,000. Then, the average annual salary of the permanent accountants exceeds the average annual salary of the temporary accountants by MOST NEARLY

    A. 25%   B. 20%   C. 75%   D. 40%

5. The average annual salary of the permanent clerks is MOST NEARLY

    A. $33,300   B. $33,900   C. $35,250   D. $35,700

6. If the temporary stenographers receive 8% of the total salaries allotted to temporary employees, then the average annual salary of the temporary stenographers is MOST NEARLY

    A. $34,500   B. $38,500   C. $36,000   D. $40,000

7. Assume that the temporary typists receive an average annual salary that is 3% less than the average annual salary that is paid to the permanent typists.
Then, the average annual salary of the temporary typists is MOST NEARLY

    A. $27,850   B. $29,250   C. $30,000   D. $32,150

8. Assume that the average annual salary of the permanent engineers exceeds the average annual salary of the temporary engineers by $30,000.
Then, the percentage of the total departmental expenditures for salaries for temporary employees that is allotted to temporary engineers is MOST NEARLY

    A. 15%   B. 20%   C. 25%   D. 30%

9. If one-half of the permanent accountants earn an average of $45,000 per annum, then the average annual salary of the other permanent accountants is MOST NEARLY

    A. $51,150   B. $51,750   C. $54,350   D. $57,100

KEY (CORRECT ANSWERS)

1. D
2. C
3. D
4. A
5. B
6. A
7. B
8. D
9. C

———

TEST 7

Questions 1-6.

DIRECTIONS: Questions 1 through 6 are to be answered SOLELY on the basis of the information contained in the five charts below.

NUMBER OF UNITS OF WORK PRODUCED IN THE BUREAU PER YEAR

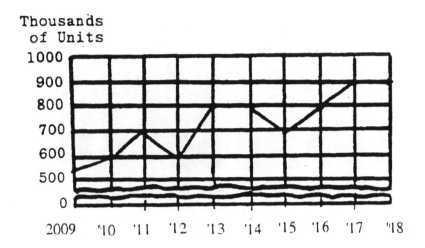

INCREASE IN THE NUMBER OF UNITS OF WORK PRODUCED IN 2018 OVER THE NUMBER PRODUCED IN 2009, BY BOROUGH

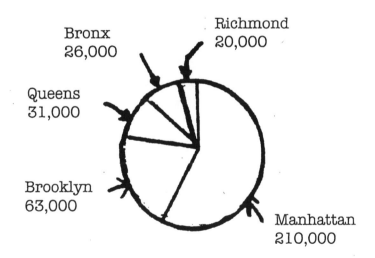

NUMBER OF MALE AND FEMALE EMPLOYEES PRODUCING THE UNITS OF WORK IN THE BUREAU PER YEAR

Number of Employees

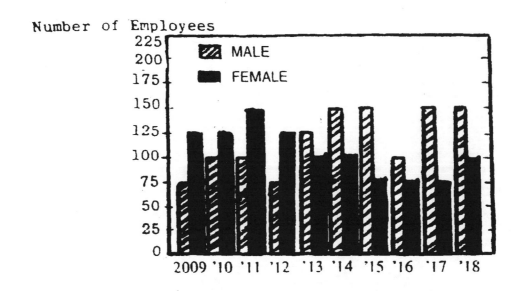

DISTRIBUTION OF THE AGES BY PERCENT OF EMPLOYEES ASSIGNED TO PRODUCE THE UNITS OF WORK IN THE YEARS 2009 AND 2018

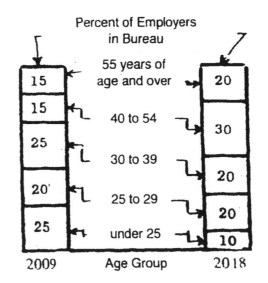

TOTAL SALARIES PAID PER YEAR TO EMPLOYEES ASSIGNED
TO PRODUCE THE UNITS OF WORK IN THE BUREAU

Thousands of Dollars

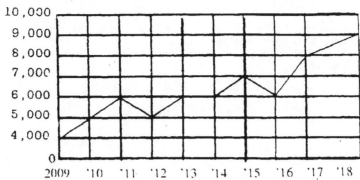

1. The information contained in the charts is sufficient to determine the   1._____

   A. amount of money paid in salaries to employees working in Richmond in 2018
   B. difference between the average annual salary of employees in the Bureau in 2018 and their average annual salary in 2017
   C. number of female employees in the Bureau between 30 and 39 years of age who were employed in 2009
   D. cost, in salary, for the average male employee in the Bureau to produce 100 units of work in 2014

2. The one of the following which was GREATER, in the Bureau, in 2014 than it was in 2012   2._____
   was the

   A. cost, in salaries, of producing a unit of work
   B. units of work produced annually per employee
   C. proportion of female employees to total number of employees
   D. average annual salary per employee

3. If, in 2018, one-half of the employees in the Bureau 55 years of age and over each   3._____
   earned an annual salary of $42,000, then the average annual salary of all the remaining
   employees in the Bureau was MOST NEARLY

   A. $31,750   B. $34,500   C. $35,300   D. $35,800

4. Assume that, in 2009, the offices in Richmond and the Bronx each produced the same   4._____
   number of units of work. Also assume that, in 2009, the offices in Brooklyn, Manhattan,
   and Queens each produced twice as many units of work as were produced in either of
   the other two boroughs.
   Then, the number of units of work produced in Brooklyn in 2008 was MOST NEARLY

   A. 69,000   B. 138,000   C. 201,000   D. 225,000

5. If, in 2016, the average annual salary of the female employees in the Bureau was four-   5._____
   fifths as large as the average annual salary of the male employees, then the average
   annual salary of the female employees in that year was

   A. $37,500   B. $31,000   C. $30,500   D. $30,000

6. Of the total number of employees in the Bureau who were 30 years of age and over in 2009, _____ must have been

    A. at least 35; females
    B. less than 75; males
    C. no more than 100; females
    D. more than 15; males

6.___

KEY (CORRECT ANSWERS)

1. B
2. B
3. C
4. C
5. D
6. A

PREPARING WRITTEN MATERIAL

PARAGRAPH REARRANGEMENT
COMMENTARY

The sentences which follow are in scrambled order. You are to rearrange them in proper order and indicate the letter choice containing the correct answer at the space at the right.

Each group of sentences in this section is actually a paragraph presented in scrambled order. Each sentence in the group has a place in that paragraph; no sentence is to be left out. You are to read each group of sentences and decide upon the best order in which to put the sentences so as to form as well-organized paragraph.

The questions in this section measure the ability to solve a problem when all the facts relevant to its solution are not given.

More specifically, certain positions of responsibility and authority require the employee to discover connections between events sometimes, apparently, unrelated. In order to do this, the employee will find it necessary to correctly infer that unspecified events have probably occurred or are likely to occur. This ability becomes especially important when action must be taken on incomplete information.

Accordingly, these questions require competitors to choose among several suggested alternatives, each of which presents a different sequential arrangement of the events. Competitors must choose the MOST logical of the suggested sequences.

In order to do so, they may be required to draw on general knowledge to infer missing concepts or events that are essential to sequencing the given events. Competitors should be careful to infer only what is essential to the sequence. The plausibility of the wrong alternatives will always require the inclusion of unlikely events or of additional chains of events which are NOT essential to sequencing the given events.

It's very important to remember that you are looking for the best of the four possible choices, and that the best choice of all may not even be one of the answers you're given to choose from.

There is no one right way to solve these problems. Many people have found it helpful to first write out the order of the sentences, as they would have arranged them, on their scrap paper before looking at the possible answers. If their optimum answer is there, this can save them some time. If it isn't, this method can still give insight into solving the problem. Others find it most helpful to just go through each of the possible choices, contrasting each as they go along. You should use whatever method feels comfortable, and works, for you.

While most of these types of questions are not that difficult, we've added a higher percentage of the difficult type, just to give you more practice. Usually there are only one or two questions on this section that contain such subtle distinctions that you're unable to answer confidently, and you then may find yourself stuck deciding between two possible choices, neither of which you're sure about.

EXAMINATION SECTION
TEST 1

DIRECTIONS: The sentences that follow are in scrambled order. You are to rearrange them in proper order and indicate the letter choice containing the correct answer. *PRINT THE LETTER OF THE CORRECT ANSWER IN THE SPACE AT THE RIGHT.*

1. Below are four statements labeled W., X., Y., and Z.   1.____
   - W.   He was a strict and fanatic drillmaster.
   - X.   The word is always used in a derogatory sense and generally shows resentment and anger on the part of the user.
   - Y.   It is from the name of this Frenchman that we derive our English word, martinet.
   - Z.   Jean Martinet was the Inspector-General of Infantry during the reign of King Louis XIV.

   The *PROPER* order in which these sentences should be placed in a paragraph is:

   A. X, Z, W, Y   B. X, Z, Y, W   C. Z, W, Y, X   D. Z, Y, W, X

2. In the following paragraph, the sentences which are numbered, have been jumbled.   2.____
   1. Since then it has undergone changes.
   2. It was incorporated in 1955 under the laws of the State of New York.
   3. Its primary purpose, a cleaner city, has, however, remained the same.
   4. The Citizens Committee works in cooperation with the Mayor's Inter-departmental Committee for a Clean City.

   The order in which these sentences should be arranged to form a well-organized paragraph is:

   A. 2, 4, 1, 3   B. 3, 4, 1, 2   C. 4, 2, 1, 3   D. 4, 3, 2, 1

Questions 3-5.

DIRECTIONS: The sentences listed below are part of a meaningful paragraph but they are not given in their proper order. You are to decide what would be the *best order* in which to put the sentences so as to form a well-organized paragraph. Each sentence has a place in the paragraph; there are no extra sentences. You are then to answer questions 3 to 5 inclusive on the basis of your rearrangements of these scrambled sentences into a properly organized paragraph.

In 1887 some insurance companies organized an Inspection Department to advise their clients on all phases of fire prevention and protection. Probably this has been due to the smaller annual fire losses in Great Britain than in the United States. It tests various fire prevention devices and appliances and determines manufacturing hazards and their safeguards. Fire research began earlier in the United States and is more advanced than in Great Britain. Later they established a laboratory specializing in electrical, mechanical, hydraulic, and chemical fields.

3. When the five sentences are arranged in proper order, the paragraph starts with the sentence which begins   3.___

     A. "In 1887 ..."   B. "Probably this ..."   C. "It tests ..."
     D. "Fire research ..."   E. "Later they ..."

4. In the last sentence listed above, "they" refers to   4.___

     A. insurance companies
     B. the United States and Great Britain
     C. the Inspection Department
     D. clients
     E. technicians

5. When the above paragraph is properly arranged, it ends with the words   5.___

     A. "... and protection."   B. "... the United States."
     C. "... their safeguards."   D. "... in Great Britain."
     E. "... chemical fields."

KEY (CORRECT ANSWERS)

1. C
2. C
3. D
4. A
5. C

TEST 2

DIRECTIONS: In each of the questions numbered 1 through 5, several sentences are given. For each question, choose as your answer the group of numbers that represents the *most logical* order of these sentences if they were arranged in paragraph form. *PRINT THE LETTER OF THE CORRECT ANSWER IN THE SPACE AT THE RIGHT.*

1.   1. It is established when one shows that the landlord has prevented the tenant's enjoyment of his interest in the property leased.
     2. Constructive eviction is the result of a breach of the covenant of quiet enjoyment implied in all leases.
     3. In some parts of the United States, it is not complete until the tenant vacates within a reasonable time.
     4. Generally, the acts must be of such serious and permanent character as to deny the tenant the enjoyment of his possessing rights.
     5. In this event, upon abandonment of the premises, the tenant's liability for that ceases.
   The CORRECT answer is:

   A. 2, 1, 4, 3, 5   B. 5, 2, 3, 1, 4   C. 4, 3, 1, 2, 5
   D. 1, 3, 5, 4, 2

1.____

2.   1. The powerlessness before private and public authorities that is the typical experience of the slum tenant is reminiscent of the situation of blue-collar workers all through the nineteenth century.
     2. Similarly, in recent years, this chapter of history has been reopened by anti-poverty groups which have attempted to organize slum tenants to enable them to bargain collectively with their landlords about the conditions of their tenancies.
     3. It is familiar history that many of the workers remedied their condition by joining together and presenting their demands collectively.
     4. Like the workers, tenants are forced by the conditions of modern life into substantial dependence on these who possess great political arid economic power.
     5. What's more, the very fact of dependence coupled with an absence of education and self-confidence makes them hesitant and unable to stand up for what they need from those in power.
   The CORRECT answer is:

   A. 5, 4, 1, 2, 3   B. 2, 3, 1, 5, 4   C. 3, 1, 5, 4, 2
   D. 1, 4, 5, 3, 2

2.____

3.   1. A railroad, for example, when not acting as a common carrier may contract away responsibility for its own negligence.
     2. As to a landlord, however, no decision has been found relating to the legal effect of a clause shifting the statutory duty of repair to the tenant.
     3. The courts have not passed on the validity of clauses relieving the landlord of this duty and liability.
     4. They have, however, upheld the validity of exculpatory clauses in other types of contracts.
     5. Housing regulations impose a duty upon the landlord to maintain leased premises in safe condition.

3.____

6. As another example, a bailee may limit his liability except for gross negligence, willful acts, or fraud.

The CORRECT answer is:

A. 2, 1, 6, 4, 3, 5   B. 1, 3, 4, 5, 6, 2   C. 3, 5, 1, 4, 2, 6
D. 5, 3, 4, 1, 6, 2

4. 1. Since there are only samples in the building, retail or consumer sales are generally   4.___
        eschewed by mart occupants, and in some instances, rigid controls are maintained
        to limit entrance to the mart only to those persons engaged in retailing.
    2. Since World War I, in many larger cities, there has developed a new type of
        property, called the mart building.
    3. It can, therefore, be used by wholesalers and jobbers for the display of sample
        merchandise.
    4. This type of building is most frequently a multi-storied, finished interior property
        which is a cross between a retail arcade and a loft building.
    5. This limitation enables the mart occupants to ship the orders from another loca-
        tion after the retailer or dealer makes his selection from the samples.

The CORRECT answer is:

A. 2, 4, 3, 1, 5   B. 4, 3, 5, 1, 2   C. 1, 3, 2, 4, 5
D. 1, 4, 2, 3, 5

5. 1. In general, staff-line friction reduces the distinctive contribution of staff personnel.   5.___
    2. The conflicts, however, introduce an uncontrolled element into the managerial
        system.
    3. On the other hand, the natural resistance of the line to staff innovations probably
        usefully restrains over-eager efforts to apply untested procedures on a large
        scale.
    4. Under such conditions, it is difficult to know when valuable ideas are being sacri-
        ficed.
    5. The relatively weak position of staff, requiring accommodation to the line, tends
        to restrict their ability to engage in free, experimental innovation.

The CORRECT answer is:

A. 4, 2, 3, 1, 3   B. 1, 5, 3, 2, 4   C. 5, 3, 1, 2, 4
D. 2, 1, 4, 5, 3

KEY (CORRECT ANSWERS)

1. A
2. D
3. D
4. A
5. B

TEST 3

DIRECTIONS: Questions 1 through 4 consist of six sentences which can be arranged in a logical sequence. For each question, select the choice which places the numbered sentences in the *most logical* sequence. *PRINT THE LETTER OF THE CORRECT ANSWER IN THE SPACE AT THE RIGHT.*

1.   1. The burden of proof as to each issue is determined before trial and remains upon   1.____
       the same party throughout the trial.
    2. The jury is at liberty to believe one witness' testimony as against a number of contradictory witnesses.
    3. In a civil case, the party bearing the burden of proof is required to prove his contention by a fair preponderance of the evidence.
    4. However, it must be noted that a fair preponderance of evidence does not necessarily mean a greater number of witnesses.
    5. The burden of proof is the burden which rests upon one of the parties to an action to persuade the trier of the facts, generally the jury, that a proposition he asserts is true.
    6. If the evidence is equally balanced, or if it leaves the jury in such doubt as to be unable to decide the controversy either way, judgment must be given against the party upon whom the burden of proof rests.

The CORRECT answer is:

A. 3, 2, 5, 4, 1, 6   B. 1, 2, 6, 5, 3, 4   C. 3, 4, 5, 1, 2, 6
D. 5, 1, 3, 6, 4, 2

2.   1. If a parent is without assets and is unemployed, he cannot be convicted of the   2.____
       crime of non-support of a child.
    2. The term "sufficient ability" has been held to mean sufficient financial ability.
    3. It does not matter if his unemployment is by choice or unavoidable circumstances.
    4. If he fails to take any steps at all, he may be liable to prosecution for endangering the welfare of a child.
    5. Under the penal law, a parent is responsible for the support of his minor child only if the parent is "of sufficient ability."
    6. An indigent parent may meet his obligation by borrowing money or by seeking aid under the provisions of the Social Welfare Law.

The CORRECT answer is:

A. 6, 1, 5, 3, 2, 4   B. 1, 3, 5, 2, 4, 6   C. 5, 2, 1, 3, 6, 4
D. 1, 6, 4, 5, 2, 3

3.   1.   Consider, for example, the case of a rabble rouser who urges a group of twenty   3.____
            people to go out and break the windows of a nearby factory.
      2.   Therefore, the law fills the indicated gap with the crime of inciting to riot.
      3.   A person is considered guilty of inciting to riot when he urges ten or more per-
            sons to engage in tumultuous and violent conduct of a kind likely to create public
            alarm.
      4.   However, if he has not obtained the cooperation of at least four people, he can-
            not be charged with unlawful assembly.
      5.   The charge of inciting to riot was added to the law to cover types of conduct
            which cannot be classified as either the crime of "riot" or the crime of "unlawful
            assembly."
      6.   If he acquires the acquiescence of at least four of them, he is guilty of unlawful
            assembly even if the project does not materialize.
The CORRECT answer is:

A. 3, 5, 1, 6, 4, 2   B.   5, 1, 4, 6, 2, 3   C.   3, 4, 1, 5, 2, 6
D. 5, 1, 4, 6, 3, 2

4.   1.   If, however, the rebuttal evidence presents an issue of credibility, it is for the jury to   4.____
            determine whether the presumption has, in fact, been destroyed.
      2.   Once sufficient evidence to the contrary is introduced, the presumption disap-
            pears from the trial.
      3.   The effect of a presumption is to place the burden upon the adversary to come
            forward with evidence to rebut the presumption.
      4.   When a presumption is overcome and ceases to exist in the case, the fact or
            facts which gave rise to the presumption still remain.
      5.   Whether a presumption has been overcome is ordinarily a question for the court.
      6.   Such information may furnish a basis for a logical inference.
The CORRECT answer is:

A. 4, 6, 2, 5, 1, 3   B.   3, 2, 5, 1, 4, 6   C.   5, 3, 6, 4, 2, 1
D. 5, 4, 1, 2, 6, 3

———

KEY (CORRECT ANSWERS)

1. D
2. C
3. A
4. B

———

PREPARING WRITTEN MATERIAL

EXAMINATION SECTION
TEST 1

DIRECTIONS : Each of the sentences in the tests that follow may be classified under one of the following four categories:

      A. *Incorrect* because of faulty grammar or sentence structure
      B. *Incorrect* because of faulty punctuation
      C. *Incorrect* because of faulty capitalization
      D. *Correct*

    Examine each sentence carefully to determine under which of the above four options it is best classified. Then, in the space on the right, print the capital letter preceding the option which is the *BEST* of the four suggested above.
    (Each incorrect sentence contains but one type of error. Consider a sentence to be correct if it contains none of the types of errors mentioned, even though there may be other correct ways of expressing the same thought.)

1. This fact, together with those brought out at the previous meeting, prove that the schedule is satisfactory to the employees. 1.____

2. Like many employees in scientific fields, the work of bookkeepers and accountants requires accuracy and neatness. 2.____

3. "What can I do for you," the secretary asked as she motioned to the visitor to take a seat. 3.____

4. Our representative, Mr. Charles will call on you next week to determine whether or not your claim has merit. 4.____

5. We expect you to return in the spring; please do not disappoint us. 5.____

6. Any supervisor, who disregards the just complaints of his subordinates, is remiss in the performance of his duty. 6.____

7. Because she took less than an hour for lunch is no reason for permitting her to leave before five o'clock. 7.____

8. "Miss Smith," said the supervisor, "Please arrange a meeting of the staff for two o'clock on Monday." 8.____

9. A private company's vacation and sick leave allowance usually differs considerably from a public agency. 9.____

10. Therefore, in order to increase the efficiency of operations in the department, a report on the recommended changes in procedures was presented to the departmental committee in charge of the program. 10.____

11. We told him to assign the work to whoever was available. 11.____

12. Since John was the most efficient of any other employee in the bureau, he received the highest service rating. 12.____

13. Only those members of the national organization who resided in the middle West   13.____
    attended the conference in Chicago.

14. The question of whether the office manager has as yet attained, or indeed can ever hope   14.____
    to secure professional status is one which has been discussed for years.

15. No one knew who to blame for the error which, we later discovered, resulted in a consid-   15.____
    erable loss of time.

_____

KEY (CORRECT ANSWERS)

1.	A		6.	B
2.	A		7.	A
3.	B		8.	C
4.	B		9.	A
5.	D		10.	D

11. D
12. A
13. C
14. B
15. A

_____

TEST 2

DIRECTIONS : Each of the sentences in the tests that follow may be classified under one of the following four categories:

      A.   *Incorrect* because of faulty grammar or sentence structure
      B.   *Incorrect* because of faulty punctuation
      C.   *Incorrect* because of faulty capitalization
      D.   *Correct*

1. The National alliance of Businessmen is trying to persuade private businesses to hire youth in the summertime.   1.____

2. The supervisor who is on vacation, is in charge of processing vouchers.   2.____

3. The activity of the committee at its conferences is always stimulating.   3.____

4. After checking the addresses again, the letters went to the mailroom.   4.____

5. The director, as well as the employees, are interested in sharing the dividends.   5.____

———

KEY (CORRECT ANSWERS)

1. C
2. B
3. D
4. A
5. A

TEST 3

DIRECTIONS: In each of the following groups of sentences, one of the four sentences is faulty in grammar, punctuation, or capitalization. Select the incorrect sentence in each case.

1. A. Sailing down the bay was a thrilling experience for me.
   B. He was not consulted about your joining the club.
   C. This story is different than the one I told you yesterday.
   D. There is no doubt about his being the best player.

   1.____

2. A. He maintains there is but one road to world peace.
   B. It is common knowledge that a child sees much he is not supposed to see.
   C. Much of the bitterness might have been avoided if arbitration had been resorted to earlier in the meeting.
   D. The man decided it would be advisable to marry a girl somewhat younger than him.

   2.____

3. A. In this book, the incident I liked least is where the hero tries to put out the forest fire.
   B. Learning a foreign language will undoubtedly give a person a better understanding of his mother tongue.
   C. His actions made us wonder what he planned to do next.
   D. Because of the war, we were unable to travel during the summer vacation.

   3.____

4. A. The class had no sooner become interested in the lesson than the dismissal bell rang.
   B. There is little agreement about the kind of world to be planned at the peace conference.
   C. "Today," said the teacher, "we shall read 'The Wind in the Willows.' I am sure you'll like it.
   D. The terms of the legal settlement of the family quarrel handicapped both sides for many years.

   4.____

5. A. I was so suprised that I was not able to say a word.
   B. She is taller than any other member of the class.
   C. It would be much more preferable if you were never seen in his company.
   D. We had no choice but to excuse her for being late.

   5.____

KEY (CORRECT ANSWERS)

1. C
2. D
3. A
4. C
5. C

———————

TEST 4

DIRECTIONS: In each of the following groups of sentences, one of the four sentences is faulty in grammar, punctuation, or capitalization. Select the incorrect sentence in each case.

1. A. Please send me these data at the earliest opportunity. 1.____
   B. The loss of their material proved to be a severe handicap.
   C. My principal objection to this plan is that it is impracticable.
   D. The doll had laid in the rain for an hour and was ruined.

2. A. The garden scissors, left out all night in the rain, were in a badly rusted condition. 2.____
   B. The girls felt bad about the misunderstanding which had arisen.
   C. Sitting near the campfire, the old man told John and I about many exciting adventures he had had.
   D. Neither of us is in a position to undertake a task of that magnitude.

3. A. The general concluded that one of the three roads would lead to the besieged city. 3.____
   B. The children didn't, as a rule, do hardly anything beyond what they were told to do.
   C. The reason the girl gave for her negligence was that she had acted on the spur of the moment.
   D. The daffodils and tulips look beautiful in that blue vase.

4. A. If I was ten years older, I should be interested in this work. 4.____
   B. Give the prize to whoever has drawn the best picture.
   C. When you have finished reading the book, take it back to the library.
   D. My drawing is as good as or better than yours.

5. A. He asked me whether the substance was animal or vegetable. 5.____
   B. An apple which is unripe should not be eaten by a child.
   C. That was an insult to me who am your friend.
   D. Some spy must of reported the matter to the enemy.

6. A. Limited time makes quoting the entire message impossible. 6.____
   B. Who did she say was going?
   C. The girls in your class have dressed more dolls this year than we.
   D. There was such a large amount of books on the floor that I couldn't find a place for my rocking chair.

7. A. What with his sleeplessness and his ill health, he was unable to assume any responsibility for the success of the meeting. 7.____
   B. If I had been born in February, I should be celebrating my birthday soon.
   C. In order to prevent breakage, she placed a sheet of paper between each of the plates when she packed them.
   D. After the spring shower, the violets smelled very sweet.

8. A. He had laid the book down very reluctantly before the end of the lesson. 8.____
   B. The dog, I am sorry to say, had lain on the bed all night.
   C. The cloth was first lain on a flat surface; then it was pressed with a hot iron.
   D. While we were in Florida, we lay in the sun until we were noticeably tanned.

9.   A.   If John was in New York during the recent holiday season, I have no doubt he spent   9.___
                most of his time with his parents.
      B.   How could he enjoy the television program; the dog was barking and the baby
                was crying.
      C.   When the problem was explained to the class, he must have been asleep.
      D.   She wished that her new dress were finished so that she could go to the party.

10.   A.   The engine not only furnishes power but light and heat as well.   10.___
      B.   You're aware that we've forgotten whose guilt was established, aren't you?
      C.   Everybody knows that the woman made many sacrifices for her children.
      D.   A man with his dog and gun is a familiar sight in this neighborhood.

KEY (CORRECT ANSWERS)

1.	D		6.	D
2.	C		7.	B
3.	B		8.	C
4.	A		9.	B
5.	D		10.	A

TEST 5

DIRECTIONS: Each of Questions 1 to 15 consists of a sentence which may be classified appropriately under one of the following four categories:

    A. *Incorrect* because of faulty grammar
    B. *Incorrect* because of faulty punctuation
    C. *Incorrect* because of faulty spelling
    D. *Correct*

Examine each sentence carefully. Then, print, in the space on the right, the letter preceding the category which is the best of the four suggested above.

(Note: Each incorrect sentence contains only one type of error. Consider a sentence correct if it contains no errors, although there may be other correct ways of writing the sentence.)

1. Of the two employees, the one in our office is the most efficient.   1.____

2. No one can apply or even understand, the new rules and regulations.   2.____

3. A large amount of supplies were stored in the empty office.   3.____

4. If an employee is occassionally asked to work overtime, he should do so willingly.   4.____

5. It is true that the new procedures are difficult to use but, we are certain that you will learn them quickly.   5.____

6. The office manager said that he did not know who would be given a large allotment under the new plan.   6.____

7. It was at the supervisor's request that the clerk agreed to postpone his vacation.   7.____

8. We do not believe that it is necessary for both he and the clerk to attend the conference.   8.____

9. All employees, who display perseverance, will be given adequate recognition.   9.____

10. He regrets that some of us employees are dissatisfied with our new assignments.   10.____

11. "Do you think that the raise was merited," asked the supervisor?   11.____

12. The new manual of procedure is a valuable supplament to our rules and regulations.   12.____

13. The typist admitted that she had attempted to pursuade the other employees to assist her in her work.   13.____

14. The supervisor asked that all amendments to the regulations be handled by you and I.   14.____

15. The custodian seen the boy who broke the window.   15.____

KEY (CORRECT ANSWERS)

1. A
2. B
3. A
4. C
5. B

6. D
7. D
8. A
9. B
10. D

11. B
12. C
13. C
14. A
15. A

———

PHILOSOPHY, PRINCIPLES, PRACTICES AND TECHNICS
OF
SUPERVISION, ADMINISTRATION, MANAGEMENT AND ORGANIZATION

TABLE OF CONTENTS

PHILOSOPHY, PRINCIPLES, PRACTICES, AND TECHNICS
OF
SUPERVISION, ADMINISTRATION, MANAGEMENT AND ORGANIZATION

I. MEANING OF SUPERVISION

The extension of the democratic philosophy has been accompanied by an extension in the scope of supervision. Modern leaders and supervisors no longer think of supervision in the narrow sense of being confined chiefly to visiting employees, supplying materials, or rating the staff. They regard supervision as being intimately related to all the concerned agencies of society, they speak of the supervisor's function in terms of "growth", rather than the "improvement," of employees.

This modern concept of supervision may be defined as follows:

Supervision is leadership and the development of leadership within groups which are cooperatively engaged in inspection, research, training, guidance and evaluation.

II. THE OLD AND THE NEW SUPERVISION

TRADITIONAL
1. Inspection
2. Focused on the employee
3. Visitation
4. Random and haphazard
5. Imposed and authoritarian
6. One person usually

MODERN
1. Study and analysis
2. Focused on aims, materials, methods, supervisors, employees, environment
3. Demonstrations, intervisitation, workshops, directed reading, bulletins, etc.
4. Definitely organized and planned (scientific)
5. Cooperative and democratic
6. Many persons involved (creative)

III THE EIGHT (8) BASIC PRINCIPLES OF THE NEW SUPERVISION

1. *PRINCIPLE OF RESPONSIBILITY*
   Authority to act and responsibility for acting must be joined.
   a. If you give responsibility, give authority.
   b. Define employee duties clearly.
   c. Protect employees from criticism by others.
   d. Recognize the rights as well as obligations of employees.
   e. Achieve the aims of a democratic society insofar as it is possible within the area of your work.
   f. Establish a situation favorable to training and learning.
   g. Accept ultimate responsibility for everything done in your section, unit, office, division, department.
   h. Good administration and good supervision are inseparable.

2. *PRINCIPLE OF AUTHORITY*

The success of the supervisor is measured by the extent to which the power of authority is not used.

    a. Exercise simplicity and informality in supervision.
    b. Use the simplest machinery of supervision.
    c. If it is good for the organization as a whole, it is probably justified.
    d. Seldom be arbitrary or authoritative.
    e. Do not base your work on the power of position or of personality.
    f. Permit and encourage the free expression of opinions.

3. *PRINCIPLE OF SELF-GROWTH*

The success of the supervisor is measured by the extent to which, and the speed with which, he is no longer needed.

    a. Base criticism on principles, not on specifics.
    b. Point out higher activities to employees.
    c. Train for self-thinking by employees, to meet new situations.
    d. Stimulate initiative, self-reliance and individual responsibility.
    e. Concentrate on stimulating the growth of employees rather than on removing defects.

4. *PRINCIPLE OF INDIVIDUAL WORTH*

Respect for the individual is a paramount consideration in supervision.

    a. Be human and sympathetic in dealing with employees.
    b. Don't nag about things to be done.
    c. Recognize the individual differences among employees and seek opportunities to permit best expression of each personality.

5. *PRINCIPLE OF CREATIVE LEADERSHIP*

The best supervision is that which is not apparent to the employee.

    a. Stimulate, don't drive employees to creative action.
    b. Emphasize doing good things.
    c. Encourage employees to do what they do best.
    d. Do not be too greatly concerned with details of subject or method.
    e. Do not be concerned exclusively with immediate problems and activities.
    f. Reveal higher activities and make them both desired and maximally possible.
    g. Determine procedures in the light of each situation but see that these are derived from a sound basic philosophy.
    h. Aid, inspire and lead so as to liberate the creative spirit latent in all good employees.

6. *PRINCIPLE OF SUCCESS AND FAILURE*

There are no unsuccessful employees, only unsuccessful supervisors who have failed to give proper leadership.

    a. Adapt suggestions to the capacities, attitudes, and prejudices of employees.
    b. Be gradual, be progressive, be persistent.
    c. Help the employee find the general principle; have the employee apply his own problem to the general principle.
    d. Give adequate appreciation for good work and honest effort.
    e. Anticipate employee difficulties and help to prevent them.
    f. Encourage employees to do the desirable things they will do anyway.
    g. Judge your supervision by the results it secures.

7. PRINCIPLE OF SCIENCE

Successful supervision is scientific, objective, and experimental. It is based on facts, not on prejudices.

a. Be cumulative in results.
b. Never divorce your suggestions from the goals of training.
c. Don't be impatient of results.
d. Keep all matters on a professional, not a personal level.
e. Do not be concerned exclusively with immediate problems and activities.
f. Use objective means of determining achievement and rating where possible.

8. PRINCIPLE OF COOPERATION

Supervision is a cooperative enterprise between supervisor and employee.

a. Begin with conditions as they are.
b. Ask opinions of all involved when formulating policies.
c. Organization is as good as its weakest link.
d. Let employees help to determine policies and department programs.
e. Be approachable and accessible - physically and mentally.
f. Develop pleasant social relationships.

IV. WHAT IS ADMINISTRATION?

Administration is concerned with providing the environment, the material facilities, and the operational procedures that will promote the maximum growth and development of supervisors and employees. (Organization is an aspect, and a concomitant, of administration.)

There is no sharp line of demarcation between supervision and administration; these functions are intimately interrelated and, often, overlapping. They are complementary activities.

1. PRACTICES COMMONLY CLASSED AS "SUPERVISORY"

a. Conducting employees conferences
b. Visiting sections, units, offices, divisions, departments
c. Arranging for demonstrations
d. Examining plans
e. Suggesting professional reading
f. Interpreting bulletins
g. Recommending in-service training courses
h. Encouraging experimentation
i. Appraising employee morale
j. Providing for intervisitation

2. PRACTICES COMMONLY CLASSIFIED AS "ADMINISTRATIVE"

a. Management of the office
b. Arrangement of schedules for extra duties
c. Assignment of rooms or areas
d. Distribution of supplies
e. Keeping records and reports
f. Care of audio-visual materials
g. Keeping inventory records
h. Checking record cards and books
i. Programming special activities
j. Checking on the attendance and punctuality of employees

3. *PRACTICES COMMONLY CLASSIFIED AS BOTH "SUPERVISORY" AND "ADMINISTRATIVE"*
    a. Program construction
    b. Testing or evaluating outcomes
    c. Personnel accounting
    d. Ordering instructional materials

V. RESPONSIBILITIES OF THE SUPERVISOR

A person employed in a supervisory capacity must constantly be able to improve his own efficiency and ability. He represents the employer to the employees and only continuous self-examination can make him a capable supervisor.

Leadership and training are the supervisor's responsibility. An efficient working unit is one in which the employees work with the supervisor. It is his job to bring out the best in his employees. He must always be relaxed, courteous and calm in his association with his employees. Their feelings are important, and a harsh attitude does not develop the most efficient employees.

VI. COMPETENCIES OF THE SUPERVISOR

1. Complete knowledge of the duties and responsibilities of his position.
2. To be able to organize a job, plan ahead and carry through.
3. To have self-confidence and initiative.
4. To be able to handle the unexpected situation and make quick decisions.
5. To be able to properly train subordinates in the positions they are best suited for.
6. To be able to keep good human relations among his subordinates.
7. To be able to keep good human relations between his subordinates and himself and to earn their respect and trust.

VII. THE PROFESSIONAL SUPERVISOR-EMPLOYEE RELATIONSHIP

There are two kinds of efficiency: one kind is only apparent and is produced in organizations through the exercise of mere discipline; this is but a simulation of the second, or true, efficiency which springs from spontaneous cooperation. If you are a manager, no matter how great or small your responsibility, it is your job, in the final analysis, to create and develop this involuntary cooperation among the people whom you supervise. For, no matter how powerful a combination of money, machines, and materials a company may have, this is a dead and sterile thing without a team of willing, thinking and articulate people to guide it.

The following 21 points are presented as indicative of the exemplary basic relationship that should exist between supervisor and employee:

1. Each person wants to be liked and respected by his fellow employee and wants to be treated with consideration and respect by his superior.
2. The most competent employee will make an error. However, in a unit where good relations exist between the supervisor and his employees, tenseness and fear do not exist. Thus, errors are not hidden or covered up and the efficiency of a unit is not impaired.
3. Subordinates resent rules, regulations, or orders that are unreasonable or unexplained.
4. Subordinates are quick to resent unfairness, harshness, injustices and favoritism.
5. An employee will accept responsibility if he knows that he will be complimented for a job well done, and not too harshly chastised for failure; that his supervisor will check the cause of the failure, and, if it was the supervisor's fault, he will assume the blame therefore. If it was the employee's fault, his supervisor will explain the correct method or means of handling the responsibility.

6. An employee wants to receive credit for a suggestion he has made, that is used. If a suggestion cannot be used, the employee is entitled to an explanation. The supervisor should not say "no" and close the subject.
7. Fear and worry slow up a worker's ability. Poor working environment can impair his physical and mental health. A good supervisor avoids forceful methods, threats and arguments to get a job done.
8. A forceful supervisor is able to train his employees individually and as a team, and is able to motivate them in the proper channels.
9. A mature supervisor is able to properly evaluate his subordinates and to keep them happy and satisfied.
10. A sensitive supervisor will never patronize his subordinates.
11. A worthy supervisor will respect his employees' confidences.
12. Definite and clear-cut responsibilities should be assigned to each executive.
13. Responsibility should always be coupled with corresponding authority.
14. No change should be made in the scope or responsibilities of a position without a definite understanding to that effect on the part of all persons concerned.
15. No executive or employee, occupying a single position in the organization, should be subject to definite orders from more than one source.
16. Orders should never be given to subordinates over the head of a responsible executive. Rather than do this, the officer in question should be supplanted.
17. Criticisms of subordinates should, whoever possible, be made privately, and in no case should a subordinate be criticized in the presence of executives or employees of equal or lower rank.
18. No dispute or difference between executives or employees as to authority or responsibilities should be considered too trivial for prompt and careful adjudication.
19. Promotions, wage changes, and disciplinary action should always be approved by the executive immediately superior to the one directly responsible.
20. No executive or employee should ever be required, or expected, to be at the same time an assistant to, and critic of, another.
21. Any executive whose work is subject to regular inspection should, whever practicable, be given the assistance and facilities necessary to enable him to maintain an independent check of the quality of his work.

VIII. MINI-TEXT IN SUPERVISION, ADMINISTRATION, MANAGEMENT, AND ORGANIZATION

A. BRIEF HIGHLIGHTS

Listed concisely and sequentially are major headings and important data in the field for quick recall and review.

1. LEVELS OF MANAGEMENT
Any organization of some size has several levels of management. In terms of a ladder the levels are:

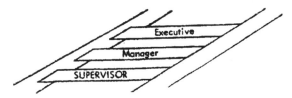

The first level is very important because it is the beginning point of management leadership.

- 6 -

2. WHAT THE SUPERVISOR MUST LEARN
A supervisor must learn to:
(1) Deal with people and their differences
(2) Get the job done through people
(3) Recognize the problems when they exist
(4) Overcome obstacles to good performance
(5) Evaluate the performance of people
(6) Check his own performance in terms of accomplishment

3. A DEFINITION OF SUPERVISOR
The term supervisor means any individual having authority, in the interests of the employer, to hire, transfer, suspend, lay-off, recall, promote, discharge, assign, reward, or discipline other employees or responsibility to direct them, or to adjust their grievances, or effectively to recommend such action, if, in connection with the foregoing, exercise of such authority is not of a merely routine or clerical nature but requires the use of independent judgment.

4. ELEMENTS OF THE TEAM CONCEPT
What is involved in teamwork? The component parts are:

(1) Members	(3) Goals	(5) Cooperation
(2) A leader	(4) Plans	(6) Spirit

5. PRINCIPLES OF ORGANIZATION
(1) A team member must know what his job is.
(2) Be sure that the nature and scope of a job are understood.
(3) Authority and responsibility should be carefully spelled out.
(4) A supervisor should be permitted to make the maximum number of decisions affecting his employees.
(5) Employees should report to only one supervisor.
(6) A supervisor should direct only as many employees as he can handle effectively.
(7) An organization plan should be flexible.
(8) Inspection and performance of work should be separate.
(9) Organizational problems should receive immediate attention.
(10) Assign work in line with ability and experience.

6. THE FOUR IMPORTANT PARTS OF EVERY JOB
(1) Inherent in every job is the *accountability* for results.
(2) A second set of factors in every job is *responsibilities.*
(3) Along with duties and responsibilities one must have the *authority* to act within certain limits without obtaining permission to proceed.
(4) No job exists in a vacuum. The supervisor is surrounded by key *relationships.*

7. PRINCIPLES OF DELEGATION
Where work is delegated for the first time, the supervisor should think in terms of these questions:
(1) Who is best qualified to do this?
(2) Can an employee improve his abilities by doing this?
(3) How long should an employee spend on this?
(4) Are there any special problems for which he will need guidance?
(5) How broad a delegation can I make?

174

8. PRINCIPLES OF EFFECTIVE COMMUNICATIONS
(1) Determine the media
(2) To whom directed?
(3) Identification and source authority
(4) Is communication understood?

9. PRINCIPLES OF WORK IMPROVEMENT
(1) Most people usually do only the work which is assigned to them
(2) Workers are likely to fit assigned work into the time available to perform it
(3) A good workload usually stimulates output
(4) People usually do their best work when they know that results will be reviewed or inspected
(5) Employees usually feel that someone else is responsible for conditions of work, workplace layout, job methods, type of tools/equipment, and other such factors
(6) Employees are usually defensive about their job security
(7) Employees have natural resistance to change
(8) Employees can support or destroy a supervisor
(9) A supervisor usually earns the respect of his people through his personal example of diligence and efficiency

10. AREAS OF JOB IMPROVEMENT
The areas of job improvement are quite numerous, but the most common ones which a supervisor can identify and utilize are:
(1) Departmental layout
(2) Flow of work
(3) Workplace layout
(4) Utilization of manpower
(5) Work methods
(6) Materials handling
(7) Utilization
(8) Motion economy

11. SEVEN KEY POINTS IN MAKING IMPROVEMENTS
(1) Select the job to be improved
(2) Study how it is being done now
(3) Question the present method
(4) Determine actions to be taken
(5) Chart proposed method
(6) Get approval and apply
(7) Solicit worker participation

12. CORRECTIVE TECHNIQUES OF JOB IMPROVEMENT

Specific Problems	General Improvement	Corrective Techniques
(1) Size of workload	(1) Departmental layout	(1) Study with scale model
(2) Inability to meet schedules	(2) Flow of work	(2) Flow chart study
(3) Strain and fatigue	(3) Work plan layout	(3) Motion analysis
(4) Improper use of men and skills	(4) Utilization of manpower	(4) Comparison of units produced to standard allowance
(5) Waste, poor quality, unsafe conditions	(5) Work methods	(5) Methods analysis
(6) Bottleneck conditions that hinder output	(6) Materials handling	(6) Flow chart & equipment study
(7) Poor utilization of equipment and machine	(7) Utilization of equipment	(7) Down time vs. running time
(8) Efficiency and productivity of labor	(8) Motion economy	(8) Motion analysis

13. A *PLANNING CHECKLIST*

(1) Objectives	(6) Resources	(11) Safety
(2) Controls	(7) Manpower	(12) Money
(3) Delegations	(8) Equipment	(13) Work
(4) Communications	(9) Supplies and materials	(14) Timing of improvements
(5) Resources	(10) Utilization of time	

14. *FIVE CHARACTERISTICS OF GOOD DIRECTIONS*

In order to get results, directions must be:

(1) Possible of accomplishment	(3) Related to mission	(5) Unmistakably clear
(2) Agreeable with worker interests	(4) Planned and complete	

15. *TYPES OF DIRECTIONS*

(1) Demands or direct orders	(3) Suggestion or implication
(2) Requests	(4) Volunteering

16. *CONTROLS*

A typical listing of the overall areas in which the supervisor should establish controls might be:

(1) Manpower	(3) Quality of work	(5) Time	(7) Money
(2) Materials	(4) Quantity of work	(6) Space	(8) Methods

17. *ORIENTING THE NEW EMPLOYEE*

(1) Prepare for him	(3) Orientation for the job
(2) Welcome the new employee	(4) Follow-up

18. *CHECKLIST FOR ORIENTING NEW EMPLOYEES*

	Yes	No
(1) Do your appreciate the feelings of new employees when they first report for work?	___	___
(2) Are you aware of the fact that the new employee must make a big adjustment to his job?	___	___
(3) Have you given him good reasons for liking the job and the organization?	___	___
(4) Have you prepared for his first day on the job?		
(5) Did you welcome him cordially and make him feel needed?		
(6) Did you establish rapport with him so that he feels free to talk and discuss matters with you?	___	___
(7) Did you explain his job to him and his relationship to you?	___	___
(8) Does he know that his work will be evaluated periodically on a basis that is fair and objective?	___	___
(9) Did you introduce him to his fellow workers in such a way that they are likely to accept him?	___	___
(10) Does he know what employee benefits he will receive?		
(11) Does he understand the importance of being on the job and what to do if he must leave his duty station?	___	___
(12) Has he been impressed with the importance of accident prevention and safe practice?	___	___
(13) Does he generally know his way around the department?	___	___
(14) Is he under the guidance of a sponsor who will teach the right ways of doing things?	___	___
(15) Do you plan to follow-up so that he will continue to adjust successfully to his job?	___	___

19. *PRINCIPLES OF LEARNING*
        (1) Motivation   (2) Demonstration or explanation   (3) Practice

20. *CAUSES OF POOR PERFORMANCE*
        (1) Improper training for job
        (2) Wrong tools
        (3) Inadequate directions
        (4) Lack of supervisory follow-up
        (5) Poor communications
        (6) Lack of standards of performance
        (7) Wrong work habits
        (8) Low morale
        (9) Other

21. *FOUR MAJOR STEPS IN ON-THE-JOB INSTRUCTION*
        (1) Prepare the worker
        (2) Present the operation
        (3) Tryout performance
        (4) Follow-up

22. *EMPLOYEES WANT FIVE THINGS*
        (1) Security (2) Opportunity (3) Recognition (4) Inclusion (5) Expression

23. *SOME DON'TS IN REGARD TO PRAISE*
        (1) Don't praise a person for something he hasn't done
        (2) Don't praise a person unless you can be sincere
        (3) Don't be sparing in praise just because your superior withholds it from you
        (4) Don't let too much time elapse between good performance and recognition of it

24. *HOW TO GAIN YOUR WORKERS' CONFIDENCE*
    Methods of developing confidence include such things as:
        (1) Knowing the interests, habits, hobbies of employees
        (2) Admitting your own inadequacies
        (3) Sharing and telling of confidence in others
        (4) Supporting people when they are in trouble
        (5) Delegating matters that can be well handled
        (6) Being frank and straightforward about problems and working conditions
        (7) Encouraging others to bring their problems to you
        (8) Taking action on problems which impede worker progress

25. *SOURCES OF EMPLOYEE PROBLEMS*
    On-the-job causes might be such things as:
        (1) A feeling that favoritism is exercised in assignments
        (2) Assignment of overtime
        (3) An undue amount of supervision
        (4) Changing methods or systems
        (5) Stealing of ideas or trade secrets
        (6) Lack of interest in job
        (7) Threat of reduction in force
        (8) Ignorance or lack of communications
        (9) Poor equipment
       (10) Lack of knowing how supervisor feels toward employee
       (11) Shift assignments

    Off-the-job problems might have to do with:
        (1) Health   (2) Finances   (3) Housing   (4) Family

26. *THE SUPERVISOR'S KEY TO DISCIPLINE*

There are several key points about discipline which the supervisor should keep in mind:

(1) Job discipline is one of the disciplines of life and is directed by the supervisor.
(2) It is more important to correct an employee fault than to fix blame for it.
(3) Employee performance is affected by problems both on the job and off.
(4) Sudden or abrupt changes in behavior can be indications of important employee problems.
(5) Problems should be dealt with as soon as possible after they are identified.
(6) The attitude of the supervisor may have more to do with solving problems than the techniques of problem solving.
(7) Correction of employee behavior should be resorted to only after the supervisor is sure that training or counseling will not be helpful.
(8) Be sure to document your disciplinary actions.
(9) Make sure that you are disciplining on the basis of facts rather than personal feelings.
(10) Take each disciplinary step in order, being careful not to make snap judgments, or decisions based on impatience.

27. *FIVE IMPORTANT PROCESSES OF MANAGEMENT*

(1) Planning   (2) Organizing   (3) Scheduling
(4) Controlling   (5) Motivating

28. *WHEN THE SUPERVISOR FAILS TO PLAN*

(1) Supervisor creates impression of not knowing his job
(2) May lead to excessive overtime
(3) Job runs itself -- supervisor lacks control
(4) Deadlines and appointments missed
(5) Parts of the work go undone
(6) Work interrupted by emergencies
(7) Sets a bad example
(8) Uneven workload creates peaks and valleys
(9) Too much time on minor details at expense of more important tasks

29. *FOURTEEN GENERAL PRINCIPLES OF MANAGEMENT*

(1) Division of work
(2) Authority and responsibility
(3) Discipline
(4) Unity of command
(5) Unity of direction
(6) Subordination of individual interest to general interest
(7) Remuneration of personnel
(8) Centralization
(9) Scalar chain
(10) Order
(11) Equity
(12) Stability of tenure of personnel
(13) Initiative
(14) Esprit de corps

30. *CHANGE*

Bringing about change is perhaps attempted more often, and yet less well understood, than anything else the supervisor does. How do people generally react to change? (People tend to resist change that is imposed upon them by other individuals or circumstances.

Change is characteristic of every situation. It is a part of every real endeavor where the efforts of people are concerned.

A. Why do people resist change?
People may resist change because of:
(1) Fear of the unknown
(2) Implied criticism
(3) Unpleasant experiences in the past
(4) Fear of loss of status
(5) Threat to the ego
(6) Fear of loss of economic stability

B. How can we best overcome the resistance to change?
In initiating change, take these steps:
(1) Get ready to sell
(2) Identify sources of help
(3) Anticipate objections
(4) Sell benefits
(5) Listen in depth
(6) Follow up

B. BRIEF TOPICAL SUMMARIES

I. WHO/WHAT IS THE SUPERVISOR?
1. The supervisor is often called the "highest level employee and the lowest level manager."
2. A supervisor is a member of both management and the work group. He acts as a bridge between the two.
3. Most problems in supervision are in the area of human relations, or people problems.
4. Employees expect: Respect, opportunity to learn and to advance, and a sense of belonging, and so forth.
5. Supervisors are responsible for directing people and organizing work. Planning is of paramount importance.
6. A position description is a set of duties and responsibilities inherent to a given position.
7. It is important to keep the position description up-to-date and to provide each employee with his own copy.

II. THE SOCIOLOGY OF WORK
1. People are alike in many ways; however, each individual is unique.
2. The supervisor is challenged in getting to know employee differences. Acquiring skills in evaluating individuals is an asset.
3. Maintaining meaningful working relationships in the organization is of great importance.
4. The supervisor has an obligation to help individuals to develop to their fullest potential.
5. Job rotation on a planned basis helps to build versatility and to maintain interest and enthusiasm in work groups.
6. Cross training (job rotation) provides backup skills.
7. The supervisor can help reduce tension by maintaining a sense of humor, providing guidance to employees, and by making reasonable and timely decisions. Employees respond favorably to working under reasonably predictable circumstances.
8. Change is characteristic of all managerial behavior. The supervisor must adjust to changes in procedures, new methods, technological changes, and to a number of new and sometimes challenging situations.
9. To overcome the natural tendency for people to resist change, the supervisor should become more skillful in initiating change.

III. PRINCIPLES AND PRACTICES OF SUPERVISION

1. Employees should be required to answer to only one superior.
2. A supervisor can effectively direct only a limited number of employees, depending upon the complexity, variety, and proximity of the jobs involved.
3. The organizational chart presents the organization in graphic form. It reflects lines of authority and responsibility as well as interrelationships of units within the organization.
4. Distribution of work can be improved through an analysis using the "Work Distribution Chart."
5. The "Work Distribution Chart" reflects the division of work within a unit in understandable form.
6. When related tasks are given to an employee, he has a better chance of increasing his skills through training.
7. The individual who is given the responsibility for tasks must also be given the appropriate authority to insure adequate results.
8. The supervisor should delegate repetitive, routine work. Preparation of recurring reports, maintaining leave and attendance records are some examples.
9. Good discipline is essential to good task performance. Discipline is reflected in the actions of employees on the job in the absence of supervision.
10. Disciplinary action may have to be taken when the positive aspects of discipline have failed. Reprimand, warning, and suspension are examples of disciplinary action.
11. If a situation calls for a reprimand, be sure it is deserved and remember it is to be done in private.

IV. DYNAMIC LEADERSHIP

1. A style is a personal method or manner of exerting influence.
2. Authoritarian leaders often see themselves as the source of power and authority.
3. The democratic leader often perceives the group as the source of authority and power.
4. Supervisors tend to do better when using the pattern of leadership that is most natural for them.
5. Social scientists suggest that the effective supervisor use the leadership style that best fits the problem or circumstances involved.
6. All four styles -- telling, selling, consulting, joining -- have their place. Using one does not preclude using the other at another time.
7. The theory X point of view assumes that the average person dislikes work, will avoid it whenever possible, and must be coerced to achieve organizational objectives.
8. The theory Y point of view assumes that the average person considers work to be as natural as play, and, when the individual is committed, he requires little supervision or direction to accomplish desired objectives.
9. The leader's basic assumptions concerning human behavior and human nature affect his actions, decisions, and other managerial practices.
10. Dissatisfaction among employees is often present, but difficult to isolate. The supervisor should seek to weaken dissatisfaction by keeping promises, being sincere and considerate, keeping employees informed, and so forth.
11. Constructive suggestions should be encouraged during the natural progress of the work.

V. PROCESSES FOR SOLVING PROBLEMS

1. People find their daily tasks more meaningful and satisfying when they can improve them.
2. The causes of problems, or the key factors, are often hidden in the background. Ability to solve problems often involves the ability to isolate them from their backgrounds. There is some substance to the cliché that some persons "can't see the forest for the trees."
3. New procedures are often developed from old ones. Problems should be broken down into manageable parts. New ideas can be adapted from old ones.

4. People think differently in problem-solving situations. Using a logical, patterned approach is often useful. One approach found to be useful includes these steps:

    (a) Define the problem   (d) Weigh and decide
    (b) Establish objectives   (e) Take action
    (c) Get the facts   (f) Evaluate action

VI. TRAINING FOR RESULTS

1. Participants respond best when they feel training is important to them.
2. The supervisor has responsibility for the training and development of those who report to him.
3. When training is delegated to others, great care must be exercised to insure the trainer has knowledge, aptitude, and interest for his work as a trainer.
4. Training (learning) of some type goes on continually. The most successful supervisor makes certain the learning contributes in a productive manner to operational goals.
5. New employees are particularly susceptible to training. Older employees facing new job situations require specific training, as well as having need for development and growth opportunities.
6. Training needs require continuous monitoring.
7. The training officer of an agency is a professional with a responsibility to assist supervisors in solving training problems.
8. Many of the self-development steps important to the supervisor's own growth are equally important to the development of peers and subordinates. Knowledge of these is important when the supervisor consults with others on development and growth opportunities.

VII. HEALTH, SAFETY, AND ACCIDENT PREVENTION

1. Management-minded supervisors take appropriate measures to assist employees in maintaining health and in assuring safe practices in the work environment.
2. Effective safety training and practices help to avoid injury and accidents.
3. Safety should be a management goal. All infractions of safety which are observed should be corrected without exception.
4. Employees' safety attitude, training and instruction, provision of safe tools and equipment, supervision, and leadership are considered highly important factors which contribute to safety and which can be influenced directly by supervisors.
5. When accidents do occur they should be investigated promptly for very important reasons, including the fact that information which is gained can be used to prevent accidents in the future.

VIII. EQUAL EMPLOYMENT OPPORTUNITY

1. The supervisor should endeavor to treat all employees fairly, without regard to religion, race, sex, or national origin.
2. Groups tend to reflect the attitude of the leader. Prejudice can be detected even in very subtle form. Supervisors must strive to create a feeling of mutual respect and confidence in every employee.
3. Complete utilization of all human resources is a national goal. Equitable consideration should be accorded women in the work force, minority-group members, the physically and mentally handicapped, and the older employee. The important question is: "Who can do the job?"
4. Training opportunities, recognition for performance, overtime assignments, promotional opportunities, and all other personnel actions are to be handled on an equitable basis.

IX. IMPROVING COMMUNICATIONS

1. Communications is achieving understanding between the sender and the receiver of a message. It also means sharing information -- the creation of understanding.
2. Communication is basic to all human activity. Words are means of conveying meanings; however, real meanings are in people.
3. There are very practical differences in the effectiveness of one-way, impersonal, and two-way communications. Words spoken face-to-face are better understood. Telephone conversations are effective, but lack the rapport of person-to-person exchanges. The whole person communicates.
4. Cooperation and communication in an organization go hand in hand. When there is a mutual respect between people, spelling out rules and procedures for communicating is unnecessary.
5. There are several barriers to effective communications. These include failure to listen with respect and understanding, lack of skill in feedback, and misinterpreting the meanings of words used by the speaker. It is also common practice to listen to what we want to hear, and tune out things we do not want to hear.
6. Communication is management's chief problem. The supervisor should accept the challenge to communicate more effectively and to improve interagency and intra-agency communications.
7. The supervisor may often plan for and conduct meetings. The planning phase is critical and may determine the success or the failure of a meeting.
8. Speaking before groups usually requires extra effort. Stage fright may never disappear completely, but it can be controlled.

X. SELF-DEVELOPMENT

1. Every employee is responsible for his own self-development.
2. Toastmaster and toastmistress clubs offer opportunities to improve skills in oral communications.
3. Planning for one's own self-development is of vital importance. Supervisors know their own strengths and limitations better than anyone else.
4. Many opportunities are open to aid the supervisor in his developmental efforts, including job assignments; training opportunities, both governmental and non-governmental -- to include universities and professional conferences and seminars.
5. Programmed instruction offers a means of studying at one's own rate.
6. Where difficulties may arise from a supervisor's being away from his work for training, he may participate in televised home study or correspondence courses to meet his self-develop- ment needs.

XI. TEACHING AND TRAINING

A. The Teaching Process

Teaching is encouraging and guiding the learning activities of students toward established goals. In most cases this process consists in five steps: preparation, presentation, summarization, evaluation, and application.

1. Preparation

Preparation is twofold in nature; that of the supervisor and the employee.

Preparation by the supervisor is absolutely essential to success. He must know what, when, where, how, and whom he will teach. Some of the factors that should be considered are:

(1) The objectives
(2) The materials needed
(3) The methods to be used
(4) Employee participation
(5) Employee interest
(6) Training aids
(7) Evaluation
(8) Summarization

Employee preparation consists in preparing the employee to receive the material. Probably the most important single factor in the preparation of the employee is arousing and maintaining his interest. He must know the objectives of the training, why he is there, how the material can be used, and its importance to him.

2. Presentation

In presentation, have a carefully designed plan and follow it.

The plan should be accurate and complete, yet flexible enough to meet situations as they arise. The method of presentation will be determined by the particular situation and objectives.

3. Summary

A summary should be made at the end of every training unit and program. In addition, there may be internal summaries depending on the nature of the material being taught. The important thing is that the trainee must always be able to understand how each part of the new material relates to the whole.

4. Application

The supervisor must arrange work so the employee will be given a chance to apply new knowledge or skills while the material is still clear in his mind and interest is high. The trainee does not really know whether he has learned the material until he has been given a chance to apply it. If the material is not applied, it loses most of its value.

5. Evaluation

The purpose of all training is to promote learning. To determine whether the training has been a success or failure, the supervisor must evaluate this learning.

In the broadest sense evaluation includes all the devices, methods, skills, and techniques used by the supervisor to keep him self and the employees informed as to their progress toward the objectives they are pursuing. The extent to which the employee has mastered the knowledge, skills, and abilities, or changed his attitudes, as determined by the program objectives, is the extent to which instruction has succeeded or failed.

Evaluation should not be confined to the end of the lesson, day, or program but should be used continuously. We shall note later the way this relates to the rest of the teaching process.

B. Teaching Methods

A teaching method is a pattern of identifiable student and instructor activity used in presenting training material.

All supervisors are faced with the problem of deciding which method should be used at a given time.

As with all methods, there are certain advantages and disadvantages to each method.

1. Lecture

The lecture is direct oral presentation of material by the supervisor. The present trend is to place less emphasis on the trainer's activity and more on that of the trainee.

2. Discussion

Teaching by discussion or conference involves using questions and other techniques to arouse interest and focus attention upon certain areas, and by doing so creating a learning situation. This can be one of the most valuable methods because it gives the employees 'an opportunity to express their ideas and pool their knowledge.

3. Demonstration

The demonstration is used to teach how something works or how to do something. It can be used to show a principle or what the results of a series of actions will be. A well-staged demonstration is particularly effective because it shows proper methods of performance in a realistic manner.

4. Performance

Performance is one of the most fundamental of all learning techniques or teaching methods. The trainee may be able to tell how a specific operation should be performed but he cannot be sure he knows how to perform the operation until he has done so.

5. Which Method to Use

Moreover, there are other methods and techniques of teaching. It is difficult to use any method without other methods entering into it. In any learning situation a combination of methods is usually more effective than anyone method alone.

Finally, evaluation must be integrated into the other aspects of the teaching-learning process.
It must be used in the motivation of the trainees; it must be used to assist in developing understanding during the training; and it must be related to employee application of the results of training.
This is distinctly the role of the supervisor.

———

GLOSSARY OF PROJECT MANAGEMENT

A

Agile software development is a set of fundamental principles about how software should be developed based on an agile way of working in contrast to previous heavy-handed software development methodologies.

Aggregate planning is an operational activity which does an aggregate plan for the production process, in advance of 2 to 18 months, to give an idea to management as to what quantity of materials and other resources are to be procured and when, so that the total cost of operations of the organization is kept to the minimum over that period.

Allocation is the assignment of available resources in an economic way.

B

Budget generally refers to a list of all planned expenses and revenues.

Budgeted cost of work performed (BCWP) measures the budgeted cost of work that has actually been performed, rather than the cost of work scheduled.

Budgeted cost of work scheduled (BCWS) the approved budget that has been allocated to complete a scheduled task (or Work Breakdown Structure (WBS) component) during a specific time period.

Business model is a profit-producing system that has an important degree of independence from the other systems within an enterprise.

Business analysis is the set of tasks, knowledge, and techniques required to identify business needs and determine solutions to business problems. Solutions often include a systems development component, but may also consist of process improvement or organizational change.

Business operations are those ongoing recurring activities involved in the running of a business for the purpose of producing value for the stakeholders. They are contrasted with project management, and consist of business processes.

Business process is a collection of related, structured activities or tasks that produce a specific service or product (serve a particular goal) for a particular customer or customers. There are three types of business processes: Management processes, Operational processes, and Supporting processes.

Business Process Modeling (BPM) is the activity of representing processes of an enterprise, so that the current ("as is") process may be analyzed and improved in future ("to be").

C

Capability Maturity Model.

Capability Maturity Model (CMM) in software engineering is a model of the maturity of the capability of certain business processes. A maturity model can be described as a structured collection of elements that describe certain aspects of maturity in an organization, and aids in the definition and understanding of an organization's processes.

Change control is the procedures used to ensure that changes (normally, but not necessarily, to IT systems) are introduced in a controlled and coordinated manner. Change control is a major aspect of the broader discipline of change management.

Change management is a field of management focused on organizational changes. It aims to ensure that methods and procedures are used for efficient and prompt handling of all changes to controlled IT infrastructure, in order to minimize the number and impact of any related incidents upon service.

Case study is a research method which involves an in-depth, longitudinal examination of a single instance or event: a case. They provide a systematic way of looking at events, collecting data, analyzing information, and reporting the results.

Certified Associate in Project Management is an entry-level certification for project practitioners offered by Project Management Institute.

Communications Log is an on-going documentation of communication events between any identified project stakeholders, managed and collected by the project manager that describes: the sender and receiver of the communication event; where, when and for how long the communication event elapsed; in what form the communication event took place; a summary of what information was communicated; what actions/outcomes should be taken as a result of the communication event; and to what level of priority should the actions/outcomes of the communication event be graded

Constructability is a project management technique to review the construction processes from start to finish during pre-construction phrase. It will identify obstacles before a project is actually built to reduce or prevent error, delays, and cost overrun.

Costs in economics, business, and accounting are the value of money that has been used up to produce something, and hence is not available for use anymore. In business, the cost may be one of acquisition, in which case the amount of money expended to acquire it is counted as cost.

Cost engineering is the area of engineering practice where engineering judgment and experience are used in the application of scientific principles and techniques to problems of cost estimating, cost control, business planning and management science, profitability analysis, project management, and planning and scheduling."[

Construction, in the fields of architecture and civil engineering, is a process that consists of the building or assembling of infrastructure. Far from being a single activity, large scale construction is a feat of multitasking. Normally the job is managed by the project manager and supervised by the construction manager, design engineer, construction engineer or project architect.

Cost overrun is defined as excess of actual cost over budget.

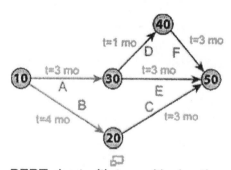

PERT chart with two critical paths.

Critical path method (CPM) is a mathematically based modeling technique for scheduling a set of project activities, used in project management.

Critical chain project management (CCPM) is a method of planning and managing projects that puts more emphasis on the resources required to execute project tasks.

D

Dependency in a project network is a link amongst a project's terminal elements.

Dynamic Systems Development Method (DSDM) is a software development methodology originally based upon the Rapid Application Development methodology. DSDM is an iterative and incremental approach that emphasizes continuous user involvement.

Duration of a project's terminal element is the number of calendar periods it takes from the time the execution of element starts to the moment it is completed.

Deliverable A contractually required work product, produced and delivered to a required state. A deliverable may be a document, hardware, software or other tangible product.

E

Earned schedule (ES) is an extension to earned value management (EVM), which renames two traditional measures, to indicate clearly they are in units of currency or quantity, not time.

Earned value management (EVM) is a project management technique for measuring project progress in an objective manner, with a combination of measuring scope, schedule, and cost in a single integrated system.

Effort management is a project management subdiscipline for effective and efficient use of time and resources to perform activities regarding quantity, quality and direction.

Enterprise modeling is the process of understanding an enterprise business and improving its performance through creation of enterprise models. This includes the modelling of the relevant business domain (usually relatively stable), business processes (usually more volatile), and Information technology

Estimation in project management is the processes of making accurate estimates using the appropriate techniques.

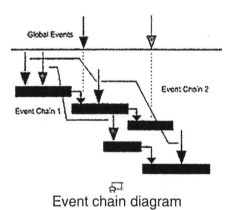
Event chain diagram

Event chain diagram : diagram that show the relationships between events and tasks and how the events affect each other.

Event chain methodology is an uncertainty modeling and schedule network analysis technique that is focused on identifying and managing events and event chains that affect project schedules.

Extreme project management (XPM) refers to a method of managing very complex and very uncertain projects.

F

Float in a project network is the amount of time that a task in a project network can be delayed without causing a delay to subsequent tasks and or the project completion date.

Focused improvement in Theory of Constraints is the ensemble of activities aimed at elevating the performance of any system, especially a business system, with respect to its goal by eliminating its constraints one by one and by not working on non-constraints.

Fordism, named after Henry Ford, refers to various social theories. It has varying but related meanings in different fields, and for Marxist and non-Marxist scholars.

G

Henry Gantt was an American mechanical engineer and management consultant, who developed the Gantt chart in the 1910s.

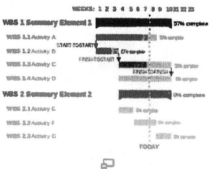

A Gantt chart.

Gantt chart is a type of bar chart that illustrates a project schedule. It illustrate the start and finish dates of the terminal elements and summary elements of a project. Terminal elements and summary elements comprise the work breakdown structure of the project.

Goal or objective consists of a projected state of affairs which a person or a system plans or intends to achieve or bring about — a personal or organizational desired end-point in some sort of assumed development. Many people endeavor to reach goals within a finite time by setting deadlines

Goal setting involves establishing specific, measurable and time targeted objectives

Graphical Evaluation and Review Technique (GERT) is a network analysis technique that allows probabilistic treatment of both network logic and activity duration estimated.

H

Hammock activity is a grouping of subtasks that "hangs" between two end dates it is tied to (or the two end-events it is fixed to).

HERMES is a Project Management Method developed by the Swiss Government, based on the German V-Modell. The first domain of application was software projects.

I

Integrated Master Plan (IMP) is an event-based, top level plan, consisting of a hierarchy of Program Events.

ISO 10006 is a guidelines for quality management in projects, is an international standard developed by the International Organization for Standardization.

Iterative and Incremental development is a cyclic software development process developed in response to the weaknesses of the waterfall model. It starts with an initial planning and ends with deployment with the cyclic interaction in between

K

Kickoff meeting is the first meeting with the project team and the client of the project.

L

Level of Effort (LOE) is qualified as a support type activity which doesn't lend itself to measurement of a discrete accomplishment. Examples of such an activity may be project budget accounting, customer liaison, etc.

Linear scheduling method (LSM) is a graphical scheduling method focusing on continuous resource utilization in repetitive activities. It is believed that it originally adopted the idea of Line-Of-Balance method.

Lean manufacturing or lean production, which is often known simply as "Lean", is the practice of a theory of production that considers the expenditure of resources for any means other than the creation of value for the presumed customer to be wasteful, and thus a target for elimination.

M

Management in business and human organization activity is simply the act of getting people together to accomplish desired goals. Management comprises planning, organizing, staffing, leading or directing, and controlling an organization (a group of one or more people or entities) or effort for the purpose of accomplishing a goal.

Management process is a process of planning and controlling the performance or execution of any type of activity.

Management science (MS), is the discipline of using mathematical modeling and other analytical methods, to help make better business management decisions.

Megaproject is an extremely large-scale investment project.

Motivation is the set of reasons that prompts one to engage in a particular behavior.

N

Nonlinear Management (NLM) is a superset of management techniques and strategies that allows order to emerge by giving organizations the space to self-organize, evolve and adapt, encompassing Agile, Evolutionary and Lean approaches, as well as many others.

O

Operations management is an area of business that is concerned with the production of good quality goods and services, and involves the responsibility of ensuring that business operations are efficient and effective. It is the management of resources, the distribution of goods and services to customers, and the analysis of queue systems.

Operations, see **Business operations**

Operations Research (OR) is an interdisciplinary branch of applied mathematics and formal science that uses methods such as mathematical modeling, statistics, and algorithms to arrive at optimal or near optimal solutions to complex problems.

Organization is a social arrangement which pursues collective goals, which controls its own performance, and which has a boundary separating it from its environment.

Organization development (OD) is a planned, structured, organization-wide effort to increase the organization's effectiveness and health.

P

Planning in organizations and public policy is both the organizational process of creating and maintaining a plan; and the psychological process of thinking about the activities required to create a desired goal on some scale.

Portfolio in finance is an appropriate mix of or collection of investments held by an institution or a private individual.

PRINCE2 : PRINCE2 is a project management methodology. The planning, monitoring and control of all aspects of the project and the motivation of all those involved in it to achieve the project objectives on time and to the specified cost, quality and performance.

Process is an ongoing collection of activities, with an inputs, outputs and the energy required to transform inputs to outputs.

Process architecture is the structural design of general process systems and applies to fields such as computers (software, hardware, networks, etc.), business processes (enterprise architecture, policy and procedures, logistics, project management, etc.), and any other process system of varying degrees of complexity.

Process management is the ensemble of activities of planning and monitoring the performance of a process, especially in the sense of business process, often confused with reengineering.

Product breakdown structure (PBS) in project management is an exhaustive, hierarchical tree structure of components that make up an item, arranged in whole-part relationship.

Product description in project management is a structured format of presenting information about a project product

Program Evaluation and Review Technique (PERT) is a statistical tool, used in project management, designed to analyze and represent the tasks involved in completing a given project.

Program Management is the process of managing multiple ongoing inter-dependent projects. An example would be that of designing, manufacturing and providing support infrastructure for an automobile manufacturer.

Project : A temporary endeavor undertaken to create a unique product, service, or result.

Project accounting Is the practice of creating financial reports specifically designed to track the financial progress of projects, which can then be used by managers to aid project management.

Project Cost Management A method of managing a project in real-time from the estimating stage to project control; through the use of technology cost, schedule and productivity is monitored.

Project management : The complete set of tasks, techniques, tools applied during project execution'.

Project Management Body of Knowledge (PMBOK) : The sum of knowledge within the profession of project management that is standardized by ISO.

Project management office: The Project management office in a business or professional enterprise is the department or group that defines and maintains the standards of process, generally related to project management, within the organization. The PMO strives to standardize and introduce economies of repetition in the execution of projects. The PMO is the source of documentation, guidance and metrics on the practice of project management and execution.

Project management process is the management process of planning and controlling the performance or execution of a project.

Project Management Professional is a certificated professional in project management.

Project Management Simulators are computer-based tools used in project management training programs. Usually, project management simulation is a group exercise. The computer-based simulation is an interactive learning activity.

Project management software is a type of software, including scheduling, cost control and budget management, resource allocation, collaboration software, communication, quality management and documentation or administration systems, which are used to deal with the complexity of large projects.

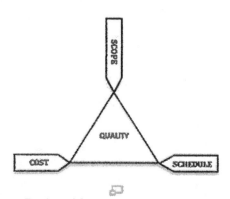
Project Management Triangle

Project Management Triangle is a model of the constraints of project management.

Project manager : professional in the field of project management. Project managers can have the responsibility of the planning, execution, and closing of any project, typically relating to construction industry, architecture, computer networking, telecommunications or software development.

Project network is a graph (flow chart) depicting the sequence in which a project's terminal elements are to be completed by showing terminal elements and their dependencies.

Project plan is a formal, approved document used to guide both *project execution* and *project control*. The primary uses of the project plan are to document planning assumptions and decisions, facilitate communication among *stakeholders*, and document approved scope, cost, and schedule *baselines*. A project plan may be summary or detailed.

Project planning is part of project management, which relates to the use of schedules such as Gantt charts to plan and subsequently report progress within the project environment.

Project stakeholders are those entities within or without an organization which sponsor a project or, have an interest or a gain upon a successful completion of a project.

Project team is the management team leading the project, and provide services to the project. Projects often bring together a variety number of problems. Stakeholders have important issues with others.

Proport refers to the combination of the unique skills of an organisation's members for collective advantage.

Q

Quality can mean a high degree of excellence ("a quality product"), a degree of excellence or the lack of it ("work of average quality"), or a property of something ("the addictive quality of alcohol").[1] Distinct from the vernacular, the subject of this article is the business interpretation of quality.

Quality, Cost, Delivery(QCD) as used in lean manufacturing measures a businesses activity and develops Key performance indicators. QCD analysis often forms a part of continuous improvement programs

R

Reengineering is radical redesign of an organization's processes, especially its business processes. Rather than organizing a firm into functional specialties (like production, accounting, marketing, etc.) and considering the tasks that each function performs; complete processes from materials acquisition, to production, to marketing and distribution should be considered. The firm should be re-engineered into a series of processes.

Resources are what is required to carry out a project's tasks. They can be people, equipment, facilities, funding, or anything else capable of definition (usually other than labour) required for the completion of a project activity.

Risk is the precise probability of specific eventualities.

Risk management is a management specialism aiming to reduce different risks related to a preselected domain to the level accepted by society. It may refer to numerous types of threats caused by environment, technology, humans, organizations and politics.

Risk register is a tool commonly used in project planning and organizational risk assessments.

S

Schedules in project management consists of a list of a project's terminal elements with intended start and finish dates.

Scientific management is a theory of management that analyzes and synthesizes workflow processes, improving labor productivity.

Scope of a project in project management is the sum total of all of its products and their requirements or features.

Scope creep refers to uncontrolled changes in a project's scope. This phenomenon can occur when the scope of a project is not properly defined, documented, or controlled. It is generally considered a negative occurrence that is to be avoided.

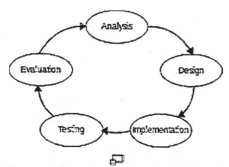

The systems development life cycle.

Scrum is an iterative incremental process of software development commonly used with agile software development. Despite the fact that "Scrum" is not an acronym, some companies implementing the process have been known to adhere to an all capital letter expression of the word, i.e. SCRUM.

Six Sigma is a business management strategy, originally developed by Motorola, that today enjoys widespread application in many sectors of industry.

Software engineering is the application of a systematic, disciplined, quantifiable approach to the development, operation, and maintenance of software.[1]

Systems Development Life Cycle (SDLC) is any logical process used by a systems analyst to develop an information system, including requirements, validation, training, and user ownership. An SDLC should result in a high quality system that meets or exceeds customer expectations, within time and cost estimates, works effectively and efficiently in the current and planned Information Technology infrastructure, and is cheap to maintain and cost-effective to enhance.

Systems engineering is an interdisciplinary field of engineering that focuses on how complex engineering projects should be designed and managed.

T

Task is part of a set of actions which accomplish a job, problem or assignment.

Tasks in project management are activity that needs to be accomplished within a defined period of time.

Task analysis is the analysis or a breakdown of exactly how a task is accomplished, such as what sub-tasks are required

Timeline is a graphical representation of a chronological sequence of events, also referred to as a chronology. It can also mean a schedule of activities, such as a timetable.

U

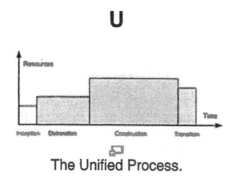

The Unified Process.

Unified Process: The Unified process is a popular iterative and incremental software development process framework. The best-known and extensively documented refinement of the Unified Process is the Rational Unified Process (RUP).

V

Value engineering (VE) is a systematic method to improve the "value" of goods and services by using an examination of function. Value, as defined, is the ratio of function to cost. Value can therefore be increased by either improving the function or reducing the cost. It is a primary tenet of value engineering that basic functions be preserved and not be reduced as a consequence of pursuing value improvements.

Vertical slice is a type of milestone, benchmark, or deadline, with emphasis on demonstrating progress across all components of a project.

Virtual Design and Construction (VDC) is the use of integrated multi-disciplinary performance models of design-construction projects, including the Product (i.e., facilities), Work Processes and Organization of the design - construction - operation team in order to support explicit and public business objectives.

W

Wideband Delphi is a consensus-based estimation technique for estimating effort.

Work in project management is the amount of effort applied to produce a deliverable or to accomplish a task (a terminal element).

A work breakdown structure.

Work Breakdown Structure (WBS) is a tool that defines a project and groups the project's discrete work elements in a way that helps organize and define the total work scope of the project. A Work breakdown structure element may be a product, data, a service, or any combination. WBS also provides the necessary framework for detailed cost estimating and control along with providing guidance for schedule development and control.

Work package is a subset of a project that can be assigned to a specific party for execution. Because of the similarity, work packages are often misidentified as projects.

Workstream is a set of associated activities, focused around a particular scope that follow a path from initiation to completion.

GLOSSARY OF COMPUTER TERMS

Contents

GLOSSARY OF COMPUTER TERMS

Basic

application & app
An application (often called "app" for short) is simply a program with a GUI. Note that it is different from an applet.

boot
Starting up an OS is booting it. If the computer is already running, it is more often called rebooting.

browser
A browser is a program used to browse the web. Some common browsers include Netscape, MSIE (Microsoft Internet Explorer), Safari, Lynx, Mosaic, Amaya, Arena, Chimera, Opera, Cyberdog, HotJava, etc.

bug
A bug is a mistake in the design of something, especially software. A really severe bug can cause something to crash.

chat
Chatting is like e-mail, only it is done instantaneously and can directly involve multiple people at once. While e-mail now relies on one more or less standard protocol, chatting still has a couple competing ones. Of particular note are IRC and Instant Messenger. One step beyond chatting is called MUDding.

click
To press a mouse button. When done twice in rapid succession, it is referred to as a double-click.

cursor
A point of attention on the computer screen, often marked with a flashing line or block. Text typed into the computer will usually appear at the cursor.

database
A database is a collection of data, typically organized to make common retrievals easy and efficient. Some common database programs include Oracle, Sybase, Postgres, Informix, Filemaker, Adabas, etc.

desktop
A desktop system is a computer designed to sit in one position on a desk somewhere and not move around. Most general purpose computers are desktop systems. Calling a system a desktop implies nothing about its platform. The fastest desktop system at any given time is typically either an Alpha or PowerPC based system, but the SPARC and PA-RISC based systems are also often in the running. Industrial strength desktops are typically called workstations.

directory
Also called "folder", a directory is a collection of files typically created for organizational purposes. Note that a directory is itself a file, so a directory can generally contain other directories. It differs in this way from a partition.

disk
A disk is a physical object used for storing data. It will not forget its data when it loses power. It is always used in conjunction with a disk drive. Some disks can be removed from their drives, some cannot. Generally it is possible to write new information to a disk in addition to reading data from it, but this is not always the case.

drive

A device for storing and/or retrieving data. Some drives (such as disk drives, zip drives, and tape drives) are typically capable of having new data written to them, but some others (like CD-ROMs or DVD-ROMs) are not. Some drives have random access (like disk drives, zip drives, CD-ROMs, and DVD-ROMs), while others only have sequential access (like tape drives).

e-book

The concept behind an e-book is that it should provide all the functionality of an ordinary book but in a manner that is (overall) less expensive and more environmentally friendly. The actual term e-book is somewhat confusingly used to refer to a variety of things: custom software to play e-book titles, dedicated hardware to play e-book titles, and the e-book titles themselves. Individual e-book titles can be free or commercial (but will always be less expensive than their printed counterparts) and have to be loaded into a player to be read. Players vary wildly in capability level. Basic ones allow simple reading and bookmarking; better ones include various features like hypertext, illustrations, audio, and even limited video. Other optional features allow the user to mark-up sections of text, leave notes, circle or diagram things, highlight passages, program or customize settings, and even use interactive fiction. There are many types of e-book; a couple popular ones include the Newton book and Palm DOC.

e-mail

E-mail is short for electronic mail. It allows for the transfer of information from one computer to another, provided that they are hooked up via some sort of network (often the Internet. E-mail works similarly to FAXing, but its contents typically get printed out on the other end only on demand, not immediately and automatically as with FAX. A machine receiving e-mail will also not reject other incoming mail messages as a busy FAX machine will; rather they will instead be queued up to be received after the current batch has been completed. E-mail is only seven-bit clean, meaning that you should not expect anything other than ASCII data to go through uncorrupted without prior conversion via something like uucode or bcode. Some mailers will do some conversion automatically, but unless you know your mailer is one of them, you may want to do the encoding manually.

file

A file is a unit of (usually named) information stored on a computer.

firmware

Sort of in-between hardware and software, firmware consists of modifiable programs embedded in hardware. Firmware updates should be treated with care since they can literally destroy the underlying hardare if done improperly. There are also cases where neglecting to apply a firmware update can destroy the underlying hardware, so user beware.

floppy

An extremely common type of removable disk. Floppies do not hold too much data, but most computers are capable of reading them. Note though that there are different competing format used for floppies, so that a floppy written by one type of computer might not directly work on another. Also sometimes called "diskette".

format

The manner in which data is stored; its organization. For example, VHS, SVHS, and Beta are three different formats of video tape. They are not 100% compatible with each other, but information can be transferred from one to the other with the proper equipment (but not always without loss; SVHS contains more information than either of the other two). Computer information can be stored in literally hundreds of different formats, and can represent text, sounds, graphics, animations, etc. Computer information can be exchanged via different computer types provided both computers can interpret the format used.

function keys

On a computer keyboard, the keys that start with an "F" that are usually (but not always) found on the top row. They are meant to perform user-defined tasks.

graphics

Anything visually displayed on a computer that is not text.

hardware

The physical portion of the computer.

hypertext

A hypertext document is like a text document with the ability to contain pointers to other regions of (possibly other) hypertext documents.

Internet

The Internet is the world-wide network of computers. There is only one Internet, and thus it is typically capitalized (although it is sometimes referred to as "the 'net"). It is different from an intranet.

keyboard

A keyboard on a computer is almost identical to a keyboard on a typewriter. Computer keyboards will typically have extra keys, however. Some of these keys (common examples include Control, Alt, and Meta) are meant to be used in conjunction with other keys just like shift on a regular typewriter. Other keys (common examples include Insert, Delete, Home, End, Help, function keys,etc.) are meant to be used independently and often perform editing tasks. Keyboards on different platforms will often look slightly different and have somewhat different collections of keys. Some keyboards even have independent shift lock and caps lock keys. Smaller keyboards with only math-related keys are typically called "keypads".

language

Computer programs can be written in a variety of different languages. Different languages are optimized for different tasks. Common languages include Java, C, C++, ForTran, Pascal, Lisp, and BASIC. Some people classify languages into two categories, higher-level and lower-level. These people would consider assembly language and machine language lower-level languages and all other languages higher-level. In general, higher-level languages can be either interpreted or compiled; many languages allow both, but some are restricted to one or the other. Many people do not consider machine language and assembly language at all when talking about programming languages.

laptop

A laptop is any computer designed to do pretty much anything a desktop system can do but run for a short time (usually two to five hours) on batteries. They are designed to be carried around but are not particularly convenient to carry around. They are significantly more expensive than desktop systems and have far worse battery life than PDAs. Calling a system a laptop implies nothing about its platform. By far the fastest laptops are the PowerPC based Macintoshes.

memory

Computer memory is used to temporarily store data. In reality, computer memory is only capable of remembering sequences of zeros and ones, but by utilizing the binary number system it is possible to produce arbitrary rational numbers and through clever formatting all manner of representations of pictures, sounds, and animations. The most common types of memory are RAM, ROM, and flash.

MHz & megahertz

One megahertz is equivalent to 1000 kilohertz, or 1,000,000 hertz. The clock speed of the main processor of many computers is measured in MHz, and is sometimes (quite misleadingly) used to represent the overall speed of a computer. In fact, a computer's speed is based upon many factors, and since MHz only reveals how many clock cycles the main processor has per second (saying nothing about how much is actually accomplished per cycle), it can really only accurately be used to gauge two computers with the same generation and family of processor plus similar configurations of memory, co-processors, and other peripheral hardware.

modem

A modem allows two computers to communicate over ordinary phone lines. It derives its name

4

from **mod**ulate / **dem**odulate, the process by which it converts digital computer data back and forth for use with an analog phone line.

monitor

The screen for viewing computer information is called a monitor.

mouse

In computer parlance a mouse can be both the physical object moved around to control a pointer on the screen, and the pointer itself. Unlike the animal, the proper plural of computer mouse is "mouses".

multimedia

This originally indicated a capability to work with and integrate various types of things including audio, still graphics, and especially video. Now it is more of a marketing term and has little real meaning. Historically the Amiga was the first multimedia machine. Today in addition to AmigaOS, IRIX and Solaris are popular choices for high-end multimedia work.

NC

The term **n**etwork **c**omputer refers to any (usually desktop) computer system that is designed to work as part of a network rather than as a stand-alone machine. This saves money on hardware, software, and maintenance by taking advantage of facilities already available on the network. The term "Internet appliance" is often used interchangeably with NC.

network

A network (as applied to computers) typically means a group of computers working together. It can also refer to the physical wire etc. connecting the computers.

notebook

A notebook is a small laptop with similar price, performance, and battery life.

organizer

An organizer is a tiny computer used primarily to store names, addresses, phone numbers, and date book information. They usually have some ability to exchange information with desktop systems. They boast even better battery life than PDAs but are far less capable. They are extremely inexpensive but are typically incapable of running any special purpose applications and are thus of limited use.

OS

The **o**perating **s**ystem is the program that manages a computer's resources. Common OSes include Windows '95, MacOS, Linux, Solaris, AmigaOS, AIX, Windows NT, etc.

PC

The term **p**ersonal **c**omputer properly refers to any desktop, laptop, or notebook computer system. Its use is inconsistent, though, and some use it to specifically refer to x86 based systems running MS-DOS, MS-Windows, GEOS, or OS/2. This latter use is similar to what is meant by a WinTel system.

PDA

A **p**ersonal **d**igital **a**ssistant is a small battery-powered computer intended to be carried around by the user rather than left on a desk. This means that the processor used ought to be power-efficient as well as fast, and the OS ought to be optimized for hand-held use. PDAs typically have an instant-on feature (they would be useless without it) and most are grayscale rather than color because of battery life issues. Most have a pen interface and come with a detachable stylus. None use mouses. All have some ability to exchange data with desktop systems. In terms of raw capabilities, a PDA is more capable than an organizer and less capable than a laptop (although some high-end PDAs beat out some low-end laptops). By far the most popular PDA is the Pilot, but other common types include Newtons, Psions, Zauri, Zoomers, and Windows CE hand-helds. By far the fastest current PDA is the Newton (based around a StrongARM RISC processor). Other PDAs are optimized for other tasks; few computers are as personal as PDAs and care must be taken in their purchase. Feneric's PDA / Handheld Comparison Page is perhaps the most detailed comparison of PDAs and handheld computers to be found anywhere on the web.

platform

Roughly speaking, a platform represents a computer's family. It is defined by both the processor type on the hardware side and the OS type on the software side. Computers belonging to different platforms cannot typically run each other's programs (unless the programs are written in a language like Java).

portable

If something is portable it can be easily moved from one type of computer to another. The verb "to port" indicates the moving itself.

printer

A printer is a piece of hardware that will print computer information onto paper.

processor

The processor (also called central processing unit, or CPU) is the part of the computer that actually works with the data and runs the programs. There are two main processor types in common usage today: CISC and RISC. Some computers have more than one processor and are thus called "multiprocessor". This is distinct from multitasking. Advertisers often use megahertz numbers as a means of showing a processor's speed. This is often extremely misleading; megahertz numbers are more or less meaningless when compared across different types of processors.

program

A program is a series of instructions for a computer, telling it what to do or how to behave. The terms "application" and "app" mean almost the same thing (albeit applications generally have GUIs). It is however different from an applet. Program is also the verb that means to create a program, and a programmer is one who programs.

run

Running a program is how it is made to do something. The term "execute" means the same thing.

software

The non-physical portion of the computer; the part that exists only as data; the programs. Another term meaning much the same is "code".

spreadsheet

An program used to perform various calculations. It is especially popular for financial applications. Some common spreadsheets include Lotus 123, Excel, OpenOffice Spreadsheet, Octave, Gnumeric, AppleWorks Spreadsheet, Oleo, and GeoCalc.

user

The operator of a computer.

word processor

A program designed to help with the production of textual documents, like letters and memos. Heavier duty work can be done with a desktop publisher. Some common word processors include MS-Word, OpenOffice Write, WordPerfect, AbiWord, AppleWorks Write, and GeoWrite.

www

The World-Wide-Web refers more or less to all the publically accessible documents on the Internet. It is used quite loosely, and sometimes indicates only HTML files and sometimes FTP and Gopher files, too. It is also sometimes just referred to as "the web".

65xx

The 65xx series of processors includes the 6502, 65C02, 6510, 8502, 65C816, 65C816S, etc. It is a CISC design and is not being used in too many new stand-alone computer systems, but is still being used in embedded systems, game systems (such as the Super NES), and processor enhancement add-ons for older systems. It was originally designed by MOS Technologies, but is now produced by The Western Design Center, Inc. It was the primary processor for many extremely popular systems no longer being produced, including the Commodore 64, the Commodore 128, and all the Apple][series machines.

68xx

The 68xx series of processors includes the 6800, 6805, 6809, 68000, 68020, 68030, 68040, 68060, etc. It is a CISC design and is not being used in too many new stand-alone computer systems, but is still being used heavily in embedded systems. It was originally designed by Motorola and was the primary processor for older generations of many current machines, including Macintoshes, Amigas, Sun workstations, HP workstations, etc. and the primary processor for many systems no longer being produced, such as the TRS-80. The PowerPC was designed in part to be its replacement.

a11y

Commonly used to abbreviate the word "accessibility". There are eleven letters between the "a" and the "y".

ADA

An object-oriented language at one point popular for military and some academic software. Lately C++ and Java have been getting more attention.

AI

Artificial intelligence is the concept of making computers do tasks once considered to require thinking. AI makes computers play chess, recognize handwriting and speech, helps suggest prescriptions to doctors for patients based on imput symptoms, and many other tasks, both mundane and not.

AIX

The industrial strength OS designed by IBM to run on PowerPC and x86 based machines. It is a variant of UNIX and is meant to provide more power than OS/2.

AJaX

AJaX is a little like DHTML, but it adds asynchronous communication between the browser and Web site via either XML or JSON to achieve performance that often rivals desktop applications.

Alpha

An Alpha is a RISC processor invented by Digital and currently produced by Digital/Compaq and Samsung. A few different OSes run on Alpha based machines including Digital UNIX, Windows NT, Linux, NetBSD, and AmigaOS. Historically, at any given time, the fastest processor in the world has usually been either an Alpha or a PowerPC (with sometimes SPARCs and PA-RISCs making the list), but Compaq has recently announced that there will be no further development of this superb processor instead banking on the release of the somewhat suspect Merced.

AltiVec

AltiVec (also called the "Velocity Engine") is a special extension built into some PowerPC CPUs to provide better performance for certain operations, most notably graphics and sound. It is similar to MMX on the x86 CPUs. Like MMX, it requires special software for full performance benefits to be realized.

Amiga

A platform originally created and only produced by Commodore, but now owned by Gateway 2000 and produced by it and a few smaller companies. It was historically the first multimedia machine and gave the world of computing many innovations. It is now primarily used for audio / video applications; in fact, a decent Amiga system is less expensive than a less capable video editing system. Many music videos were created on Amigas, and a few television series and movies had their special effects generated on Amigas. Also, Amigas can be readily synchronized with video cameras, so typically when a computer screen appears on television or in a movie and it is not flickering wildly, it is probably an Amiga in disguise. Furthermore, many coin-operated arcade games are really Amigas packaged in stand-up boxes. Amigas have AmigaOS for their OS. New Amigas have either a PowerPC or an Alpha for their main processor and a 68xx processor dedicated to graphics manipulation. Older (and low end) Amigas do everything with just a 68xx processor.

AmigaOS

The OS used by Amigas. AmigaOS combines the functionality of an OS and a window manager and is fully multitasking. AmigaOS boasts a pretty good selection of games (many arcade games are in fact written on Amigas) but has limited driver support. AmigaOS will run on 68xx, Alpha, and PowerPC based machines.

Apple][

The Apple][computer sold millions of units and is generally considered to have been the first home computer with a 1977 release date. It is based on the 65xx family of processors. The earlier Apple I was only available as a build-it-yourself kit.

AppleScript

A scripting language for Mac OS computers.

applet

An applet differs from an application in that is not meant to be run stand-alone but rather with the assistance of another program, usually a browser.

AppleTalk

AppleTalk is a protocol for computer networks. It is arguably inferior to TCP/IP.

Aqua

The default window manager for Mac OS X.

Archie

Archie is a system for searching through FTP archives for particular files. It tends not to be used too much anymore as more general modern search engines are significantly more capable.

ARM

An ARM is a RISC processor invented by Advanced RISC Machines, currently owned by Intel, and currently produced by both the above and Digital/Compaq. ARMs are different from most other processors in that they were not designed to maximize speed but rather to maximize speed per power consumed. Thus ARMs find most of their use on hand-held machines and PDAs. A few different OSes run on ARM based machines including Newton OS, JavaOS, and (soon) Windows CE and Linux. The StrongARM is a more recent design of the original ARM, and it is both faster and more power efficient than the original.

ASCII

The ASCII character set is the most popular one in common use. People will often refer to a bare text file without complicated embedded format instructions as an ASCII file, and such files can usually be transferred from one computer system to another with relative ease. Unfortunately there are a few minor variations of it that pop up here and there, and if you receive a text file that seems subtly messed up with punctuation marks altered or upper and lower case reversed, you are probably encountering one of the ASCII variants. It is usually fairly straightforward to translate from one ASCII variant to another, though. The ASCII character set is seven bit while pure binary is usually eight bit, so transferring a binary file through ASCII channels will result in corruption and loss of data. Note also that the ASCII character set is a subset of the Unicode character set.

ASK

A protocol for an infrared communications port on a device. It predates the IrDA compliant infrared communications protocol and is not compatible with it. Many devices with infrared communications support both, but some only support one or the other.

assembly language

Assembly language is essentially machine language that has had some of the numbers replaced by somewhat easier to remember mnemonics in an attempt to make it more human-readable. The program that converts assembly language to machine language is called an assembler. While assembly language predates FORTRAN, it is not typically what people think of when they discuss computer languages.

Atom

Atom is an intended replacement for RSS and like it is used for syndicating a web site's content. It is currently not nearly as popular or well-supported by software applications, however.

authoring system

Any GUIs method of designing new software can be called an authoring system. Any computer language name with the word "visual" in front of it is probably a version of that language built with some authoring system capabilities. It appears that the first serious effort to produce a commercial quality authoring system took place in the mid eighties for the Amiga.

AWK

AWK is an interpreted language developed in 1977 by Aho, Weinberger, & Kernighan. It gets its name from its creators' initials. It is not particularly fast, but it was designed for creating small throwaway programs rather than full-blown applications -- it is designed to make the writing of the program fast, not the program itself. It is quite portable with versions existing for numerous platforms, including a free GNU version. Plus, virtually every version of UNIX in the world comes with AWK built-in.

BASIC

The Beginners' All-purpose Symbolic Instruction Code is a computer language developed by Kemeny & Kurtz in 1964. Although it is traditionally interpreted, compilers exist for many platforms. While the interpreted form is typically fairly slow, the compiled form is often quite fast, usually faster than Pascal. The biggest problem with BASIC is portability; versions for different machines are often completely unlike each other; Amiga BASIC at first glance looks more like Pascal, for example. Portability problems actually go beyond even the cross platform level; in fact, most machines have multiple versions of incompatible BASICs available for use. The most popular version of BASIC today is called Visual BASIC. Like all BASICs it has portability issues, but it has some of the advantages of an authoring system so it is relatively easy to use.

baud

A measure of communications speed, used typically for modems indicating how many bits per second can be transmitted.

BBS

A bulletin board system is a computer that can be directly connected to via modem and provides various services like e-mail, chatting, newsgroups, and file downloading. BBSs have waned in popularity as more and more people are instead connecting to the Internet, but they are still used for product support and local area access. Most current BBSs provide some sort of gateway connection to the Internet.

bcode

Identical in intent to uucode, bcode is slightly more efficient and more portable across different computer types. It is the preferred method used by MIME.

BeOS

A lightweight OS available for both PowerPC and x86 based machines. It is often referred to simply as "Be".

beta

A beta version of something is not yet ready for prime time but still possibly useful to related developers and other interested parties. Expect beta software to crash more than properly released software does. Traditionally beta versions (of commercial software) are distributed only to selected testers who are often then given a discount on the proper version after its release in exchange for their testing work. Beta versions of non-commercial software are more often freely available to anyone who has an interest.

binary

There are two meanings for binary in common computer usage. The first is the name of the number system in which there are only zeros and ones. This is important to computers because all computer data is ultimately a series of zeros and ones, and thus can be represented by binary numbers. The second is an offshoot of the first; data that is not meant to be intepreted through a common character set (like ASCII) is typically referred to as binary data. Pure binary data is typically eight bit data, and transferring a binary file through ASCII channels without prior modification will result in corruption and loss of data. Binary data can be turned into ASCII data via uucoding or bcoding.

bit

A bit can either be on or off; one or zero. All computer data can ultimately be reduced to a series of bits. The term is also used as a (very rough) measure of sound quality, color quality, and even procesor capability by considering the fact that series of bits can represent binary numbers. For example (without getting too technical), an eight bit image can contain at most 256 distinct colors while a sixteen bit image can contain at most 65,536 distinct colors.

bitmap

A bitmap is a simplistic representation of an image on a computer, simply indicating whether or not pixels are on or off, and sometimes indicating their color. Often fonts are represented as bitmaps. The term "pixmap" is sometimes used similarly; typically when a distinction is made, pixmap refers to color images and bitmap refers to monochrome images.

blog

Short for web log, a blog (or weblog, or less commonly, 'blog) is a web site containing periodic (usually frequent) posts. Blogs are usually syndicated via either some type of RSS or Atom and often supports TrackBacks. It is not uncommon for blogs to function much like newspaper columns. A blogger is someone who writes for and maintains a blog.

boolean

Boolean algebra is the mathematics of base two numbers. Since base two numbers have only two values, zero and one, there is a good analogy between base two numbers and the logical values "true" & "false". In common usage, booleans are therefore considered to be simple logical values like true & false and the operations that relate them, most typically "and", "or" and "not". Since everyone has a basic understanding of the concepts of true & false and basic conjunctions, everyone also has a basic understanding of boolean concepts -- they just may not realize it.

byte

A byte is a grouping of bits. It is typically eight bits, but there are those who use non-standard byte sizes. Bytes are usually measured in large groups, and the term "kilobyte" (often abbreviated as K) means one-thousand twenty-four (1024) bytes; the term "megabyte" (often abbreviated as M) means one-thousand twenty-four (1024) K; the term gigabyte (often abbreviated as G) means one-thousand twenty-four (1024) M; and the term "terabyte" (often abbreviated as T) means one-thousand twenty-four (1024) G. Memory is typically measured in kilobytes or megabytes, and disk space is typically measured in megabytes or gigabytes. Note that the multipliers here are 1024 instead of the more common 1000 as would be used in the metric system. This is to make it easier to work with the binary number system. Note also that some hardware manufacturers will use the smaller 1000 multiplier on M & G quantities to make their disk drives seem larger than they really are; buyer beware.

bytecode

Sometimes computer languages that are said to be either interpreted or compiled are in fact neither and are more accurately said to be somewhere in between. Such languages are compiled into bytecode which is then interpreted on the target system. Bytecode tends to be binary but will work on any machine with the appropriate runtime environment (or virtual machine) for it.

C

C is one of the most popular computer languages in the world, and quite possibly *the* most popular. It is a compiled langauge widely supported on many platforms. It tends to be more portable than FORTRAN but less portable than Java; it has been standardized by ANSI as "ANSI C" -- older versions are called either "K&R C" or "Kernighan and Ritchie C" (in honor of C's creators), or sometimes just "classic C". Fast and simple, it can be applied to all manner of general purpose tasks. C compilers are made by several companies, but the free GNU version (gcc) is still considered one of the best. Newer C-like object-oriented languages include both Java and C++.

C#

C# is a compiled object-oriented language based heavily on C++ with some Java features.

C++

C++ is a compiled object-oriented language. Based heavily on C, C++ is nearly as fast and can often be thought of as being just C with added features. It is currently probably the second most popular object-oriented language, but it has the drawback of being fairly complex -- the much simpler but somewhat slower Java is probably the most popular object-oriented language. Note that C++ was developed independently of the somewhat similar Objective-C; it is however related to Objective-C++.

C64/128

The Commodore 64 computer to this day holds the record for being the most successful model of computer ever made with even the lowest estimates being in the tens of millions. Its big brother, the Commodore 128, was not quite as popular but still sold several million units. Both units sported ROM-based BASIC and used it as a default "OS". The C128 also came with CP/M (it was a not-often-exercized option on the C64). In their later days they were also packaged with GEOS. Both are based on 65xx family processors. They are still in use today and boast a friendly and surprisingly active user community. There is even a current effort to port Linux to the C64 and C128 machines.

CDE

The **c**ommon **d**esktop **e**nvironment is a popular commercial window manager (and much more -- as its name touts, it is more of a desktop environment) that runs under X-Windows. Free work-alike versions are also available.

chain

Some computer devices support chaining, the ability to string multiple devices in a sequence plugged into just one computer port. Often, but not always, such a chain will require some sort of terminator to mark the end. For an example, a SCSI scanner may be plugged into a SCSI CD-ROM drive that is plugged into a SCSI hard drive that is in turn plugged into the main computer. For all these components to work properly, the scanner would also have to have a proper terminator in use. Device chaining has been around a long time, and it is interesting to note that C64/128 serial devices supported it from the very beginning. Today the most common low-cost chainable devices in use support USB while the fastest low-cost chainable devices in use support FireWire.

character set

Since in reality all a computer can store are series of zeros and ones, representing common things like text takes a little work. The solution is to view the series of zeros and ones instead as a sequence of bytes, and map each one to a particular letter, number, or symbol. The full mapping is called a character set. The most popular character set is commonly referred to as ASCII. The second most popular character set these days is Unicode (and it will probably eventually surpass ASCII). Other fairly common character sets include EBCDIC and PETSCII. They are generally quite different from one another; programs exist to convert between them on most platforms, though. Usually EBCDIC is only found on really old machines.

CISC

Complex **i**nstruction **s**et **c**omputing is one of the two main types of processor design in use today. It is slowly losing popularity to RISC designs; currently all the fastest processors in the world are RISC. The most popular current CISC processor is the x86, but there are also still some 68xx, 65xx, and Z80s in use.

CLI

A command-line interface is a text-based means of communicating with a program, especially an OS. This is the sort of interface used by MS-DOS, or a UNIX shell window.

COBOL

The **Com**mon **B**usiness **O**riented **L**anguage is a language developed back in 1959 and still used by some businesses. While it is relatively portable, it is still disliked by many professional programmers simply because COBOL programs tend to be physically longer than equivalent programs written in almost any other language in common use.

compiled

If a program is compiled, its original human-readable source has been converted into a form more easily used by a computer prior to it being run. Such programs will generally run more quickly than interpreted programs, because time was pre-spent in the compilation phase. A program that compiles other programs is called a compiler.

compression

It is often possible to remove redundant information or capitalize on patterns in data to make a file smaller. Usually when a file has been compressed, it cannot be used until it is uncompressed. Image files are common exceptions, though, as many popular image file formats have compression built-in.

cookie

A cookie is a small file that a web page on another machine writes to your personal machine's disk to store various bits of information. Many people strongly detest cookies and the whole idea of them, and most browsers allow the reception of cookies to be disabled or at least selectively disabled, but it should be noted that both Netscape and MSIE have silent cookie reception enabled by default. Sites that maintain shopping carts or remember a reader's last position have legitimate uses for cookies. Sites without such functionality that still spew cookies with distant (or worse, non-existent) expiration dates should perhaps be treated with a little caution.

CP/M

An early DOS for desktops, CP/M runs on both Z80 and the x86 based machines. CP/M provides only a CLI and there really is not any standard way to get a window manager to run on top of it. It is fairly complex and tricky to use. In spite of all this, CP/M was once the most popular DOS and is still in use today.

crash

If a bug in a program is severe enough, it can cause that program to crash, or to become inoperable without being restarted. On machines that are not multitasking, the entire machine will crash and have to be rebooted. On machines that are only partially multitasking the entire machine will sometimes crash and have to be rebooted. On machines that are fully multitasking, the machine should never crash and require a reboot.

Cray

A Cray is a high-end computer used for research and frequently heavy-duty graphics applications. Modern Crays typically have Solaris for their OS and sport sixty-four RISC processors; older ones had various other configurations. Current top-of-the-line Crays can have over 2000 processors.

crippleware

Crippleware is a variant of shareware that will either self-destruct after its trial period or has built-in limitations to its functionality that get removed after its purchase.

CSS

Cascading style sheets are used in conjunction with HTML and XHTML to define the layout of web pages. While CSS is how current web pages declare how they should be displayed, it tends not to be supported well (if at all) by ancient browsers. XSL performs this same function more generally.

desktop publisher

A program for creating newspapers, magazines, books, etc. Some common desktop publishing programs include FrameMaker, PageMaker, InDesign, and GeoPublish.

DHTML

Dynamic **HTML** is simply the combined use of both CSS and JavaScript together in the same document; a more extreme form is called AJaX. Note that DHTML is quite different from the similarly named DTML.

dict

A protocol used for looking up definitions across a network (in particular the Internet).

digital camera

A digital camera looks and behaves like a regular camera, except instead of using film, it stores the image it sees in memory as a file for later transfer to a computer. Many digital cameras offer additional storage besides their own internal memory; a few sport some sort of disk but the majority utilize some sort of flash card. Digital cameras currently lack the resolution and color palette of real cameras, but are usually much more convenient for computer applications. Another related device is called a scanner.

DIMM

A physical component used to add RAM to a computer. Similar to, but incompatible with, SIMMs.

DNS

Domain name service is the means by which a name (like www.saugus.net or ftp.saugus.net) gets converted into a real Internet address that points to a particular machine.

DoS

In a denial of service attack, many individual (usually compromised) computers are used to try and simultaneously access the same public resource with the intent of overburdening it so that it will not be able to adequately serve its normal users.

DOS

A disk operating system manages disks and other system resources. Sort of a subset of OSes, sort of an archaic term for the same. MS-DOS is the most popular program currently calling itself a DOS. CP/M was the most popular prior to MS-DOS.

download

To download a file is to copy it from a remote computer to your own. The opposite is upload.

DR-DOS

The DOS currently produced by Caldera (originally produced by Design Research as a successor to CP/M) designed to work like MS-DOS. While similar to CP/M in many ways, it utilizes simpler commands. It provides only a CLI, but either Windows 3.1 or GEOS may be run on top of it to provide a GUI. It only runs on x86 based machines.

driver

A driver is a piece of software that works with the OS to control a particular piece of hardware, like a printer or a scanner or a mouse or whatever.

DRM

Depending upon whom you ask, DRM can stand for either Digital Rights Management or Digital Restrictions Management. In either case, DRM is used to place restrictions upon the usage of digital media ranging from software to music to video.

DTML

The **D**ocument **T**emplate **M**ark-up **L**anguage is a subset of SGML and a superset of HTML used for creating documents that dynamically adapt to external conditions using its own custom tags and a little bit of Python. Note that it is quite different from the similarly named DHTML.

EDBIC

The EDBIC character set is similar to (but less popular than) the ASCII character set in concept, but is significantly different in layout. It tends to be found only on old machines..

emacs

Emacs is both one of the most powerful and one of the most popular text editing programs in existence. Versions can be found for most platforms, and in fact multiple companies make versions, so for a given platform there might even be a choice. There is even a free GNU version available. The drawback with emacs is that it is not in the least bit lightweight. In fact, it goes so far in the other direction that even its advocates will occasionally joke about it. It is however extremely capable. Almost anything that one would need to relating to text can be done with emacs and is probably built-in. Even if one manages to find something that emacs was not built to do, emacs has a built-in Lisp interpreter capable of not only extending its text editing capabilities, but even of being used as a scripting language in its own right.

embedded

An embedded system is a computer that lives inside another device and acts as a component of that device. For example, current cars have an embedded computer under the hood that helps regulate much of their day to day operation.

An embedded file is a file that lives inside another and acts as a portion of that file. This is frequently seen with HTML files having embedded audio files; audio files often embedded in HTML include AU files, MIDI files, SID files, WAV files, AIFF files, and MOD files. Most browsers will ignore these files unless an appropriate plug-in is present.

emulator

An emulator is a program that allows one computer platform to mimic another for the purposes of running its software. Typically (but not always) running a program through an emulator will not be quite as pleasent an experience as running it on the real system.

endian

A processor will be either "big endian" or "little endian" based upon the manner in which it encodes multiple byte values. There is no difference in performance between the two encoding methods, but it is one of the sources of difficulty when reading binary data on different platforms.

environment

An environment (sometimes also called a runtime environment) is a collection of external variable items or parameters that a program can access when run. Information about the computer's hardware and the user can often be found in the environment.

EPOC

EPOC is a lightweight OS. It is most commonly found on the Psion PDA.

extension

Filename extensions originate back in the days of CP/M and basically allow a very rough grouping of different file types by putting a tag at the end of the name. To further complicate matters, the tag is sometimes separated by the name proper by a period "." and sometimes by a tab. While extensions are semi-enforced on CP/M, MS-DOS, and MS-Windows, they have no real meaning aside from convention on other platforms and are only optional.

FAQ

A frequently asked questions file attempts to provide answers for all commonly asked questions related to a given topic.

FireWire

An incredibly fast type of serial port that offers many of the best features of SCSI at a lower price. Faster than most types of parallel port, a single FireWire port is capable of chaining many devices without the need of a terminator. FireWire is similar in many respects to USB but is significantly faster and somewhat more expensive. It is heavily used for connecting audio/video devices to computers, but is also used for connecting storage devices like drives and other assorted devices like printers and scanners.

fixed width

As applied to a font, fixed width means that every character takes up the same amount of space. That is, an "i" will be just as wide as an "m" with empty space being used for padding. The opposite is variable width. The most common fixed width font is Courier.

flash

Flash memory is similar to RAM. It has one significant advantage: it does not lose its contents when power is lost; it has two main disadvantages: it is slower, and it eventually wears out. Flash memory is frequently found in PCMCIA cards.

font

In a simplistic sense, a font can be thought of as the physical description of a character set. While the character set will define what sets of bits map to what letters, numbers, and other symbols, the font will define what each letter, number, and other symbol looks like. Fonts can be either fixed width or variable width and independently, either bitmapped or vectored. The size of the large characters in a font is typically measured in points.

Forth

A language developed in 1970 by Moore. Forth is fairly portable and has versions on many different platforms. While it is no longer an very popular language, many of its ideas and concepts have been carried into other computer programs. In particular, some programs for doing heavy-duty mathematical and engineering work use Forth-like interfaces.

FORTRAN

FORTRAN stands for **for**mula **tran**slation and is the oldest computer language in the world. It is typically compiled and is quite fast. Its primary drawbacks are portability and ease-of-use -- often different FORTRAN compilers on different platforms behave quite differently in spite of standardization efforts in 1966 (FORTRAN 66 or FORTRAN IV), 1978 (FORTRAN 77), and 1991 (FORTRAN 90). Today languages like C and Java are more popular, but FORTRAN is still heavily used in military software. It is somewhat amusing to note that when FORTRAN was first released back in 1958 its advocates thought that it would mean the end of software bugs. In truth of course by making the creation of more complex software practical, computer languages have merely created new types of software bugs.

FreeBSD

A free variant of Berkeley UNIX available for Alpha and x86 based machines. It is not as popular as Linux.

freeware

Freeware is software that is available for free with no strings attached. The quality is often superb as the authors are also generally users.

FTP

The **f**ile **t**ransfer **p**rotocol is one of the most commonly used methods of copying files across the Internet. It has its origins on UNIX machines, but has been adapted to almost every type of computer in existence and is built into many browsers. Most FTP programs have two modes of operation, ASCII, and binary. Transmitting an ASCII file via the ASCII mode of operation is more efficient and cleaner. Transmitting a binary file via the ASCII mode of operation will result in a broken binary file. Thus the FTP programs that do not support both modes of operation will typically only do the binary mode, as binary transfers are capable of transferring both kinds of data without corruption.

gateway

A gateway connects otherwise separate computer networks.

GEOS

The **g**raphic **e**nvironment **o**perating **s**ystem is a lightweight OS with a GUI. It runs on several different processors, including the 65xx (different versions for different machines -- there are versions for the C64, the C128, and the Apple][, each utilizing the relevant custom chip sets), the x86 (although the x86 version is made to run on top of MS-DOS (or PC-DOS or DR-DOS) and is not strictly a full OS or a window manager, rather it is somewhat in between, like Windows 3.1) and numerous different PDAs, embedded devices, and hand-held machines. It was originally designed by Berkeley Softworks (no real relation to the Berkeley of UNIX fame) but is currently in a more interesting state: the company GeoWorks develops and promotes development of GEOS for hand-held devices, PDAs, & and embedded devices and owns (but has ceased further development on) the x86 version. The other versions are owned (and possibly still being developed) by the company CMD.

GHz & **gigahertz**

One gigahertz is equivalent to 1000 megahertz, or 1,000,000,000 hertz.

Glulx

A virtual machine optimized for running interactive fiction, interactive tutorials, and other interactive things of a primarily textual nature. Glulx has been ported to several platforms, and in in many ways an upgrade to the Z-machine.

GNOME

The **GNU** **n**etwork **o**bject **m**odel environment is a popular free window manager (and much more -- as its name touts, it is more of a desktop environment) that runs under X-Windows. It is a part of the GNU project.

GNU

GNU stands for **GNU's** **n**ot **UNIX** and is thus a recursive acronym (and unlike the animal name, the "G" here is pronounced). At any rate, the GNU project is an effort by the Free Software Foundation (FSF) to make all of the traditional UNIX utilities free for whoever wants them. The Free Software Foundation programmers know their stuff, and the quality of the GNU software is on par with the best produced commercially, and often better. All of the GNU software can be downloaded for free or obtained on CD-ROM for a small service fee. Documentation for all GNU software can be downloaded for free or obtained in book form for a small service fee. The Free Software Foundation pays its bills from the collection of service fees and the sale of T-shirts, and exists mostly through volunteer effort. It is based in Cambridge, MA.

gopher

Though not as popular as FTP or http, the gopher protocol is implemented by many browsers and numerous other programs and allows the transfer of files across networks. In some respects it can be thought of as a hybrid between FTP and http, although it tends not to be as good at raw file transfer as FTP and is not as flexible as http. The collection of documents available through gopher is often called "gopherspace", and it should be noted that gopherspace is older than the web. It should also be noted that gopher is not getting as much attention as it once did, and surfing through gopherspace is a little like exploring a ghost town, but there is an interesting VR interface available for it, and some things in gopherspace still have not been copied onto the web.

GUI

A **g**raphical **u**ser **i**nterface is a graphics-based means of communicating with a program, especially an OS or window manager. In fact, a window manager can be thought of as a GUI for a CLI OS.

HP-UX

HP-UX is the version of UNIX designed by Hewlett-Packard to work with their PA-RISC and

68xx based machines.
HTML
The **Hypertext Mark-up Language** is the language currently most frequently used to express web pages (although it is rapidly being replaced by XHTML). Every browser has the built-in ability to understand HTML. Some browsers can additionally understand Java and browse FTP areas. HTML is a proper subset of SGML.
http
The **hypertext transfer protocol** is the native protocol of browsers and is most typically used to transfer HTML formatted files. The secure version is called "https".
Hurd
The Hurd is the official GNU OS. It is still in development and is not yet supported on too many different processors, but promises to be the most powerful OS available. It (like all the GNU software) is free.
Hz & hertz
Hertz means cycles per second, and makes no assumptions about what is cycling. So, for example, if a fluorescent light flickers once per jiffy, it has a 60 Hz flicker. More typical for computers would be a program that runs once per jiffy and thus has a 60 Hz frequency, or larger units of hertz like kHz, MHz, GHz, or THz.
i18n
Commonly used to abbreviate the word "internationalization". There are eighteen letters between the "i" and the "n". Similar to (and often used along with) i18n.
iCalendar
The iCalendar standard refers to the format used to store calendar type information (including events, to-do items, and journal entries) on the Internet. iCalendar data can be found on some World-Wide-Web pages or attached to e-mail messages.
icon
A small graphical display representing an object, action, or modifier of some sort.
IDE
Loosely speaking, a disk format sometimes used by MS-Windows, Mac OS, AmigaOS, and (rarely) UNIX. EIDE is enhanced IDE; it is much faster. Generally IDE is inferior (but less expensive) to SCSI, but it varies somewhat with system load and the individual IDE and SCSI components themselves. The quick rundown is that: SCSI-I and SCSI-II will almost always outperform IDE; EIDE will almost always outperform SCSI-I and SCSI-II; SCSI-III and UltraSCSI will almost always outperform EIDE; and heavy system loads give an advantage to SCSI. Note that although loosely speaking it is just a format difference, it is deep down a hardware difference.
Inform
A compiled, object-oriented language optimized for creating interactive fiction.
infrared communications
A device with an infrared port can communicate with other devices at a distance by beaming infrared light signals. Two incompatible protocols are used for infrared communications: IrDA and ASK. Many devices support both.
Instant Messenger
AOL's Instant Messenger is is a means of chatting over the Internet in real-time. It allows both open group discussions and private conversations. Instant Messenger uses a different, proprietary protocol from the more standard IRC, and is not supported on as many platforms.
interactive fiction
Interactive fiction (often abbreviated "IF" or "I-F") is a form of literature unique to the computer. While the reader cannot influence the direction of a typical story, the reader plays a more active role in an interactive fiction story and completely controls its direction. Interactive fiction works come in all the sizes and genres available to standard fiction, and in fact are not always even

fiction per se (interactive tutorials exist and are slowly becoming more common).

interpreted

If a program is interpreted, its actual human-readable source is read as it is run by the computer. This is generally a slower process than if the program being run has already been compiled.

intranet

An intranet is a private network. There are many intranets scattered all over the world. Some are connected to the Internet via gateways.

IP

IP is the family of protocols that makes up the Internet. The two most common flavors are TCP/IP and UDP/IP.

IRC

Internet relay chat is a means of chatting over the Internet in real-time. It allows both open group discussions and private conversations. IRC programs are provided by many different companies and will work on many different platforms. AOL's Instant Messenger utilizes a separate incompatible protocol but is otherwise very similar.

IrDA

The Infrared Data Association (IrDA) is a voluntary organization of various manufacturers working together to ensure that the infrared communications between different computers, PDAs, printers, digital cameras, remote controls, etc. are all compatible with each other regardless of brand. The term is also often used to designate an IrDA compliant infrared communications port on a device. Informally, a device able to communicate via IrDA compliant infrared is sometimes simply said to "have IrDA". There is also an earlier, incompatible, and usually slower type of infrared communications still in use called ASK.

IRI

An Internationalized Resource Identifier is just a URI with i18n.

IRIX

The variant of UNIX designed by Silicon Graphics, Inc. IRIX machines are known for their graphics capabilities and were initially optimized for multimedia applications.

ISDN

An integrated service digital network line can be simply looked at as a digital phone line. ISDN connections to the Internet can be four times faster than the fastest regular phone connection, and because it is a digital connection a modem is not needed. Any computer hooked up to ISDN will typically require other special equipment in lieu of the modem, however. Also, both phone companies and ISPs charge more for ISDN connections than regular modem connections.

ISP

An Internet service provider is a company that provides Internet support for other entities. AOL (America Online) is a well-known ISP.

Java

A computer language designed to be both fairly lightweight and extremely portable. It is tightly bound to the web as it is the primary language for web applets. There has also been an OS based on Java for use on small hand-held, embedded, and network computers. It is called JavaOS. Java can be either interpreted or compiled. For web applet use it is almost always interpreted. While its interpreted form tends not to be very fast, its compiled form can often rival languages like C++ for speed. It is important to note however that speed is not Java's primary purpose -- raw speed is considered secondary to portabilty and ease of use.

JavaScript

JavaScript (in spite of its name) has nothing whatsoever to do with Java (in fact, it's arguably more like Newton Script than Java). JavaScript is an interpreted language built into a browser to provide a relatively simple means of adding interactivity to web pages. It is only supported on a few different browsers, and tends not to work exactly the same on different versions. Thus its use on the Internet is somewhat restricted to fairly simple programs. On intranets where there are usually fewer browser versions in use, JavaScript has been used to implement much more complex and impressive programs.

jiffy

A jiffy is 1/60 of a second. Jiffies are to seconds as seconds are to minutes.

joystick

A joystick is a physical device typically used to control objects on a computer screen. It is frequently used for games and sometimes used in place of a mouse.

JSON

The JSON is used for data interchange between programs, an area in which the ubiquitous XML is not too well-suited. JSON is lightweight and works extremely cleanly with languages languages including JavaScript, Python, Java, C++, and many others.

JSON-RPC

JSON-RPC is like XML-RPC but is significantly more lightweight since it uses JSON in lieu of XML.

KDE

The **K d**esktop environment is a popular free window manager (and much more -- as its name touts, it is more of a desktop environment) that runs under X-Windows.

Kerberos

Kerberos is a network authentication protocol. Basically it preserves the integrity of passwords in any untrusted network (like the Internet). Kerberized applications work hand-in-hand with sites that support Kerberos to ensure that passwords cannot be stolen.

kernel

The very heart of an OS is often called its kernel. It will usually (at minimum) provide some libraries that give programmers access to its various features.

kHz & **kilohertz**

One kilohertz is equivalent to 1000 hertz. Some older computers have clock speeds measured in kHz.

l10n

Commonly used to abbreviate the word "localization". There are ten letters between the "l" and the "n". Similar to (and often used along with) i18n.

LDAP

The **L**ightweight **D**irectory **A**ccess **P**rotocol provides a means of sharing address book type of information across an intranet or even across the Internet. Note too that "address book type of information" here is pretty broad; it often includes not just human addresses, but machine addresses, printer configurations, and similar.

library

A selection of routines used by programmers to make computers do particular things.

lightweight

Something that is lightweight will not consume computer resources (such as RAM and disk space) too much and will thus run on less expensive computer systems.

Linux

Believe it or not, one of the fastest, most robust, and powerful multitasking OSes is available for free. Linux can be downloaded for free or be purchased on CD-ROM for a small service charge. A handful of companies distribute Linux including Red Hat, Debian, Caldera, and many others. Linux is also possibly available for more hardware combinations than any other OS (with the possible exception of NetBSD. Supported processors include: Alpha, PowerPC, SPARC, x86, and 68xx. Most processors currently not supported are currently works-in-progress or even available in beta. For example, work is currently underway to provide support for PA-RISC, 65xx, StrongARM, and Z80. People have even successfully gotten Linux working on PDAs. As you may have guessed, Linux can be made quite lightweight. Linux is a variant of UNIX and as such, most of the traditional UNIX software will run on Linux. This especially includes the GNU software, most of which comes with the majority of Linux distributions. Fast, reliable, stable, and inexpensive, Linux is popular with ISPs, software developers, and home hobbyists alike.

Lisp

Lisp stands for **lis**t **p**rocessing and is the second oldest computer language in the world. Being developed in 1959, it lost the title to FORTRAN by only a few months. It is typically interpreted, but compilers are available for some platforms. Attempts were made to standardize the language, and the standard version is called "Common Lisp". There have also been efforts to simplify the language, and the results of these efforts is another language called Scheme. Lisp is a fairly portable language, but is not particularly fast. Today, Lisp is most widely used with AI software.

load

There are two popular meanings for load. The first means to fetch some data or a program from a disk and store it in memory. The second indicates the amount of work a component (especially a processor) is being made to do.

Logo

Logo is an interpreted language designed by Papert in 1966 to be a tool for helping people (especially kids) learn computer programming concepts. In addition to being used for that purpose, it is often used as a language for controlling mechanical robots and other similar devices. Logo interfaces even exist for building block / toy robot sets. Logo uses a special graphics cursor called "the turtle", and Logo is itself sometimes called "Turtle Graphics". Logo is quite portable but not particularly fast. Versions can be found on almost every computer platform in the world. Additionally, some other languages (notably some Pascal versions) provide Logo-like interfaces for graphics-intensive programming.

lossy

If a process is lossy, it means that a little quality is lost when it is performed. If a format is lossy, it means that putting data into that format (or possibly even manipulating it in that format) will cause some slight loss. Lossy processes and formats are typically used for performance or resource utilization reasons. The opposite of lossy is lossless.

Lua

Lua is a simple interpreted language. It is extremely portable, and free versions exist for most platforms.

Mac OS

Mac OS is the OS used on Macintosh computers. There are two distinctively different versions of it; everything prior to version 10 (sometimes called Mac OS Classic) and everything version 10 or later (called Mac OS X).

Mac OS Classic

The OS created by Apple and originally used by Macs is frequently (albeit slightly incorrectly) referred to as Mac OS Classic (officially Mac OS Classic is this original OS running under the modern Mac OS X in emulation. Mac OS combines the functionality of both an OS and a window manager and is often considered to be the easiest OS to use. It is partially multitasking but will still sometimes crash when dealing with a buggy program. It is probably the second most popular OS, next only to Windows 'XP (although it is quickly losing ground to Mac OS X) and has excellent driver support and boasts a fair selection of games. Mac OS will run on PowerPC and 68xx based machines.

Mac OS X

Mac OS X (originally called Rhapsody) is the industrial strength OS produced by Apple to run on both PowerPC and x86 systems (replacing what is often referred to as Mac OS Classic. Mac OS X is at its heart a variant of UNIX and possesses its underlying power (and the ability to run many of the traditional UNIX tools, including the GNU tools). It also was designed to mimic other OSes on demand via what it originally refered to as "boxes" (actually high-performance emulators); it has the built-in capability to run programs written for older Mac OS (via its "BlueBox", officially called Mac OS Classic) and work was started on making it also run Windows '95 / '98 / ME software (via what was called its "YellowBox"). There are also a few rumors going around that future versions may even be able to run Newton software (via the "GreenBox"). It provides a selection of two window managers built-in: Aqua and X-Windows (with Aqua being the default).

machine language

Machine language consists of the raw numbers that can be directly understood by a particular processor. Each processor's machine language will be different from other processors' machine language. Although called "machine language", it is not usually what people think of when talking about computer languages. Machine language dressed up with mnemonics to make it a bit more human-readable is called assembly language.

Macintosh

A Macintosh (or a Mac for short) is a computer system that has Mac OS for its OS. There are a few different companies that have produced Macs, but by far the largest is Apple. The oldest Macs are based on the 68xx processor; somewhat more recent Macs on the PowerPC processor, and current Macs on the x86 processor. The Macintosh was really the first general purpose computer to employ a GUI.

MacTel

An x86 based system running some flavor of Mac OS.

mainframe

A mainframe is any computer larger than a small piece of furniture. A modern mainframe is more powerful than a modern workstation, but more expensive and more difficult to maintain.

MathML

The **Math M**ark-up **L**anguage is a subset of XML used to represent mathematical formulae and equations. Typically it is found embedded within XHTML documents, although as of this writing not all popular browsers support it.

megahertz

A million cycles per second, abbreviated MHz. This is often used misleadingly to indicate processor speed, because while one might expect that a higher number would indicate a faster processor, that logic only holds true within a given type of processors as different types of processors are capable of doing different amounts of work within a cycle. For a current example, either a 200 MHz PowerPC or a 270 MHz SPARC will outperform a 300 MHz Pentium.

Merced

The Merced is a RISC processor developed by Intel with help from Hewlett-Packard and possibly Sun. It is just starting to be released, but is intended to eventually replace both the x86 and PA-RISC processors. Curiously, HP is recommending that everyone hold off using the first release and instead wait for the second one. It is expected some day to be roughly as fast as an Alpha or PowerPC. It is expected to be supported by future versions of Solaris, Windows-NT, HP-UX, Mac OS X, and Linux. The current semi-available Merced processor is called the Itanium. Its overall schedule is way behind, and some analysts predict that it never will really be released in significant quanitities.

MFM

Loosely speaking, An old disk format sometimes used by CP/M, MS-DOS, and MS-Windows. No longer too common as it cannot deliver close to the performance of either SCSI or IDE.

middleware

Software designed to sit in between an OS and applications. Common examples are Java and Tcl/Tk.

MIME

The **m**ulti-purpose **I**nternet **m**ail **e**xtensions specification describes a means of sending non-

ASCII data (such as images, sounds, foreign symbols, etc.) through e-mail. It commonly utilizes bcode.

MMX

Multimedia extensions were built into some x86 CPUs to provide better performance for certain operations, most notably graphics and sound. It is similar to AltiVec on the PowerPC CPUs. Like AltiVec, it requires special software for full performance benefits to be realized.

MOB

A **mo**vable **ob**ject is a graphical object that is manipulated separately from the background. These are seen all the time in computer games. When implemented in hardware, MOBs are sometimes called sprites.

Modula-2 & Modula-3

Modula-2 is a procedural language based on Pascal by its original author in around the 1977 - 1979 time period. Modula-3 is an intended successor that adds support for object-oriented constructs (among other things). Modula-2 can be either compiled or interpreted, while Modula-3 tends to be just a compiled language.

MOTD

A **m**essage **of t**he **d**ay. Many computers (particularly more capable ones) are configured to display a MOTD when accessed remotely.

Motif

Motif is a popular commercial window manager that runs under X-Windows. Free work-alike versions are also available.

MS-DOS

The DOS produced by Microsoft. Early versions of it bear striking similarities to the earlier CP/M, but it utilizes simpler commands. It provides only a CLI, but either OS/2, Windows 3.1, Windows '95, Windows '98, Windows ME, or GEOS may be run on top of it to provide a GUI. It only runs on x86 based machines.

MS-Windows

MS-Windows is the name collectively given to several somewhat incompatible OSes all produced by Microsoft. They are: Windows CE, Windows NT, Windows 3.1, Windows '95, Windows '98, Windows ME, Windows 2000, and Windows XP.

MUD

A **m**ulti-**u**ser **d**imension (also sometimes called multi-user dungeon, but in either case abbreviated to "MUD") is sort of a combination between the online chatting abilities provided by something like IRC and a role-playing game. A MUD built with object oriented principles in mind is called a "Multi-user dimension object-oriented", or MOO. Yet another variant is called a "multi-user shell", or MUSH. Still other variants are called multi-user role-playing environments (MURPE) and multi-user environments (MUSE). There are probably more. In all cases the differences will be mostly academic to the regular user, as the same software is used to connect to all of them. Software to connect to MUDs can be found for most platforms, and there are even Java based ones that can run from within a browser.

multitasking

Some OSes have built into them the ability to do several things at once. This is called multitasking, and has been in use since the late sixties / early seventies. Since this ability is built into the software, the overall system will be slower running two things at once than it will be running just one thing. A system may have more than one processor built into it though, and such a system will be capable of running multiple things at once with less of a performance hit.

nagware

Nagware is a variant of shareware that will frequently remind its users to register.

NetBSD

A free variant of Berkeley UNIX available for Alpha, x86, 68xx, PA-RISC, SPARC, PowerPC, ARM, and many other types of machines. Its emphasis is on portability.

netiquette
The established conventions of online politeness are called netiquette. Some conventions vary from site to site or online medium to online medium; others are pretty standard everywhere. Newbies are often unfamiliar with the conventional rules of netiquette and sometimes embarrass themselves accordingly. Be sure not to send that incredibly important e-mail message before reading about netiquette.

newbie
A newbie is a novice to the online world or computers in general.

news
Usenet news can generally be thought of as public e-mail as that is generally the way it behaves. In reality, it is implemented by different software and is often accessed by different programs. Different newsgroups adhere to different topics, and some are "moderated", meaning that humans will try to manually remove off-topic posts, especially spam. Most established newsgroups have a FAQ, and people are strongly encouraged to read the FAQ prior to posting.

Newton
Although Newton is officially the name of the lightweight OS developed by Apple to run on its MessagePad line of PDAs, it is often used to mean the MessagePads (and compatible PDAs) themselves and thus the term "Newton OS" is often used for clarity. The Newton OS is remarkably powerful; it is fully multitasking in spite of the fact that it was designed for small machines. It is optimized for hand-held use, but will readily transfer data to all manner of desktop machines. Historically it was the first PDA. Recently Apple announced that it will discontinue further development of the Newton platform, but will instead work to base future hand-held devices on either Mac OS or Mac OS X with some effort dedicated to making the new devices capable of running current Newton programs.

Newton book
Newton books provide all the functionality of ordinary books but add searching and hypertext capabilities. The format was invented for the Newton to provide a means of making volumes of data portable, and is particularly popular in the medical community as most medical references are available as Newton books and carrying around a one pound Newton is preferable to carrying around twenty pounds of books, especially when it comes to looking up something. In addition to medical books, numerous references, most of the classics, and many contemporary works of fiction are available as Newton books. Most fiction is available for free, most references cost money. Newton books are somewhat more capable than the similar Palm DOC; both are specific types of e-books.

Newton Script
A intepreted, object-oriented language for Newton MessagePad computers.

nybble
A nybble is half a byte, or four bits. It is a case of computer whimsy; it only stands to reason that a small byte should be called a nybble. Some authors spell it with an "i" instead of the "y", but the "y" is the original form.

object-oriented
While the specifics are well beyond the scope of this document, the term "object-oriented" applies to a philosophy of software creation. Often this philosophy is referred to as object-oriented design (sometimes abbreviated as OOD), and programs written with it in mind are referred to as object-oriented programs (often abbreviated OOP). Programming languages designed to help facilitate it are called object-oriented languages (sometimes abbreviated as OOL) and databases built with it in mind are called object-oriented databases (sometimes abbreviated as OODB or less fortunately OOD). The general notion is that an object-oriented approach to creating software starts with modeling the real-world problems trying to be solved in familiar real-world ways, and carries the analogy all the way down to structure of the program. This is of course a great over-simplification. Numerous object-oriented programming languages

exist including: Java, C++, Modula-2, Newton Script, and ADA.

Objective-C & ObjC

Objective-C (often called "ObjC" for short) is a compiled object-oriented language. Based heavily on C, Objective-C is nearly as fast and can often be thought of as being just C with added features. Note that it was developed independently of C++; its object-oriented extensions are more in the style of Smalltalk. It is however related to Objective-C++.

Objective-C++ & ObjC++

Objective-C++ (often called "ObjC++" for short) is a curious hybrid of Objective-C and C++, allowing the syntax of both to coexist in the same source files.

office suite

An office suite is a collection of programs including at minimum a word processor, spreadsheet, drawing program, and minimal database program. Some common office suites include MS-Office, AppleWorks, ClarisWorks, GeoWorks, Applixware, Corel Office, and StarOffice.

open source

Open source software goes one step beyond freeware. Not only does it provide the software for free, it provides the original source code used to create the software. Thus, curious users can poke around with it to see how it works, and advanced users can modify it to make it work better for them. By its nature, open souce software is pretty well immune to all types of computer virus.

OpenBSD

A free variant of Berkeley UNIX available for Alpha, x86, 68xx, PA-RISC, SPARC, and PowerPC based machines. Its emphasis is on security.

OpenDocument & ODF

OpenDocument (or ODF for short) is the suite of open, XML-based office suite application formats defined by the OASIS consortium. It defines a platform-neutral, non-proprietary way of storing documents.

OpenGL

A low-level 3D graphics library with an emphasis on speed developed by SGI.

OS/2

OS/2 is the OS designed by IBM to run on x86 based machines. It is semi-compatible with MS-Windows. IBM's more industrial strength OS is called AIX.

PA-RISC

The PA-RISC is a RISC processor developed by Hewlett-Packard. It is currently produced only by HP. At the moment only one OS runs on PA-RISC based machines: HP-UX. There is an effort underway to port Linux to them, though.

Palm DOC

Palm DOC files are quite similar to (but slightly less capable than) Newton books. They were designed for Palm Pilots but can now be read on a couple other platforms, too. They are a specific type of e-book.

Palm Pilot

The Palm Pilot (also called both just Palm and just Pilot, officially now just Palm) is the most popular PDA currently in use. It is one of the least capable PDAs, but it is also one of the smallest and least expensive. While not as full featured as many of the other PDAs (such as the Newton) it performs what features it does have quite well and still remains truly pocket-sized.

parallel

Loosely speaking, parallel implies a situation where multiple things can be done simultaneously, like having multiple check-out lines each serving people all at once. Parallel connections are by their nature more expensive than serial ones, but usually faster. Also, in a related use of the word, often multitasking computers are said to be capable of running multiple programs in parallel.

partition

Sometimes due to hardware limitations, disks have to be divided into smaller pieces. These pieces are called partitions.

Pascal

Named after the mathematician Blaise Pascal, Pascal is a language designed by Niklaus Wirth originally in 1968 (and heavily revised in 1972) mostly for purposes of education and training people how to write computer programs. It is a typically compiled language but is still usually slower than C or FORTRAN. Wirth also created a more powerful object-oriented Pascal-like language called Modula-2.

PC-DOS

The DOS produced by IBM designed to work like MS-DOS. Early versions of it bear striking similarities to the earlier CP/M, but it utilizes simpler commands. It provides only a CLI, but either Windows 3.1 or GEOS may be run on top of it to provide a GUI. It only runs on x86 based machines.

PCMCIA

The **P**ersonal **C**omputer **M**emory **C**ard **I**nternational **A**ssociation is a standards body that concern themselves with PC Card technology. Often the PC Cards themselves are referred to as "PCMCIA cards". Frequently flash memory can be found in PC card form.

Perl

Perl is an interpreted language extremely popular for web applications.

PET

The Commodore PET (**P**ersonal **E**lectronic **T**ransactor) is an early (circa 1977-1980, around the same time as the Apple][) home computer featuring a ROM-based BASIC developed by Microsoft which it uses as a default "OS". It is based on the 65xx family of processors and is the precursor to the VIC-20.

PETSCII

The PETSCII character set gets its name from "**PET A**SCII; it is a variant of the ASCII character set originally developed for the Commodore PET that swaps the upper and lower case characters and adds over a hundred graphic characters in addition to other small changes. If you encounter some text that seems to have uppercase where lowercase is expected and vice-versa, it is probably a PETSCII file.

PHP

Named with a recursive acronym (PHP: Hypertext Preprocessor), PHP provides a means of creating web pages that dynamically modify themselves on the fly.

ping

Ping is a protocol designed to check across a network to see if a particular computer is "alive" or not. Computers that recognize the ping will report back their status. Computers that are down will not report back anything at all.

pixel

The smallest distinct point on a computer display is called a pixel.

plug-in

A plug-in is a piece of software designed not to run on its own but rather work in cooperation with a separate application to increase that application's abilities.

point

There are two common meanings for this word. The first is in the geometric sense; a position in space without size. Of course as applied to computers it must take up some space in practise (even if not in theory) and it is thus sometimes synonomous with pixel. The other meaning is related most typically to fonts and regards size. The exact meaning of it in this sense will unfortunately vary somewhat from person to person, but will often mean 1/72 of an inch. Even when it does not exactly mean 1/72 of an inch, larger point sizes always indicate larger fonts.

PowerPC

The PowerPC is a RISC processor developed in a collaborative effort between IBM, Apple, and Motorola. It is currently produced by a few different companies, of course including its original developers. A few different OSes run on PowerPC based machines, including Mac OS, AIX, Solaris, Windows NT, Linux, Mac OS X, BeOS, and AmigaOS. At any given time, the fastest processor in the world is usually either a PowerPC or an Alpha, but sometimes SPARCs and PA-RISCs make the list, too.

proprietary

This simply means to be supplied by only one vendor. It is commonly misused. Currently, most processors are non-proprietary, some systems are non-proprietary, and every OS (except for arguably Linux) is proprietary.

protocol

A protocol is a means of communication used between computers. As long as both computers recognize the same protocol, they can communicate without too much difficulty over the same network or even via a simple direct modem connection regardless whether or not they are themselves of the same type. This means that WinTel boxes, Macs, Amigas, UNIX machines, etc., can all talk with one another provided they agree on a common protocol first.

Psion

The Psion is a fairly popular brand of PDA. Generally, it is in between a Palm and a Newton in capability. It runs the EPOC OS.

Python

Python is an interpreted, object-oriented language popular for Internet applications. It is extremely portable with free versions existing for virtually every platform.

queue

A queue is a waiting list of things to be processed. Many computers provide printing queues, for example. If something is being printed and the user requests that another item be printed, the second item will sit in the printer queue until the first item finishes printing at which point it will be removed from the queue and get printed itself.

QuickDraw

A high-level 3D graphics library with an emphasis on quick development time created by Apple.

RAM

Random access memory is the short-term memory of a computer. Any information stored in RAM will be lost if power goes out, but the computer can read from RAM far more quickly than from a drive.

random access

Also called "dynamic access" this indicates that data can be selected without having to skip over earlier data first. This is the way that a CD, record, laserdisc, or DVD will behave -- it is easy to selectively play a particular track without having to fast forward through earlier tracks. The other common behavior is called sequential access.

RDF

The Resource Description Framework is built upon an XML base and provides a more modern means of accessing data from Internet resources. It can provide metadata (including annotations) for web pages making (among other things) searching more capable. It is also being used to refashion some existing formats like RSS and iCalendar; in the former case it is already in place (at least for newer RSS versions), but it is still experimental in the latter case.

real-time

Something that happens in real-time will keep up with the events around it and never give any sort of "please wait" message.

Rexx

The Restructured Extended Executor is an interpreted language designed primarily to be embedded in other applications in order to make them consistently programmable, but also to be easy to learn and understand.

RISC

Reduced instruction set computing is one of the two main types of processor design in use today, the other being CISC. The fastest processors in the world today are all RISC designs. There are several popular RISC processors, including Alphas, ARMs, PA-RISCs, PowerPCs, and SPARCs.

robot

A robot (or 'bot for short) in the computer sense is a program designed to automate some task, often just sending messages or collecting information. A spider is a type of robot designed to traverse the web performing some task (usually collecting data).

robust

The adjective robust is used to describe programs that are better designed, have fewer bugs, and are less likely to crash.

ROM

Read-only memory is similar to RAM only cannot be altered and does not lose its contents when power is removed.

RSS

RSS stands for either **R**ich **S**ite **S**ummary, **R**eally **S**imple **S**yndication, or **R**DF **S**ite **S**ummary, depending upon whom you ask. The general idea is that it can provide brief summaries of articles that appear in full on a web site. It is well-formed XML, and newer versions are even more specifically well-formed RDF.

Ruby

Ruby is an interpreted, object-oriented language. Ruby was fairly heavily influenced by Perl, so people familiar with that language can typically transition to Ruby easily.

scanner

A scanner is a piece of hardware that will examine a picture and produce a computer file that represents what it sees. A digital camera is a related device. Each has its own limitations.

Scheme

Scheme is a typically interpreted computer language. It was created in 1975 in an attempt to make Lisp simpler and more consistent. Scheme is a fairly portable language, but is not particularly fast.

script

A script is a series of OS commands. The term "batch file" means much the same thing, but is a bit dated. Typically the same sort of situations in which one would say DOS instead of OS, it would also be appropriate to say batch file instead of script. Scripts can be run like programs, but tend to perform simpler tasks. When a script is run, it is always interpreted.

SCSI

Loosely speaking, a disk format sometimes used by MS-Windows, Mac OS, AmigaOS, and (almost always) UNIX. Generally SCSI is superior (but more expensive) to IDE, but it varies somewhat with system load and the individual SCSI and IDE components themselves. The quick rundown is that: SCSI-I and SCSI-II will almost always outperform IDE; EIDE will almost always outperform SCSI-I and SCSI-II; SCSI-III and UltraSCSI will almost always outperform EIDE; and heavy system loads give an advantage to SCSI. Note that although loosely speaking it is just a format difference, it is deep down a hardware difference.

sequential access

This indicates that data cannot be selected without having to skip over earlier data first. This is the way that a cassette or video tape will behave. The other common behavior is called random access.

serial

Loosely speaking, serial implies something that has to be done linearly, one at a time, like people being served in a single check-out line. Serial connections are by their nature less expensive than parallel connections (including things like SCSI) but are typically slower.

server

A server is a computer designed to provide various services for an entire network. It is typically either a workstation or a mainframe because it will usually be expected to handle far greater loads than ordinary desktop systems. The load placed on servers also necessitates that they utilize robust OSes, as a crash on a system that is currently being used by many people is far worse than a crash on a system that is only being used by one person.

SGML
The **S**tandard **G**eneralized **M**ark-up **L**anguage provides an extremely generalized level of mark-up. More common mark-up languages like HTML and XML are actually just popular subsets of SGML.

shareware
Shareware is software made for profit that allows a trial period before purchase. Typically shareware can be freely downloaded, used for a period of weeks (or sometimes even months), and either purchased or discarded after it has been learned whether or not it will satisfy the user's needs.

shell
A CLI designed to simplify complex OS commands. Some OSes (like AmigaOS, the Hurd, and UNIX) have built-in support to make the concurrent use of multiple shells easy. Common shells include the Korn Shell (ksh), the Bourne Shell (sh or bsh), the Bourne-Again Shell, (bash or bsh), the C-Shell (csh), etc.

SIMM
A physical component used to add RAM to a computer. Similar to, but incompatible with, DIMMs.

Smalltalk
Smalltalk is an efficient language for writing computer programs. Historically it is one of the first object-oriented languages, and is not only used today in its pure form but shows its influence in other languages like Objective-C.

Solaris
Solaris is the commercial variant of UNIX currently produced by Sun. It is an industrial strength, nigh bulletproof, powerful multitasking OS that will run on SPARC, x86, and PowerPC based machines.

spam
Generally spam is unwanted, unrequested e-mail or Usenet news. It is typically sent out in bulk to huge address lists that were automatically generated by various robots endlessly searching the Internet and newsgroups for things that resemble e-mail addresses. The legality of spam is a topic of much debate; it is at best only borderline legal, and spammers have been successfully persecuted in some states.

SPARC
The SPARC is a RISC processor developed by Sun. The design was more or less released to the world, and it is currently produced by around a dozen different companies too numerous to even bother mentioning. It is worth noting that even computers made by Sun typically sport SPARCs made by other companies. A couple different OSes run on SPARC based machines, including Solaris, SunOS, and Linux. Some of the newer SPARC models are called UltraSPARCs.

sprite
The term sprite originally referred to a small MOB, usually implemented in hardware. Lately it is also being used to refer to a single image used piecemeal within a Web site in order to avoid incurring the time penalty of downloading multiple files.

SQL
SQL (pronounced **Sequel**) is an interpreted language specially designed for database access. It is supported by virtually every major modern database system.

Sugar
The window manager used by the OLPC XO. It is made to run on top of Linux.

SunOS

SunOS is the commercial variant of UNIX formerly produced (but still supported) by Sun.

SVG

Scalable Vector Graphics data is an XML file that is used to hold graphical data that can be resized without loss of quality. SVG data can be kept in its own file, or even embedded within a web page (although not all browsers are capable of displaying such data).

Tcl/Tk

The Tool Command Language is a portable interpreted computer language designed to be easy to use. Tk is a GUI toolkit for Tcl. Tcl is a fairly popular language for both integrating existing applications and for creating Web applets (note that applets written in Tcl are often called Tcklets). Tcl/Tk is available for free for most platforms, and plug-ins are available to enable many browsers to play Tcklets.

TCP/IP

TCP/IP is a protocol for computer networks. The Internet is largely built on top of TCP/IP (it is the more reliable of the two primary Internet Protocols -- TCP stands for Transmission Control Protocol).

terminator

A terminator is a dedicated device used to mark the end of a device chain (as is most typically found with SCSI devices). If such a chain is not properly terminated, weird results can occur.

TEX

TEX (pronounced "tek") is a freely available, industrial strength typesetting program that can be run on many different platforms. These qualities make it exceptionally popular in schools, and frequently software developed at a university will have its documentation in TEX format. TEX is not limited to educational use, though; many professional books were typeset with TEX. TEX's primary drawback is that it can be quite difficult to set up initially.

THz & terahertz

One terahertz is equivalent to 1000 gigahertz.

TrackBack

TrackBacks essentially provide a means whereby different web sites can post messages to one another not just to inform each other about citations, but also to alert one another of related resources. Typically, a blog may display quotations from another blog through the use of TrackBacks.

UDP/IP

UDP/IP is a protocol for computer networks. It is the faster of the two primary Internet Protocols. UDP stands for User Datagram Protocol.

Unicode

The Unicode character set is a superset of the ASCII character set with provisions made for handling international symbols and characters from other languages. Unicode is sixteen bit, so takes up roughly twice the space as simple ASCII, but is correspondingly more flexible.

UNIX

UNIX is a family of OSes, each being made by a different company or organization but all offering a very similar look and feel. It can not quite be considered non-proprietary, however, as the differences between different vendor's versions can be significant (it is still generally possible to switch from one vendor's UNIX to another without too much effort; today the differences between different UNIXes are similar to the differences between the different MS-Windows; historically there were two different UNIX camps, Berkeley / BSD and AT&T / System V, but the assorted vendors have worked together to minimalize the differences). The free variant Linux is one of the closest things to a current, non-proprietary OS; its development is controlled by a non-profit organization and its distribution is provided by several companies. UNIX is powerful; it is fully multitasking and can do pretty much anything that any OS can do (look to the Hurd if you need a more powerful OS). With power comes complexity, however, and

UNIX tends not to be overly friendly to beginners (although those who think UNIX is difficult or cryptic apparently have not used CP/M). Window managers are available for UNIX (running under X-Windows) and once properly configured common operations will be almost as simple on a UNIX machine as on a Mac. Out of all the OSes in current use, UNIX has the greatest range of hardware support. It will run on machines built around many different processors. Lightweight versions of UNIX have been made to run on PDAs, and in the other direction, full featured versions make full advantage of all the resources on large, multi-processor machines. Some different UNIX versions include Solaris, Linux, IRIX, AIX, SunOS, FreeBSD, Digital UNIX, HP-UX, NetBSD, OpenBSD, etc.

upload

To upload a file is to copy it from your computer to a remote computer. The opposite is download.

UPS

An uninterrupted power supply uses heavy duty batteries to help smooth out its input power source.

URI

A **U**niform **R**esource **I**dentifier is basically just a unique address for almost any type of resource. It is similar to but more general than a URL; in fact, it may also be a URN.

URL

A **U**niform **R**esource **L**ocator is basically just an address for a file that can be given to a browser. It starts with a protocol type (such as http, ftp, or gopher) and is followed by a colon, machine name, and file name in UNIX style. Optionally an octothorpe character "#" and and arguments will follow the file name; this can be used to further define position within a page and perform a few other tricks. Similar to but less general than a URI.

URN

A **U**niform **R**esource **N**ame is basically just a unique address for almost any type of resource unlike a URL it will probably not resolve with a browser.

USB

A really fast type of serial port that offers many of the best features of SCSI without the price. Faster than many types of parallel port, a single USB port is capable of chaining many devices without the need of a terminator. USB is much slower (but somewhat less expensive) than FireWire.

uucode

The point of uucode is to allow 8-bit binary data to be transferred through the more common 7-bit ASCII channels (most especially e-mail). The facilities for dealing with uucoded files exist for many different machine types, and the most common programs are called "uuencode" for encoding the original binary file into a 7-bit file and "uudecode" for restoring the original binary file from the encoded one. Sometimes different uuencode and uudecode programs will work in subtly different manners causing annoying compatibility problems. Bcode was invented to provide the same service as uucode but to maintain a tighter standard.

variable width

As applied to a font, variable width means that different characters will have different widths as appropriate. For example, an "i" will take up much less space than an "m". The opposite of variable width is fixed width. The terms "proportional width" and "proportionally spaced" mean the same thing as variable width. Some common variable width fonts include Times, Helvetica, and Bookman.

VAX

The VAX is a computer platform developed by Digital. Its plural is VAXen. VAXen are large expensive machines that were once quite popular in large businesses; today modern UNIX workstations have all the capability of VAXen but take up much less space. Their OS is called VMS.

vector

This term has two common meanings. The first is in the geometric sense: a vector defines a direction and magnitude. The second concerns the formatting of fonts and images. If a font is a vector font or an image is a vector image, it is defined as lines of relative size and direction rather than as collections of pixels (the method used in bitmapped fonts and images). This makes it easier to change the size of the font or image, but puts a bigger load on the device that has to display the font or image. The term "outline font" means the same thing as vector font.

Veronica & Veronica2

Although traditionally written as a proper name, Veronica is actually an acronym for "**v**ery **e**asy **r**odent-**o**riented **n**etwide **i**ndex to **c**omputerized **a**rchives", where the "rodent" refers to gopher. The acronym was obviously a little forced to go along with the pre-existing (and now largely unused) Archie, in order to have a little fun with a comic book reference. Regardless, Veronica (or these days more likely Veronica2) is essentially a search engine for gopher resources.

VIC-20

The Commodore VIC-20 computer sold millions of units and is generally considered to have been the first affordable home computer. It features a ROM-based BASIC and uses it as a default "OS". It is based on the 65xx family of processors. VIC (in case you are wondering) can stand for either video interface **c** or video interface **c**omputer. The VIC-20 is the precursor to the C64/128.

virtual machine

A virtual machine is a machine completely defined and implemented in software rather than hardware. It is often referred to as a "runtime environment"; code compiled for such a machine is typically called bytecode.

virtual memory

This is a scheme by which disk space is made to substitute for the more expensive RAM space. Using it will often enable a comptuer to do things it could not do without it, but it will also often result in an overall slowing down of the system. The concept of swap space is very similar.

virtual reality

Virtual reality (often called VR for short) is generally speaking an attempt to provide more natural, human interfaces to software. It can be as simple as a pseudo 3D interface or as elaborate as an isolated room in which the computer can control the user's senses of vision, hearing, and even smell and touch.

virus

A virus is a program that will seek to duplicate itself in memory and on disks, but in a subtle way that will not immediately be noticed. A computer on the same network as an infected computer or that uses an infected disk (even a floppy) or that downloads and runs an infected program can itself become infected. A virus can only spread to computers of the same platform. For example, on a network consisting of a WinTel box, a Mac, and a Linux box, if one machine acquires a virus the other two will probably still be safe. Note also that different platforms have different general levels of resistance; UNIX machines are almost immune, Win '95 / '98 / ME / XP is quite vulnerable, and most others lie somewhere in between.

VMS

The industrial strength OS that runs on VAXen.

VoIP

VoIP means "Voice over IP" and it is quite simply a way of utilizing the Internet (or even in some cases intranets) for telephone conversations. The primary motivations for doing so are cost and convenience as VoIP is significantly less expensive than typical telephone long distance packages, plus one high speed Internet connection can serve for multiple phone lines.

VRML

A **V**irtual **R**eality **M**odeling **L**anguage file is used to represent VR objects. It has essentially been superceded by X3D.

W3C

The World Wide Web Consortium (usually abbreviated W3C) is a non-profit, advisory body that makes suggestions on the future direction of the World Wide Web, HTML, CSS, and browsers.

Waba

An extremely lightweight subset of Java optimized for use on PDAs.

WebDAV

WebDAV stands for Web-based Distributed Authoring and Versioning, and is designed to provide a way of editing Web-based resources in place. It serves as a more modern (and often more secure) replacement for FTP in many cases.

WebTV

A WebTV box hooks up to an ordinary television set and displays web pages. It will not display them as well as a dedicated computer.

window manager

A window manager is a program that acts as a graphical go-between for a user and an OS. It provides a GUI for the OS. Some OSes incorporate the window manager into their own internal code, but many do not for reasons of efficiency. Some OSes partially make the division. Some common true window managers include CDE (Common Desktop Environment), GNOME, KDE, Aqua, OpenWindows, Motif, FVWM, Sugar, and Enlightenment. Some common hybrid window managers with OS extensions include Windows ME, Windows 98, Windows 95, Windows 3.1, OS/2 and GEOS.

Windows '95

Windows '95 is currently the second most popular variant of MS-Windows. It was designed to be the replacement Windows 3.1 but has not yet done so completely partly because of suspected security problems but even more because it is not as lightweight and will not work on all the machines that Windows 3.1 will. It is more capable than Windows 3.1 though and now has excellent driver support and more games available for it than any other platform. It is made to run on top of MS-DOS and will not do much of anything if MS-DOS is not on the system. It is thus not strictly an OS per se, but nor is it a true window manager either; rather the combination of MS-DOS and Windows '95 result in a full OS with GUI. It is partially multitasking but has a much greater chance of crashing than Windows NT does (or probably even Mac OS) if faced with a buggy program. Windows '95 runs only on x86 based machines. Currently Windows '95 has several Y2K issues, some of which have patches that can be downloaded for free, and some of which do not yet have fixes at all.

Windows '98

Windows '98 is quite possibly the second most popular form of MS-Windows, in spite of the fact that its official release is currently a point of legal debate with at least nineteen states, the federal government, and a handful of foreign countries as it has a few questionable features that might restrict the novice computer user and/or unfairly compete with other computer companies. It also has some specific issues with the version of Java that comes prepackaged with it that has never been adequately fixed, and it still has several Y2K issues, most of which have patches that can be downloaded for free (in fact, Microsoft guarantees that it will work properly through 2000 with the proper patches), but some of which do not yet have fixes at all (it won't work properly through 2001 at this point). In any case, it was designed to replace Windows '95.

Windows 2000

Windows 2000 was the intended replacement for Windows NT and in that capacity received relatively lukewarm support. Being based on Windows NT, it inherits some of its driver support problems. Originally it was also supposed to replace Windows '98, but Windows ME was made to do that instead, and the merger between Windows NT and Windows '98 was postponed until Windows XP.

Windows 3.1

Windows 3.1 remains a surprisingly popular variant of MS-Windows. It is lighter weight than either Windows '95 or Windows NT (but not lighter weight than GEOS) but less capable than the other two. It is made to run on top of MS-DOS and will not do much of anything if MS-DOS is not on the system. It is thus not strictly an OS per se, but nor is it a true window manager, either; rather the combination of MS-DOS and Windows 3.1 result in a full OS with GUI. Its driver support is good, but its game selection is limited. Windows 3.1 runs only on x86 based machines. It has some severe Y2K issues that may or may not be fixed.

Windows CE

Windows CE is the lightweight variant of MS-Windows. It offers the general look and feel of Windows '95 but is targetted primarily for hand-held devices, PDAs, NCs, and embedded devices. It does not have all the features of either Windows '95 or Windows NT and is very different from Windows 3.1. In particular, it will not run any software made for any of the other versions of MS-Windows. Special versions of each program must be made. Furthermore, there are actually a few slightly different variants of Windows CE, and no variant is guaranteed to be able to run software made specifically for another one. Driver support is also fairly poor for all types, and few games are made for it. Windows CE will run on a few different processor types, including the x86 and several different processors dedicated to PDAs, embedded systems, and hand-held devices.

Windows ME

Windows ME is yet another flavor of MS-Windows (specifically the planned replacement for Windows '98). Windows ME currently runs only on the x86 processor.

Windows NT

Windows NT is the industrial-strength variant of MS-Windows. Current revisions offer the look and feel of Windows '95 and older revisions offer the look and feel of Windows 3.1. It is the most robust flavor of MS-Windows and is fully multitasking. It is also by far the most expensive flavor of MS-Windows and has far less software available for it than Windows '95 or '98. In particular, do not expect to play many games on a Windows NT machine, and expect some difficulty in obtaining good drivers. Windows NT will run on a few different processor types, including the x86, the Alpha, and the PowerPC. Plans are in place to port Windows NT to the Merced when it becomes available.

Windows Vista

Windows Vista is the newest flavor of MS-Windows (specifically the planned replacement for Windows XP). Windows Vista (originally known as Longhorn) currently only runs on x86 processors.

Windows XP

Windows XP is yet another flavor of MS-Windows (specifically the planned replacement for both Windows ME and Windows 2000). Windows XP currently only runs on the x86 processors. Windows XP is currently the most popular form of MS-Windows.

WinTel

An x86 based system running some flavor of MS-Windows.

workstation

Depending upon whom you ask, a workstation is either an industrial strength desktop computer or its own category above the desktops. Workstations typically have some flavor of UNIX for their OS, but there has been a recent trend to call high-end Windows NT and Windows 2000 machines workstations, too.

WYSIWYG

What you see is what you get; an adjective applied to a program that attempts to exactly represent printed output on the screen. Related to WYSIWYM but quite different.

WYSIWYM

What you see is what you mean; an adjective applied to a program that does not attempt to exactly represent printed output on the screen, but rather defines how things are used and so will adapt to different paper sizes, etc. Related to WYSIWYG but quite different.

X-Face

X-Faces are small monochrome images embedded in headers for both provides a e-mail and news messages. Better mail and news applications will display them (sometimes automatically, sometimes only per request).

X-Windows

X-Windows provides a GUI for most UNIX systems, but can also be found as an add-on library for other computers. Numerous window managers run on top of it. It is often just called "X".

X3D

Extensible **3D** Graphics data is an XML file that is used to hold three-dimensional graphical data. It is the successor to VRML.

x86

The x86 series of processors includes the Pentium, Pentium Pro, Pentium II, Pentium III, Celeron, and Athlon as well as the 786, 686, 586, 486, 386, 286, 8086, 8088, etc. It is an exceptionally popular design (by far the most popular CISC series) in spite of the fact that even its fastest model is significantly slower than the assorted RISC processors. Many different OSes run on machines built around x86 processors, including MS-DOS, Windows 3.1, Windows '95, Windows '98, Windows ME, Windows NT, Windows 2000, Windows CE, Windows XP, GEOS, Linux, Solaris, OpenBSD, NetBSD, FreeBSD, Mac OS X, OS/2, BeOS, CP/M, etc. A couple different companies produce x86 processors, but the bulk of them are produced by Intel. It is expected that this processor will eventually be completely replaced by the Merced, but the Merced development schedule is somewhat behind. Also, it should be noted that the Pentium III processor has stirred some controversy by including a "fingerprint" that will enable individual computer usage of web pages etc. to be accurately tracked.

XBL

An XML Binding Language document is used to associate executable content with an XML tag. It is itself an XML file, and is used most frequently (although not exclusively) in conjunction with XUL.

XHTML

The Extensible **H**ypertext **M**ark-up **L**anguage is essentially a cleaner, stricter version of HTML. It is a proper subset of XML.

XML

The Extensible **M**ark-up **L**anguage is a subset of SGML and a superset of XHTML. It is used for numerous things including (among many others) RSS and RDF.

XML-RPC

XML-RPC provides a fairly lightweight means by which one computer can execute a program on a co-operating machine across a network like the Internet. It is based on XML and is used for everything from fetching stock quotes to checking weather forcasts.

XO

The energy-efficient, kid-friendly laptop produced by the OLPC project. It runs Sugar for its window manager and Linux for its OS. It sports numerous built-in features like wireless networking, a video camera & microphone, a few USB ports, and audio in/out jacks. It comes with several educational applications (which it refers to as "Activities"), most of which are written in Python.

XSL

The Extensible Stylesheet Language is like CSS for XML. It provides a means of describing how an XML resource should be displayed.

XSLT

XSL Transformations are used to transform one type of XML into another. It is a component of XSL that can be (and often is) used independently.

XUL

An XML User-Interface Language document is used to define a user interface for an application using XML to specify the individual controls as well as the overall layout.

Y2K

The general class of problems resulting from the wrapping of computers' internal date timers is given this label in honor of the most obvious occurrence -- when the year changes from 1999 to 2000 (abbreviated in some programs as 99 to 00 indicating a backwards time movement). Contrary to popular belief, these problems will not all manifest themselves on the first day of 2000, but will in fact happen over a range of dates extending out beyond 2075. A computer that does not have problems prior to the beginning of 2001 is considered "Y2K compliant", and a computer that does not have problems within the next ten years or so is considered for all practical purposes to be "Y2K clean". Whether or not a given computer is "clean" depends upon both its OS and its applications (and in some unfortunate cases, its hardware). The quick rundown on common home / small business machines (roughly from best to worst) is that:

> All Mac OS systems are okay until at least the year 2040. By that time a patch should be available.

> All BeOS systems are okay until the year 2040 (2038?). By that time a patch should be available.

> Most UNIX versions are either okay or currently have free fixes available (and typically would not have major problems until 2038 or later in any case).

> NewtonOS has a problem with the year 2010, but has a free fix available.

> Newer AmigaOS systems are okay; older ones have a problem with the year 2000 but have a free fix available. They also have a year 2077 problem that does not yet have a free fix.

> Some OS/2 systems have a year 2000 problem, but free fixes are available.

> All CP/M versions have a year 2000 problem, but free fixes are available.

> PC-DOS has a year 2000 problem, but a free fix is available.

> DR-DOS has a year 2000 problem, but a free fix is available.

> Different versions of GEOS have different problems ranging from minor year 2000 problems (with fixes in the works) to larger year 2080 problems (that do not have fixes yet). The only problem that may not have a fix in time is the year 2000 problem on the Apple][version of GEOS; not only was that version discontinued, unlike the other GEOS versions it no longer has a parent company to take care of it.

> All MS-Windows versions (except possibly Windows 2000 and Windows ME) have multiple problems with the year 2000 and/or 2001, most of which have free fixes but some of which still lack free fixes as of this writing. Even new machines off the shelf that are labelled "Y2K Compliant" usually are not unless additional software is purchased and installed. Basically WinNT and WinCE can be properly patched, Windows '98 can be patched to work properly through 2000 (possibly not 2001), Windows '95 can be at least partially patched for 2000 (but not 2001) but is not being guaranteed by Microsoft, and Windows 3.1 cannot be fully patched.

> MS-DOS has problems with at least the year 2000 (and probably more). None of its problems have been addressed as of this writing. Possible fixes are to change over to either PC-DOS or DR-DOS.

Results vary wildly for common applications, so it is better to be safe than sorry and check out the ones that you use. It should also be noted that some of the biggest expected Y2K problems will be at the two ends of the computer spectrum with older legacy mainframes (such as power some large banks) and some of the various tiny embedded computers (such as power most burglar alarms and many assorted appliances). Finally, it should also be mentioned that some older WinTel boxes and Amigas may have Y2K problems in their hardware requiring a card addition or replacement.

Z-Machine

A virtual machine optimized for running interactive fiction, interactive tutorials, and other interactive things of a primarily textual nature. Z-Machines have been ported to almost every platform in use today. Z-machine bytecode is usually called Z-code. The Glulx virtual machine is of the same idea but somewhat more modern in concept.

Z80

The Z80 series of processors is a CISC design and is not being used in too many new stand-alone computer systems, but can still be occasionally found in embedded systems. It is the most popular processor for CP/M machines.

Zaurus

The Zaurus is a brand of PDA. It is generally in between a Palm and a Newton in capability.

zip

There are three common zips in the computer world that are completely different from one another. One is a type of removable removable disk slightly larger (physically) and vastly larger (capacity) than a floppy. The second is a group of programs used for running interactive fiction. The third is a group of programs used for compression.

Zoomer

The Zoomer is a type of PDA. Zoomers all use GEOS for their OS and are / were produced by numerous different companies and are thus found under numerous different names. The "classic" Zoomers are known as the Z-7000, the Z-PDA, and the GRiDpad and were made by Casio, Tandy, and AST respectively. Newer Zoomers include HP's OmniGo models, Hyundai's Gulliver (which may not have actually been released to the general public), and Nokia's Communicator line of PDA / cell phone hybrids.

———